HTML 4

FOR

DUMMIES®

5TH EDITION

HTML 4
FOR
DUMMIES®
5TH EDITION

by Ed Tittel and Mary C. Burmeister

WILEY

Wiley Publishing, Inc.

HTML 4 For Dummies, 5th Edition

Published by
Wiley Publishing, Inc.
111 River Street
Hoboken, NJ 07030-5774

www.wiley.com

Copyright © 2005 by Wiley Publishing, Inc., Indianapolis, Indiana

Published by Wiley Publishing, Inc., Indianapolis, Indiana

Published simultaneously in Canada

For general information on our other products and services, please contact our Customer Care Department within the U.S. at 800-762-2974, outside the U.S. at 317-572-3993, or fax 317-572-4002.

For technical support, please visit www.wiley.com/techsupport.

Wiley also publishes its books in a variety of electronic formats. Some content that appears in print may not be available in electronic books.

Library of Congress Control Number: 2005923232

ISBN-13: 978-0-7645-8917-1

ISBN-10: 0-7645-8917-2

Manufactured in the United States of America

10 9 8 7 6 5 4 3

5B/RR/QV/QV/IN

WILEY

About the Authors

Ed Tittel is a full-time independent writer, trainer, and consultant who works out of his home in beautiful Austin, Texas. Ed has been writing for the trade press since 1986 and has worked on more than 130 books. In addition to this title, Ed has worked on more than 35 books for Wiley, including *Networking Windows NT Server For Dummies, XML For Dummies,* and *Networking with NetWare For Dummies.*

Ed is the technology editor at *Certification* magazine, writes the "Must Know News" twice-monthly newsletter for Cramsession.com, and also writes for a variety of Web sites and magazines. When he's not busy doing all that work stuff, Ed likes to travel, shoot pool, spend time with his family (especially taking walks with young Gregory), and wrestle with his Labrador, Blackie.

You can contact Ed Tittel by e-mail at etittel@yahoo.com.

Mary Burmeister is an editor, project manager, and writer. She's edited and project managed over 75 computer-related books. Mary has contributed material to several editions of *HTML For Dummies* and *XML For Dummies* in addition to project managing and editing them. Mary spends most of her time these days project managing, editing, and writing courses for Powered, Inc.

Authors' Acknowledgments

Because this is the ninth go-round for *HTML For Dummies,* we must start by thanking our many readers for keeping this book alive. We'd also like to thank them and the Wiley editors for providing the feedback that drives the continuing improvement of this book. Please, don't stop now — tell us what you want to do, and what you like and don't like about this book.

Let me go on by thanking my sterling co-author, Mary Burmeister, for her efforts on this revision. I'd also like to thank Rich Wagner, Brock Kyle, and Chelsea Valentine, and above all, Kim Lindros for their contributions, too. I am eternally grateful for your ideas, your hard work, and your experience in reaching an audience of budding Web experts. Thanks for breathing fresh life into this project!

Next, I'd like to thank my colleagues and former coworkers at LANWrights (now part of Thomson) as well as the Wiley team for their efforts on this title. Here in Austin, my fervent thanks go to Mary Burmeister and Kim Lindros for the services provided and time spent on this book. At Wiley, I must thank Bob Woerner and Pat O'Brien for their outstanding efforts, and Marnie Knue-Merkel for their marvelous ways with our words. Other folks we need to thank include the folks in Composition Services for their artful page layouts, and the Media Development team for their assistance with the *HTML 4 For Dummies* Web site on Dummies.com.

I'd like to thank my lovely wife, Dina Kutueva-Tittel, for putting up with crazy schedules and cranky words for balky PCs during this project. I'd also like to extend a big Texas welcome to our wonderful son, Gregory, who made his debut at Seton Hospital on February 6, 2004. Thanks for all the funny faces and sleepless nights! Finally, I'd like to thank my parents, Al and Ceil, for all the great things they did for me. I remain grateful to my wonderdog, Blackie, who's always ready to pull me away from the keyboard — sometimes literally — to explore the great outdoors.

Ed Tittel

I would like to thank Ed Tittel and Kim Lindros for roping me in on this project. You're more than colleagues; you're valuable friends. I'd also like to thank my mentor, co-worker, and best friend Dawn Rader for years of friendship and guidance. Another round of thanks goes out to my wonderful family and friends — you know who you are. And last, but certainly not least...thank you to my heart and soul: Steven, I can't find the words to explain the joy and completeness you've brought to my life. I can't wait to marry you!

Mary Burmeister

Publisher's Acknowledgments

We're proud of this book; please send us your comments through our online registration form located at `www.dummies.com/register/`.

Some of the people who helped bring this book to market include the following:

Acquisitions, Editorial, and Media Development

Project Editor: Pat O'Brien

(Previous Edition: Linda Morris)

Acquisitions Editor: Bob Woerner

Copy Editor: Andy Hollandbeck

Technical Editor: Marnie Knue-Merkel

Editorial Manager: Kevin Kirschner

Media Development Manager: Laura VanWinkle

Media Development Supervisor: Richard Graves

Editorial Assistant: Amanda Foxworth

Cartoons: Rich Tennant (`www.the5thwave.com`)

Composition Services

Project Coordinator: Shannon Schiller

Layout and Graphics: Carl Byers, Andrea Dahl, Joyce Haughey, Barry Offringa, Lynsey Osborn, Heather Ryan

Proofreaders: Leeann Harney, Jessica Kramer, Carl William Pierce

Indexer: TECHBOOKS Production Services

Publishing and Editorial for Technology Dummies

    Richard Swadley, Vice President and Executive Group Publisher

    Andy Cummings, Vice President and Publisher

    Mary Bednarek, Executive Acquisitions Director

    Mary C. Corder, Editorial Director

Publishing for Consumer Dummies

    Diane Graves Steele, Vice President and Publisher

    Joyce Pepple, Acquisitions Director

Composition Services

    Gerry Fahey, Vice President of Production Services

    Debbie Stailey, Director of Composition Services

Contents at a Glance

Table of Contents

Introduction

Welcome to the wild, wacky, and wonderful possibilities of the World Wide Web, simply referred to as *the Web*. In this book, we introduce you to the mysteries of the Hypertext Markup Language (HTML) and its successor, XHTML. Because HTML and XHTML (we use *(X)HTML* in this book to refer to both versions at the same time) are used to build Web pages, learning them will bring you into the community of Web authors and content developers.

If you've tried to build your own Web pages but found it too forbidding, now you can relax. If you can dial a telephone or find your keys in the morning, you too can become an (X)HTML author. No kidding!

This book keeps the technobabble to a minimum and sticks with plain English whenever possible. Besides plain talk about hypertext, (X)HTML, and the Web, we include lots of examples, plus tag-by-tag instructions to help you build your very own Web pages with minimum muss and fuss. We also provide more examples about what to do with your Web pages after they're created so you can share them with the world. We also explain the differences between HTML 4 and XHTML, so you can decide whether you want to stick with the best-known and longest-lived Web markup language (HTML) or the latest and greatest Web markup language (XHTML).

We also have a companion Web site for this book that contains (X)HTML examples from the chapters in usable form — plus pointers to interesting widgets that you can use to embellish your own documents and astound your friends. Visit `www.dummies.com/extras` and select "HTML 4 For Dummies, 5th Edition" from the list.

About This Book

Think of this book as a friendly, approachable guide to taking up the tools of HTML and building readable, attractive pages for the Web. HTML isn't hard to learn, but it packs a lot of details. You need to handle some of these details while you build your Web pages. Topics you find in this book include

- Designing and building Web pages
- Uploading and publishing Web pages for the world to see
- Testing and debugging your Web pages

You can build Web pages without years of arduous training, advanced aesthetic capabilities, or ritual ablutions in ice-cold streams. If you can tell somebody how to drive across town to your house, you can build a useful Web document. The purpose of this book isn't to turn you into a rocket scientist (or, for that matter, a rocket scientist into a Web site). The purpose is to show you the design and technical elements you need for a good-looking, readable Web page and to give you the confidence to do it!

How to Use This Book

This book tells you how to use (X)HTML to get your Web pages up and running on the World Wide Web. We tell you what's involved in designing and building effective Web documents that can bring your ideas and information to the whole online world — if that's what you want to do — and maybe have some high-tech fun communicating them.

All (X)HTML code appears in monospaced type such as this:

```
<head><title>What's in a Title?</title></head>...
```

When you type (X)HTML tags or other related information, be sure to copy the information exactly as you see it between the angle brackets (< and >), including the angle brackets themselves, because that's part of the magic that makes (X)HTML work. Other than that, you find out how to marshal and manage the content that makes your pages special, and we tell you exactly what you need to do to mix the elements of (X)HTML with your own work.

The margins of a book don't give us the same room as the vast reaches of cyberspace. Therefore, some long lines of (X)HTML markup, or designations of Web sites (called *URLs,* for *Uniform Resource Locators*), may wrap to the next line. Remember that your computer shows such wrapped lines as a *single line of (X)HTML,* or as a single URL — so if you type that hunk of code, keep it as one line. Don't insert a hard return if you see one of these wrapped lines. We clue you in that the (X)HTML markup is supposed to be all one line by breaking the line at a slash or other appropriate character (to imply "but wait, there's more!") and by slightly indenting the overage, as in the following silly example:

```
http://www.infocadabra.transylvania.com/nexus/plexus/lexus/
       praxis/okay/this/is/a/make-believe/URL/but/some/real/
       ones/are/SERIOUSLY/long.html
```

HTML doesn't care whether you type tag text in uppercase, lowercase, or both (except for character entities, also known as character codes). XHTML, however, wants tag text only in lowercase in order to be perfectly correct. Thus, to make your own work look like ours as much as possible, enter all (X)HTML tag text in lowercase only. (If you have a previous edition of the book, this is a complete reversal of earlier instructions. The keepers of the eternal and ever-magnanimous standard of HTML, the World Wide Web Consortium (W3C), have restated the rules of this game, so we follow their lead. We don't make the rules, but we *do* know how to play the game!)

Three Presumptuous Assumptions

They say that making assumptions makes a fool out of the person who makes them and the person who is subject to those assumptions (and just who are *they,* anyway? We *assume* we know, but . . . never mind).

You don't need to be a master logician or a wizard in the arcane arts of programming, nor do you need a PhD in computer science. You don't even need a detailed sense of what's going on in the innards of your computer to deal with the material in this book.

Even so, practicality demands that we make a few assumptions about you, gentle reader: you can turn your computer on and off; you know how to use a mouse and a keyboard, and you want to build your own Web pages for fun, profit, or your job. We also assume that you already have a working connection to the Internet and a Web browser.

If you can write a sentence and know the difference between a heading and a paragraph, you can build and publish your own documents on the Web. The rest consists of details, and we help you with those!

How This Book Is Organized

This book contains seven major parts, arranged like Russian *Matrioshka* (nesting dolls). Parts contain at least three chapters, and each chapter contains several modular sections. How you use the book is up to you:

- ✔ Jump around.
- ✔ Find topics or keywords in the Index or in the Table of Contents.
- ✔ Read the whole book from cover to cover.

Part I: Getting to Know (X)HTML

This part sets the stage and includes an overview of and introduction to the Web and the software that people use to mine its treasures. This section also explains how the Web works, including the (X)HTML to which this book is devoted, and the server-side software and services that deliver information to end users (when we aren't doing battle with the innards of our systems).

(X)HTML documents, also called *Web pages,* are the fundamental units of information organization and delivery on the Web. Here, you also discover what HTML is about and how hypertext can enrich ordinary text. Next, you take a walk on the Web side and build your very first (X)HTML document.

Part II: Formatting Web Pages with (X)HTML

HTML mixes ordinary text with special strings of characters, called *markup,* used to instruct browsers how to display (X)HTML documents. In this part of the book, you find out about markup in general and (X)HTML in particular. We start with a fascinating discussion of (X)HTML document organization and structure. (Well . . . *we* think it's fascinating, and hope you do, too.) Next, we explain how text can be organized into blocks and lists. Then we tackle how the hyperlinks that put the *H* into (X)HTML work. After that, we discuss how you can find and use graphical images in your Web pages and make some fancy formatting maneuvers to spruce up those pages.

Throughout this part of the book, we include discussion of (X)HTML markup elements *(tags)* and how they work. By the time you finish Part II, expect to have a good overall idea of what HTML is and how you can use it.

Part III: Taking Precise Control Over Web Pages

Part III starts with a discussion of Cascading Style Sheets (CSS) — another form of markup language that lets (X)HTML deal purely with content while it deals with how Web pages look when they're displayed in a Web browser. After exploring CSS syntax and structures and discovering how to use them, you learn how to manipulate the color and typefaces of text, backgrounds, and more on your Web pages. You also learn about more complex collections of markup — specifically tables — as you explore and observe their capabilities in detail. We give you lots of examples to help you design and build commercial-grade (X)HTML documents. You can get started working with related (X)HTML tag syntax and structures that you need to know so you can build complex Web pages.

Part IV: Integrating Scripts with HTML

(X)HTML isn't good at snazzing up text and graphics when they're on display (which is where CSS excels). And (X)HTML really can't *do* much by itself. Web designers often build interactive, dynamic Web pages by using scripting tools to add interactivity to an (X)HTML framework.

In this part of the book, you learn about scripting languages that enable Web pages to interact with users and that also provide ways to respond to user input or actions and to grab and massage data along the way. You learn about general scripting languages, and we jump directly into the most popular of such languages — JavaScript. You can discover the basic elements of this scripting language and how to add interaction to Web pages. You can also explore a typical use for scripting that you can extend and add to your own Web site. We go on to explore how to create and extract data from Web-based data input forms and how to create and use scripts that react to a user's actions while she visits your Web pages.

Throughout this part of the book, examples, advice, and details show you how these scripting components can enhance and improve your Web site's capabilities — and your users' experiences when visiting your pages.

Part V: HTML Projects

This part tackles typical complex Web pages. You can use these as models for similar capabilities in your own Web pages. These projects include About Me and About My Company pages, an eBay auction page, a product marketing page, and even a product catalog page with its own shopping cart!

Part VI: The Part of Tens

We sum up and distill the very essence of the mystic secrets of (X)HTML. Here, you can read further about cool Web tools, get a second chance to review top do's and don'ts for HTML markup, and review how to catch and kill potential bugs and errors in your pages before anybody else sees them.

Part VII: Appendixes

This book ends with appendixes of technical terms and a Glossary.

Icons Used in This Book

This icon signals technical details that are informative and interesting but that aren't critical to writing HTML.

This icon flags useful information that makes HTML markup or other important stuff even less complicated than you feared it might be.

This icon points out information you shouldn't pass by — don't overlook these gentle reminders (the life, sanity, or page you save could be your own).

Be cautious when you see this icon. It warns you of things you shouldn't do; consequences can be severe if you ignore the accompanying bit of wisdom.

Text marked with this icon contains information about something that can be found on this book's companion Web site. You can find all the code examples in this book, for starters. Simply visit the Extras section of Dummies.com (`www.dummies.com/extras`) and click the link for this book. We also use this icon to point out great useful Web resources.

The information highlighted with this icon gives best practices — advice that we wish we'd had when we first started out! These techniques can save you time and money on migraine medication.

Where to Go from Here

This is where you pick a direction and hit the road! Where you start out doesn't matter. Don't worry. You can handle it. Who cares whether anybody else thinks you're just goofing around? We know you're getting ready to have the time of your life. Enjoy!

Part I
Getting to Know (X)HTML

The 5th Wave · By Rich Tennant

FREELANCER NED WILLIS CONSULTS WITH A MEMBER OF HIS TECHNICAL STAFF

"...and that's pretty much all there is to converting a document to an HTML file."

In this part . . .

In this part of the book, we explore and explain basic HTML document links and structures. We also explain the key role that Web browsers play in delivering all this stuff to people's desktops. We even explain where the *(X)* comes from — namely, a reworking of the original description of HTML markup using XML syntax to create XHTML — and go on to help you understand what makes XHTML different (and possibly better, according to some) than plain old HTML. We also take a look at Web page anatomy and look at the various pieces and parts that make up a Web page.

Next, we take you through the exercise of creating and viewing a simple Web page so you can understand what's involved in doing this for yourself. We also explain what's involved in making changes to an existing Web page and how to post your changes (or a new page) online.

This part concludes with a rousing exhortation to figure out what you're doing before making too much markup happen. Just as a well-built house starts with a set of blueprints and architectural drawings, so should a Web page (and site) start with a plan or a map, with some idea of where your pages will reside in cyberspace and how hordes of users can find their way to them.

Chapter 1

The Least You Need to Know about HTML and the Web

In This Chapter

▶ Creating HTML in text files

▶ Serving and browsing Web pages

▶ Understanding links and URLs

▶ Understanding basic HTML syntax

Welcome to the wonderful world of the Web and HTML. With just a little bit of knowledge, some practice, and something to say, you can either build your own little piece of cyberspace or expand on work you've already done.

This book is your down-and-dirty guide to putting together your first Web page, sprucing up an existing Web page, or creating complex and exciting pages that integrate intricate designs, multimedia, and scripting.

The best way to start working with HTML is to jump right in, so that's what this chapter does: It brings you up to speed on the basics of how HTML works behind the scenes of Web pages, introducing you to HTML's building blocks. When you're done with this chapter, you'll know how HTML works so you can start creating Web pages right away.

Web Pages in Their Natural Habitat

Web pages can contain many kinds of content, such as *text, graphics, forms, audio and video files,* and *interactive games.*

Browse the Web for just a little while and you see a buffet of information and content displayed in many ways. Every Web site is different, but most have one thing in common: the Hypertext Markup Language (HTML).

Whatever information a Web page contains, every Web page is created in HTML (or some reasonable facsimile). HTML is the mortar that holds a Web page together; the graphics, content, and other information are the bricks.

HTML files that produce Web pages are just text documents. That's why the Web works as well as it does. Text is the universal language of computers. Any text file that you create on a Windows computer, including an HTML file, works equally well on any other operating system.

But Web pages aren't *merely* text documents. They're made with a special, attention-deprived, sugar-loaded text called *HTML*. HTML is a collection of instructions that you include along with pointers to your content in a text file that specifies how your page should look and behave.

Stick with us to discover all the details you need to know about HTML!

Hypertext

Special instructions in HTML permit text to point *(link)* to something else. Such pointers are called *hyperlinks*. Hyperlinks are the glue that holds the World Wide Web together. In your Web browser, hyperlinks usually appear in blue and are underlined. When you click one, it takes you somewhere else.

Hypertext or not, a Web page is a text file. You can create and edit a Web page in any application that creates plain text (such as Notepad). When you're getting started with HTML, a text editor is the best tool to use. Just break out Notepad and you're ready to go. Some software tools have fancy options and applications (covered in Chapter 20) to help you create Web pages, but they generate the same text files that you create with plain-text editors.

The World Wide Web comes by its name honestly. It's quite literally a web of pages hosted on Web servers around the world, connected in millions of ways. Those connections are made by hyperlinks that connect one page to another. Without such links, the Web is just a bunch of standalone pages.

Much of the Web's value comes from its ability to link to pages and other resources (such as images, downloadable files, and media presentations) on either the same Web site or at another site. For example, FirstGov (`www.firstgov.gov`) is a *gateway* Web site — its sole function is to provide access to other Web sites. If you aren't sure which government agency handles first-time loans for homebuyers, or if want to know how to arrange a tour of the Capitol, visit this site (shown in Figure 1-1) to find out.

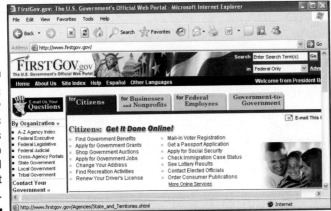

Figure 1-1:
FirstGov uses hyperlinks to help visitors find government information.

Markup

Web browsers were created specifically for the purpose of reading HTML instructions (known as *markup*) and displaying the resulting Web page.

Markup lives in a text file (with your content) to give orders to a browser.

For example, look at the page shown in Figure 1-2. You can see how the page is made up and how it is formatted by examining its underlying HTML.

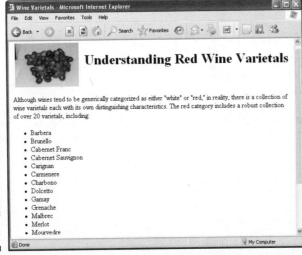

Figure 1-2:
This Web page incorporates multiple parts and numerous bits of markup.

This page includes an image, a heading that describes the page, a paragraph of text about red wine, and a list of common grape varietals.

However, different components of the page use different formatting:

- The heading at the top of the page is larger than the text in the paragraph.

- The items in the list have bullet points (big dots) before them.

The browser knows to display these components of the page in specific ways thanks to the *HTML markup,* shown in Listing 1-1.

Listing 1-1:   Sample HTML Markup

```
<!DOCTYPE html PUBLIC "-//W3C//DTD XHTML 1.0 Transitional//EN"
     "http://www.w3.org/TR/xhtml1/DTD/xhtml1-transitional.dtd">
<html xmlns="http://www.w3.org/1999/xhtml">
  <head>
    <title>Wine Varietals</title>
  </head>

  <body>
    <h1><img src="red_grapes.jpg" width="75" height="100"
        alt="Red Grapes" align="middle" hspace="5" />
        Understanding Red Wine Varietals
    </h1>
    <p>Although wines tend to be generically categorized as
        either "white" or "red," in reality, there is a
        collection of wine varietals each with its own
        distinguishing characteristics. The red category
        includes a robust collection of over 20 varietals,
        including:
    </p>
    <ul>
      <li>Barbera</li>
      <li>Brunello</li>
      <li>Cabernet Franc</li>
      <li>Cabernet Sauvignon</li>
      <li>Carignan</li>
      <li>Carmenere</li>
      <li>Charbono</li>
      <li>Dolcetto</li>
      <li>Gamay</li>
      <li>Grenache</li>
      <li>Malbrec</li>
      <li>Merlot</li>
      <li>Mourvedre</li>
      <li>Nebbiolo</li>
      <li>Petite Sirah</li>
      <li>Pinot Noir</li>
```

```
      <li>Sangiovese</li>
      <li>Syrah</li>
      <li>Tempranillo</li>
      <li>Zinfandel</li>
    </ul>
  </body>
</html>
```

Any text enclosed between less-than and greater-than signs (< >) is an HTML tag (often called the *markup*). For example, a p within brackets (<p>...</p> tags) identifies the text about red varietals as a paragraph; the li (<li>... </li> tags) markup identifies each item in a list of varietals. That's really all there is to it. You embed the markup in a text file, along with text for readers to view, to let the browser know how to display your Web page.

Tags and content between and within the tags are collectively called *elements*.

Browsers

The user's piece in the Web puzzle is a Web browser. Web browsers read instructions written in HTML and use those instructions to display a Web page's content on your screen.

A bevy of browsers

The Web world is full of browsers of many shapes and sizes — or rather versions and feature sets. Two of the more popular browsers are Microsoft Internet Explorer and Netscape Navigator. Other browsers, such as Mozilla Firefox and Opera, are widely used. As an HTML developer, you must think beyond your own browser experience and preferences. Every user has his or her own browser preferences and settings.

Each browser renders HTML a bit differently. Every browser handles JavaScript, multimedia, style sheets, and other HTML add-ins differently, too. Throw different operating systems into the mix, and things get really fun.

Usually, the differences between browsers are minor. But sometimes, a combination of HTML, text, and media brings a specific browser to its knees.

When you work with HTML, you need to test your pages on as many different browsers as you can. Install at least three different browsers on your own system for testing. We recommend the latest versions of Internet Explorer, Navigator, and Opera.

Yahoo! has a fairly complete list of browsers at

http://dir.yahoo.com/Computers_and_Internet/Software/Internet/World_Wide_Web/Browsers

You should always write your HTML with the idea that people will view the content using a Web browser. Just remember that there's more than one kind of browser out there, and each one comes in several versions.

Usually, Web browsers request and display Web pages available via the Internet from a Web server. You can also display HTML pages you've saved on your own computer before making them available on a Web server on the Internet. When you're developing your own HTML pages, you view these pages (called *local* pages) in your browser. You can use local pages to get a good idea of what people see after the page goes live on the Internet.

Each Web browser interprets HTML in its own way. The same HTML doesn't look exactly the same from one browser to the next. When you work with basic HTML, variances aren't significant, but as you integrate other elements (such as scripting and multimedia), rendering the markup can get hairy.

Chapter 2 shows how to use a Web browser to view a local copy of your first Web page.

Some people use text-only Web browsers, such as Lynx, because either

✔ They're visually impaired and can't use a graphical display.

✔ They like a lean, fast Web browser that displays only text.

Web servers

Your HTML pages aren't much good if you can't share them with the world. Web servers make that possible. A *Web server* is a computer that

✔ Connects to the Internet

✔ Runs Web server software

✔ Responds to requests from Web browsers for Web pages

Almost any computer can be a Web server, including your home computer. But Web servers generally are computers dedicated to the task. You don't need to be an Internet or computer guru to publish your Web pages, but you must find a Web server to serve your pages:

✔ If you're building pages for a company Web site, your IT department may have a Web server. (Ask your IT guru for the information.)

✔ If you're starting a new site, you need a host for your pages.

Finding an inexpensive host is easy. Chapter 3 shows how to determine your hosting needs and find the perfect provider.

Anatomy of a URL

The Web is made up of millions of resources, each of them linkable. A resource's exact location is the key to linking to it. Without an exact address (a *Uniform Resource Locator,* or *URL*), you can't use the Address bar in a Web browser to visit a Web page directly.

URLs are the standard addressing system for resources on the Web. Each resource (Web page, site, or individual file) has a unique URL. URLs work a lot like your postal address. Figure 1-3 identifies the components of a URL.

Figure 1-3: The components of a URL help it define the exact location of a file on the Web.

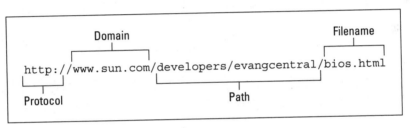

Each URL component helps define the location of a Web page or resource:

- ✔ **Protocol:** Specifies the protocol the browser follows to request the file.

  The Web page protocol is `http://` (the usual start to most URLs).

- ✔ **Domain:** Points to the general Web site (such as `www.sun.com`) where the file resides. A domain may host a few files (like a personal Web site) or millions of files (like a corporate site, such as `www.sun.com`).

- ✔ **Path:** Names the sequence of folders through which you must navigate to get to a specific file.

  For example, to get to a file in the `evangcentral` folder that resides in the `developers` folder, you use the `/developers/evangcentral/` path.

- ✔ **Filename:** Specifies which file in a directory path the browser accesses.

The URL shown in Figure 1-3 points to the Sun domain and offers a path that leads to a specific file named `bios.html`:

`http://www.sun.com/developers/evangcentral/bios.html`

Introducing Internet protocols

Interactions between browsers and servers are made possible by a set of computer-communication instructions: Hypertext Transfer Protocol (HTTP). This protocol defines how browsers should request Web pages and how Web servers should respond to those requests.

HTTP isn't the only protocol at work on the Internet. The Simple Mail Transfer Protocol (SMTP) and Post Office Protocol (POP) make e-mail exchange possible, and the File Transfer Protocol (FTP) allows you to upload, download, move, copy, and delete files and folders across the Internet. The good news is that Web browsers and servers do all of the HTTP work for you, so you only have to put your pages on a server or type a Web address into a browser.

To see how HTTP works, check Webmonkey's article, "HTTP Transactions and You":

```
http://hotwired.lycos.com/webmonkey/geektalk/97/06/index4a.html
```

Chapter 6 provides the complete details on how you use HTML and URLs to add hyperlinks to your Web pages, and Chapter 3 shows how to obtain a URL for your own Web site after you're ready move it to a Web server.

(X) HTML's Component Parts

The following section removes the mystery from the *X*. This section shows

- ✔ The differences between HTML and XHTML
- ✔ How HTML is written (its *syntax*)
- ✔ Rules that govern its use
- ✔ Names for important pieces and parts of HTML (and XHTML) markup
- ✔ How to make the best, most correct use of its capabilities

HTML and XHTML: What's the difference?

HTML is *Hypertext Markup Language,* a notation developed in the late 1980s and early 1990s for describing Web pages. HTML is now enshrined in numerous standard descriptions (*specifications*) from the World Wide Web Consortium (W3C). The last HTML specification was finalized in 1999.

HTML and XHTML specifications

The formal documents to describe HTML and XHTML are on the W3C's Web site at `www.w3.org`.

Markup languages usually include version numbers to identify them. The current version of HTML is 4.01. It dates back to December 1997; you can find the document at `www.w3.org/TR/html4`.

XHTML has gone through two major drafts, 1.0 and 1.1. The 1.1 version is more advanced than 1.0, but most Web content developers and software tools follow the 1.0 specification. An XHTML 2.0 specification is in "Working Draft" status (its authors haven't finalized its content and structure). When a W3C specification is finished, it's known as a *W3C Recommendation*.

You can find specifications for all three versions of XHTML:

✔ XHTML 2.0 Working Draft (7/4/2004)

   `www.w3.org/TR/2004/WD-xhtml2-20040722/`
✔ XHTML 1.1 Module-based XHTML Recommendation (5/31/2001)

   `www.w3.org/TR/xhtml11/`
✔ XHTML 1.0 Recommendation (1/26/2000)

   `www.w3.org/TR/xhtml11/`

Reading W3C specifications takes some learning and improves with repeated exposure. Don't let the formal language and notation of these documents put you off: After you understand what's up, you appreciate the precision and detail! But you may decide never even to look at one of these specifications — it's entirely up to you!

The HTML 4.01 specification is the rulebook of HTML, as the XHTML 1.0 specification is for XHTML — each one tells you exactly which elements you can use, which attributes go with those elements, and how you use elements in combinations to create such page structures as lists, forms, tables, and frames. This book uses the XHTML 1.0 specification as its basis.

When you put an *X* in front of *HTML* to get *XHTML,* you get a new, improved version of HTML based on the *eXtensible Markup Language (XML).* XML is designed to work and behave well with computers, software, and the Internet.

The original formulation of HTML has some irregularities that can cause heartburn for software that reads HTML documents. XHTML, on the other hand, uses an extremely regular and predictable syntax that's easier for software to handle. XHTML will replace HTML someday, but HTML keeps on ticking. This book covers both varieties and shows you the steps to put the X in front of your own HTML documents and turn them into XHTML.

✔ Most HTML and XHTML markup is identical.

✔ In a few cases, HTML and XHTML markup looks a little different.

✔ In a few cases, HTML and XHTML markup must be used differently.

This book shows how to create code that works in both HTML and XHTML.

The types of (X)HTML

The HTML and XHTML specifications use *Document Type Definitions* (DTDs) written in the Standard Generalized Markup Language (SGML) — the granddaddy of all markup — to define the details.

In its earlier versions, HTML used elements for formatting; over time, developers realized that

✔ Formatting needed its own language (now called *Cascading Style Sheets,* or CSS).

✔ HTML elements should describe only a page's structure.

This resulted in three flavors of HTML, which also apply to XHTML. These are the *XHTML DTDs:*

✔ **XHTML Transitional:** Uses HTML's elements to describe font faces and page colors. XHTML Transitional accounts for formatting elements in older versions of HTML. Formatting elements in XHTML Transitional are *deprecated* (considered obsolete) because the W3C would like developers to move away from them and to a combination of XHTML Strict and CSS. We use the XHTML Transitional DTD for the markup in this book.

✔ **XHTML Strict:** Doesn't include any elements that describe formatting. This version is designed to let CSS drive the page formatting.

The CSS-with-XHTML Strict approach is an ambitious way to build Web pages, but in practice it has its pros and cons. CSS provides more control over your page formatting, but creating style sheets that work well in all browsers can be tricky. Chapter 9 covers style sheets and the issues around using them in more detail.

✔ **XHTML Frameset:** Includes *frames,* which is markup that allows you to display more than one Web page or resource at a time in the same browser window. Frames are still used in some Web sites but are less popular today than they were in the late 1990s. Our advice is to use them only if you *must* display information from multiple HTML documents at the same time in a single browser window.

All Web browsers support all elements in HTML Transitional (and in XHTML 1.0 Transitional if proper tag formatting is used); you can choose to use elements from it or stick with (X)HTML Strict instead. If you use frames, you technically work with (X)HTML Frameset, but all elements still work the same way.

This book covers all (X)HTML tags in all versions (lumping them into one category called *(X)HTML)* because all real-world Web browsers support all three flavors.

Syntax and rules

HTML is a straightforward language for describing Web page contents. XHTML is even less demanding. Their components are easy to use — when you know how to use a little bit of (X)HTML. Both HTML and XHTML markup have three types of components:

- **Elements:** Identify different parts of an HTML page by using tags
- **Attributes:** Information about an instance of an element
- **Entities:** Non-ASCII text characters, such as copyright symbols (©) and accented letters (É)

Every bit of HTML and/or XHTML markup that describes a Web page's content includes some combination of elements, attributes, and entities.

This chapter covers the basic form and syntax for elements, attributes, and entities. Parts II and III of the book detail how elements and attributes

- Describe kinds of text (such as paragraphs or tables)
- Create an effect on the page (such as changing a font style)
- Add images and links to a page

Elements

Elements are the building blocks of (X)HTML. You use them to describe every piece of text on your page. Elements are made up of tags and the content within those tags. There are two main types of elements:

- Elements with content made up of a tag pair and whatever content sits between the opening and closing tag in the pair
- Elements that insert something into the page using a single tag

Tag pairs

Elements that describe content use a *tag pair* to mark the beginning and the end of the element. Start and end tag pairs look like this:

```
<tag>...</tag>
```

Content — such as *paragraphs, headings, tables,* and *lists* — always uses a tag pair:

- ✔ The start tag (`<tag>`) tells the browser, "The element begins here."
- ✔ The end tag (`</tag>`) tells the browser, "The element ends here."

The actual content is what occurs between the start tag and end tag. For example, the Red Wine Varietals page in Listing 1-1 uses the paragraph element (`<p>`) to surround the text of a paragraph:

```
<p>Although wines tend to be generically categorized as
   either "white" or "red," in reality, there is a
   collection of wine varietals each with its own
   distinguishing characteristics. The red category
   includes a robust collection of over 20 varietals,
   including:
</p>
```

Single tags

Elements that insert something into the page are called *empty elements* (because they enclose no content) and use just a single tag, like this:

```
<tag />
```

Images and line breaks insert something into the HTML file, so they use one tag.

One key difference between XHTML and HTML is that, in XHTML, all empty elements must end with a slash before the closing greater-than symbol. This is because XHTML is based on XML, and the XML rule is that you close empty elements with a slash, like this:

```
<tag/>
```

However, to make this kind of markup readable inside older browsers, you must insert a space before the closing slash, like this:

```
<tag />
```

This space allows older browsers to ignore the closing slash (since they don't know about XHTML). Newer browsers that understand XHTML ignore the space and interpret the tag exactly as intended, which is `<tag/>` (as per the XML rules).

HTML doesn't require a slash with empty elements, but this markup is deprecated. An HTML empty element looks like this:

```
<tag>
```

Listing 1-1 uses the image element (<img />) to include an image on the page:

```
<img src="red_grapes.jpg" width="75" height="100" alt="Red Grapes"
     align="middle" hspace="5" />
```

The <img /> element references an image. When the browser displays the page, it replaces the <img /> element with the file that it points to (it uses an attribute to do the pointing, which is shown in the next section). Following the XHTML rule introduced earlier, what appears in HTML as <img> appears in XHTML as <img /> (and this applies to all single tag elements).

You can't *make up* HTML or XHTML elements. Elements that are legal in (X)HTML are a very specific set — if you use elements that aren't part of the (X)HTML set, every browser ignores them. The elements you *can* use are defined in the HTML 4.01 or XHTML 1.0 specifications.

Nesting

Many page structures combine nested elements. Think of your nested elements as *suitcases* that fit neatly inside one another.

For example, a bulleted list uses two kinds of elements:

- ✔ The <ul> element specifies that the list is unordered (bulleted).
- ✔ The <li> elements mark each item in the list.

When you combine elements by using this method, be sure you close the inside element completely before you close the outside element:

```
<ul>
  <li>Barbera</li>
  <li>Brunello</li>
</ul>
```

Attributes

Attributes allow variety in how an element describes content or works. Attributes let you use elements differently depending on the circumstances. For example, the <img /> element uses the src attribute to specify the location of the image you want to include at a specific spot on your page:

```
<img src="red_grapes.jpg" width="75" height="100" alt="Red Grapes"
     align="middle" hspace="5" />
```

In this bit of HTML, the `<img />` element itself is a general flag to the browser that you want to include an image; the `src` attribute provides the specifics on the image you want to include — `red_grapes.jpg` in this instance. Other attributes (such as `width`, `height`, `align`, and `hspace`) provide information about how to display the image, and the `alt` attribute provides a text alternative to the image that a text-only browser can display.

Chapter 7 describes the `<img />` element and its attributes in detail.

You include attributes within the start tag of the element you want them with — after the element name but before the ending sign, like this:

```
<tag attribute="value" attribute="value">
```

XML syntax rules decree that attribute values must always appear in quotation marks, but you can include the attributes and their values in any order within the start tag or within a single tag.

Every (X)HTML element has a collection of attributes that can be used with it, and you can't mix and match attributes and elements. Some attributes can take any text as a value because the value could be anything, like the location of an image or a page you want to link to. Others have a specific list of values the attribute can take, such as your options for aligning text in a table cell.

The HTML 4.01 and XHTML 1.0 specifications define exactly which attributes you can use with any given element and which values (if explicitly defined) each attribute can take.

Each chapter in Parts II and III covers which attributes you can use with each (X)HTML element. Also, see Appendix A for complete lists of deprecated (X)HTML tags and attributes.

Entities

Text makes the Web possible, but it has limitations. *Entities* are special characters that you can display on your Web page.

Non-ASCII characters

Basic American Standard Code for Information Interchange (ASCII) text defines a fairly small number of characters. It doesn't include some special characters, such as *trademark symbols, fractions,* and *accented characters.*

For example, the list of white wine varietals in Figure 1-4 includes two accented *e* characters *(é)* and two *u* characters with umlauts *(ü).*

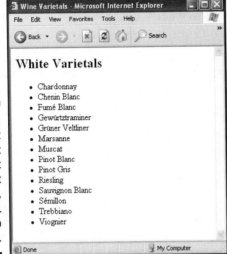

Figure 1-4:
ASCII text
can't
represent
all text
characters,
so HTML
entities do
instead.

ASCII text doesn't include either the accented *e* or the umlauted *u,* so HTML uses *entities* to represent them instead. The browser replaces the entity with the character it references. Each entity begins with an ampersand (&) and ends with a semicolon (;). The following markup shows the entities in bold:

```
<html>
<head>
<title>Wine Varietals</title>
</head>

<body bgcolor="#FFFFFF">
  <h2>White Varietals</h2>
  <ul>
    <li> Chardonnay</li>
    <li>Chenin Blanc</li>
    <li>Fum&eacute; Blanc</li>
    <li>Gew&uuml;rztraminer</li>
    <li>Gr&uuml;ner Veltliner</li>
    <li>Marsanne</li>
    <li>Muscat</li>
    <li>Pinot Blanc</li>
    <li>Pinot Gris</li>
    <li>Reisling</li>
    <li>Sauvignon Blanc</li>
    <li>S&eacute;millon</li>
    <li>Trebbiano</li>
    <li>Viognie</li>
  </ul>
</body>
</html>
```

The entity that represents the *e* with the acute accent is `&eacute;`, and the entity that represents the umlauted *u* is `&uuml;`.

(X)HTML character codes

The encodings for the ISO-Latin-1 character set are supplied by default, and related entities (a pointer to a complete table appears in Table 1-1) can be invoked and used without special contortions. But using the other encodings mentioned in Table 1-1 requires inclusion of special markup to tell the browser it must be ready to interpret Unicode character codes. (Unicode is an international standard — ISO standard 10646, in fact — that embraces enough character codes to handle most unique alphabets, plus plenty of other symbols and nonalphabetic characters as well.) This special markup takes the form `<meta http-equiv="Content-Type" content="text/html; charset=UTF 8">`; when the value for `charset` is changed to `UTF-8`, you can reference the common Unicode code charts shown in Table 1-1.

Table 1-1	Online Pointers to (X)HTML Character Codes
Name	*URL*
Unicode Code Charts	`www.unicode.org/charts/`
ISO-Latin-1 character set	`www.htmlhelp.com/reference/charset/`
Greek characters	`www.unicode.org/charts/PDF/U0370.pdf`
Currency symbols	`www.unicode.org/charts/PDF/U20A0.pdf`
Miscellaneous symbols	`www.unicode.org/charts/PDF/U2600.pdf`
Arrow characters	`www.unicode.org/charts/PDF/U27F0.pdf` `www.unicode.org/charts/PDF/U2900.pdf`
Mathematical characters	Search **math** at `www.unicode.org/charts/` (there are six different, relevant code charts)
General punctuation	`www.unicode.org/charts/PDF/U2000.pdf`

Tag characters

HTML-savvy software assumes that some HTML characters, such as the greater-than and less-than signs, are meant to be hidden and not displayed on your finished Web page. The following entities display characters that normally are part of the hidden HTML markup:

- **less-than sign** (<): `&lt;`
- **greater-than sign** (>): `&gt;`
- **ampersand** (&): `&amp;`

The 〈 and 〉 signs are used in markup, but these symbols are *instructions to the browser* and won't show up on the page. If you need these symbols on the Web page, include the entities for them in your markup, like this:

```
<p>The paragraph element identifies some text as a paragraph:</p>
<p>&lt;p&gt;This is a paragraph.&lt;/p&gt;</p>
```

In the preceding markup, the first line uses *tags* to describe a paragraph, and the second line shows how *entities* describe the 〈 and 〉 symbols.

Figure 1-5 shows these entities as characters in a browser window.

Figure 1-5:
Entities let
〈, 〉, or &
symbols
appear in a
browser
window.

Parts Is Parts: What Web Pages Are Made Of

Comments include text in (X)HTML files that isn't displayed in the final page. Each comment is identified with two special sequences of markup characters:

✔ Begin each comment with the string 〈!--
✔ End each comment with the string -->

In the following code, comments explain how each markup element functions and where it fits into the HTML markup hierarchy.

Elements are organized into a structure:

✔ Some elements can occur only inside other elements.
✔ Some elements are required for a well-structured (X)HTML document.

```
<html> <!-- This tag should always occur at or near the beginning of any
          well-formed HTML document -->
<head> <!-- The head element supplies information to label the whole HTML
          document -->
<title>Wine Varietals</title> <!-- The text in the title element appears
          in the title bar of the browser window when the page is
          viewed -->
</head> <!-- closes the head element -->

<body bgcolor="#FFFFFF"> <!-- The content that appears on any Web page
          appears or is invoked from inside the body element -->
  <h2>White Varietals</h2> <!-- heading elements start with the letter h
          followed by a number from 1 to 6 to indicate hierarchy. This
          is a level 2 heading, h2. -->
  <ul> <!-- This is an unordered list element, ul, which produces a
          bulleted list of list items, li -->
    <li> Chardonnay</li>  <!-- A whole bunch of individual list items -->
    <li>Chenin Blanc</li>
    <li>Fum&eacute; Blanc</li>
    <li>Gew&uuml;rztraminer</li>
    <li>Gr&uuml;ner Veltliner</li>
    <li>Marsanne</li>
    <li>Muscat</li>
    <li>Pinot Blanc</li>
    <li>Pinot Gris</li>
    <li>Reisling</li>
    <li>Sauvignon Blanc</li>
    <li>S&eacute;millon</li>
    <li>Trebbiano</li>
    <li>Viognie</li>
  </ul> <!-- End of the unordered/bulleted list -->
</body>  <!-- End of the body section -->
</html>  <!-- End of the HTML document -->
```

The preceding document is broken into a head and a body. Within each section, certain kinds of elements appear. Many combinations are possible, and that's what you see throughout this book!

Organizing HTML text

Beyond the division into head and body sections, text can be organized in plenty of ways in HTML documents.

Document heads

Inside the head section, you can define all kinds of labels and information besides a title, primarily to describe the document that follows, such as the character sets used, scripts to be invoked, and style information. The body section is where real content lives and most (X)HTML elements appear.

Document headings

Headings (denoted using elements h1 through h6) are different from the HTML document head. Individual headings structure the text that follows them, whereas the head identifies or describes the whole document.

In the Wine Varietals example, the h2 element titles a list of grape varieties.

Paragraphs and more

When you want running text on a Web page, the paragraph element, p (which includes the `<p>` and `</p>` tags), breaks text into paragraphs. You can also

- ✔ Force line breaks by using the break element `<br />`.
- ✔ Create horizontal rules (lines) by using the `<hr />` element.

HTML also includes all kinds of ways to emphasize or identify text inside paragraphs; Parts II and III of this book show them.

Lists

HTML permits easy definition of unordered or bulleted lists. Various mechanisms to create other kinds of lists, including numbered lists, are also available. Lists can be nested within lists to create as many levels of hierarchy as your list might need (perhaps when outlining a complex subject or modeling a table of contents with several heading levels you want to represent). Chapter 5 covers creating lists in more detail.

Tables

HTML includes markup for defining tables. Chapter 11 covers tables. Structure is part of how markup works, so within the definition of a table, you can

- ✔ Distinguish between column heads and table data
- ✔ Manage how rows and columns are laid out

Images in HTML documents

Adding an image to any HTML document is easy. Careful and well-planned use of images adds a lot to Web pages. Chapter 7 shows how to grab images from files. Chapter 9 shows how to use complex markup to position and flow text around graphics. You also discover how to select and use interesting and compelling images to add interest and information to your Web pages.

Links and navigation tools

A Web page's structure should help visitors find their way around collections of Web pages, look for (and hopefully, find) items of interest, and get where they most want to go quickly and easily. Links provide the mechanism to bring people into your Web pages, so Chapter 6 shows how to

✔ Reference external items or resources

✔ Jump from one page to the next

✔ Jump around inside a page

✔ Add structure and organization to your pages

The importance of structure and organization goes up as the amount of information that you want to present to your visitors goes up.

Navigation tools, (which establish standard mechanisms and tools for moving around inside a Web site) provide ways to create and present your Web page (and site) structure to visitors and mechanisms for users to grab and use organized menus of choices

When you add everything up, your result should be a well-organized set of information and images that's easy to understand, use, and navigate.

Chapter 2

Creating and Viewing a Web Page

Creating your very own Web page can seem a little daunting, but it's definitely fun, and our experience tells us that the best way to get started is to jump right in with both feet. You might splash around a bit at first, but you can keep your head above water without too much thrashing.

This chapter walks you through four simple steps to creating a Web page. We don't stop and explain every nuance of the markup you use — we save that for other chapters. Instead, we want to make you comfortable working with markup and content to create and view a Web page.

Before You Get Started

Creating HTML documents differs from creating word-processor documents in an application like Microsoft Word because you use two applications:

✔ You create the Web pages in your text or HTML editor.

✔ You view the results in your Web browser.

Even though many HTML editors, such as Dreamweaver and HTML-Kit, provide a browser preview, it's still important to preview your Web pages inside actual Web browsers, such as Internet Explorer and Firefox, so you can see them as your end users will. It's a bit unwieldy to edit in one application and switch to another to look at your work, but you'll be switching like a pro from text editor to browser and back in (almost) no time.

To get started on your first Web page, you need two types of software:

> ✔ **A text editor such as Notepad, TextPad, or SimpleText**
>
> Notepad is the native text editor in Windows. TextPad is a shareware text editor available from `www.textpad.com`. (TextPad is used to create most of the figures in this chapter.) SimpleText is the native text editor in the Macintosh operating system.
>
> ✔ **A Web browser**

We discuss these basic tools in more detail in Chapter 20. We recommend that you whip out your good ol' text editor to make your first page. Here are a couple of reasons why:

> ✔ An advanced HTML editor, such as FrontPage or Dreamweaver, often *hides* your HTML from you. For your first page, you want to see your HTML in all of its (limited) glory.
>
> You can make a smooth transition to a more advanced editor after you're a little more familiar with HTML markup, syntax, and document structure.
>
> ✔ *Word processors* (such as Microsoft Word) usually store a lot of extra file information behind the scenes (for example, formatting instructions to display or print files). You can't see or change the extra information, but it interferes with your HTML.

Creating a Page from Scratch

Using HTML to create a Web page from scratch involves four straightforward steps:

1. **Plan your page design.**
2. **Combine HTML and text in a text editor to make that design a reality.**
3. **Save your page.**
4. **View your page in a Web browser.**

So break out your text editor and Web browser and roll up your sleeves.

Step 1: Planning a simple design

We've discovered that a few minutes spent planning your general approach to a page at the outset of work makes the page-creation process much easier.

You don't have to create a complicated diagram or elaborate graphical display in this step. Just jot down some ideas for *what you want on the page* and *how you want it arranged*.

You don't even have to be at your desk to plan your simple design. Take a notepad and pencil outside and design in the sun, or scribble on a napkin while you're having lunch. Remember, this is supposed to be fun.

The example in this chapter is our take on the traditional "Hello World" exercise used in just about every existing programming language. That is, the first thing you learn when tackling a new programming language is how to display the phrase Hello World on-screen. In our example, we create a short letter to the world instead, so the page is a bit more substantial and gives you more text to work with. Figure 2-1 shows our basic design for this page.

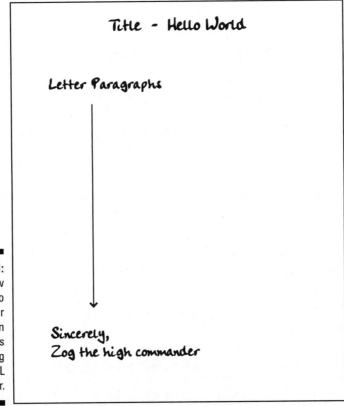

Figure 2-1:
Taking a few minutes to sketch your page design makes writing HTML easier.

The basic design for the page includes four basic components:

- ✔ A serviceable title: "Hello World"
- ✔ A few paragraphs explaining how the page's author plans to help the Earth meet its yearly quota of Znufengerbs
- ✔ A closing of "Sincerely"
- ✔ A signature

Jot down some notes about the color scheme you want to use on the page. For effect, we decided that our example page should have a black background and white text, and the title should be "Greetings From Your Future Znufengerb Minister."

When you know what kind of information you want on the page, you can move on to Step 2 — writing the markup.

Step 2: Writing some HTML

You have a couple of different options when you're ready to create your HTML. In the end, you'll probably use some combination of these:

- ✔ If you already have some text that you just want to describe with HTML, save that text as a plain-text file and add HTML markup around it.
- ✔ Start creating markup and add the content as you go.

Our example in this chapter starts with some text in Word document format. We saved the content as a text file, opened the text file in our text editor, and added markup around the text.

To save a Word file as a text document, choose File↷Save As. In the dialog box that appears, choose Text Only (*.txt) from the Save As Type drop-down list.

Figure 2-2 shows how our draft letter appears in Microsoft Word before we convert it to text for our page.

Listing 2-1:   The Complete HTML Page for the Zog Letter

```
<!DOCTYPE html PUBLIC "-//W3C//DTD XHTML 1.0 Transitional//EN"
        "http://www.w3.org/TR/xhtml1/DTD/xhtml1-transitional.dtd">
<html xmlns="http://www.w3.org/1999/xhtml">

  <head>
    <title>Greetings From Your Future Znufengerb Minister</title>
  </head>
```

```
<body bgcolor="black" text="white">

<h1>Hello World</h1>

<p>It has come to our attention that Earth has fallen well short of
    producing its yearly quota of Znufengerbs. To help you improve your
    production and establish a plentiful Znufengerb colony, I, Zog, the
    Minister of Agriculture of Grustland, will be arriving on your planet
    within the week along with my herd experts to take command of your
    Znufengerb enterprise.
</p>

<p>Do not fear, I have the highest expectations for a smooth transition
    from your current production of the creatures you call cows to our beloved
    Znufengerbs. The future of the galaxy hinges on Earth's ability to meet
    its Znufengerb quota, and I will do all in my power to make you the most
    productive source of Znufengerbs in the universe.
</p>

<p>I have studied your history extensively and feel that I am the best
    candidate for the position of Znufengerb Minister. I look forward to
    placing a Znufengerb in every home to bring you joy.
</p>

<p>Sincerely,<br />
    Zog, Minister of Agriculture
</p>

</body>
</html>
```

The complete HTML page looks like Listing 2-1.

The HTML markup includes a collection of markup elements and attributes that describe the letter's contents:

✔ The `<html>` element defines the document as an HTML document.

✔ The `<head>` element creates a header section for the document.

✔ The `<title>` element defines a document title that is displayed in the browser's title bar.

    The `<title>` element is *inside* the `<head>` element.

✔ The `<body>` element holds the text that appears in the browser window.

    The `bgcolor` and `text` attributes work with the `<body>` element. These attributes set the background color to black and the text color to white. (These attributes are deprecated, but really easy to use. Chapters 8 and 9 how to achieve the same effects by using CSS, which is the recommended method.)

✔ The `<h1>` element marks the `Hello World` text as a first-level heading.

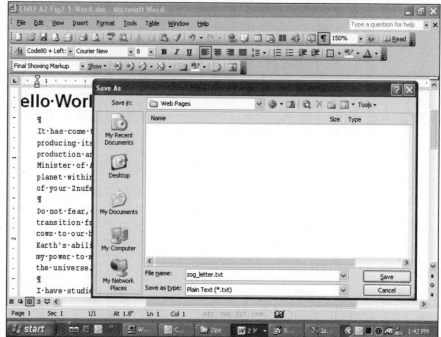

Figure 2-2:
The letter
that is the
text for our
page in
word-
processing
form.

✔ The <p> elements identify each paragraph of the document.

✔ The <br /> element adds a manual line break after Sincerely.

Don't worry about the ins and outs of how all these elements work. They are covered in detail in Chapters 4 and 5.

After you create a complete HTML page (or the first chunk of it that you want to review), you must save it before you can see your work in a browser.

Step 3: Saving your page

You use a text editor to create your HTML documents and a Web browser to view them, but before you can let your browser loose on your HTML page, you have to save that page. When you're just building a page, you should save a copy of it to your local hard drive and view it locally with your browser.

Choosing a location and name for your file

When you save your file to your hard drive, keep the following in mind:

✔ You need to be able to find it again.

Create a folder on your hard drive especially for your Web pages. Call it Web Pages or HTML (or any other name that makes sense to you), and be sure you put it somewhere easy to find.

✔ The name should make sense to you so you can identify file contents without actually opening the file.

✔ The name should work well in a Web browser.

Don't use spaces in the name. Some operating systems — most notably Unix and Linux (the most popular Web-hosting operating systems around) — don't tolerate spaces in filenames.

In our example, we saved our file in a folder called Web Pages and named it (drum roll, please) zog_letter.html, as shown in Figure 2-3.

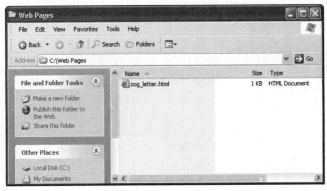

Figure 2-3:
Use a handy location and a logical filename for HTML pages.

.htm or .html

You can actually choose from one of two suffixes for your pages: .html or .htm. (Our example filename, zog_letter.html, uses the .html suffix.)

The shorter .htm is a relic from the 8.3 DOS days when filenames could only have eight characters followed by a three-character suffix that described the file's type. Today, operating systems can support long filenames and suffixes that are more than three letters long, so we suggest you stick with .html.

Web servers and Web browsers handle both .htm and .html equally well.

Stick with one filename option. .html and .htm files are treated the same by browsers and servers, but they're different suffixes, so they create different filenames. (The name zog_letter.html is different from zog_letter.htm.) This matters when you create *hyperlinks* (covered in Chapter 6).

Step 4: Viewing your page

After you save a copy of your page, you're ready to view it in a Web browser. Follow these steps to view your Web page in Internet Explorer. (Steps may be different if you're using a different browser.)

1. **If you haven't opened your browser, do that now.**

2. **Choose File⇨Open and click the Browse button.**

3. **Navigate your file system until you find your HTML file, and then select it so it appears in the File name area.**

   Figure 2-4 shows a highlighted HTML file, ready to be opened.

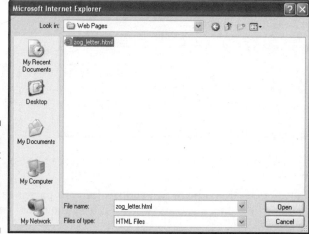

Figure 2-4: Use Internet Explorer to navigate to your Web pages.

4. **Click the Open button, and then click OK.**

   The page appears in your Web browser in all its glory, as shown in Figure 2-5.

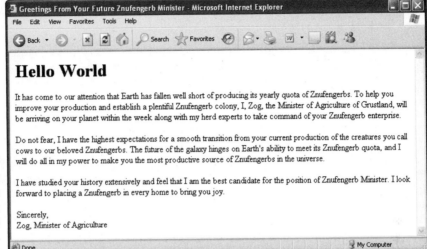

Figure 2-5:
Viewing a
local file in
your Web
browser.

You aren't actually viewing this file on the Web yet; you're just viewing a *copy* of it saved on your local hard drive. You can't give anyone the URL for this file yet, but you can edit and view the changes you make.

Editing an Existing Web Page

Chances are you'll want to change one thing (at least) about your page after you view it in a Web browser for the first time. After all, you can't really see how the page is going to look when you're creating the markup, and you might decide that a first-level heading is too big or that you really *want* purple text on a green background.

To make changes to the Web page you've created in a text editor and are viewing in a browser, repeat these steps until you're happy with the final appearance of your page:

1. **Leave the browser window with the HTML page display open and go back to the text editor.**

2. **If the HTML page isn't open in the text editor, open it.**

   You should have the same file open in both the browser and the text editor, as shown in Figure 2-6.

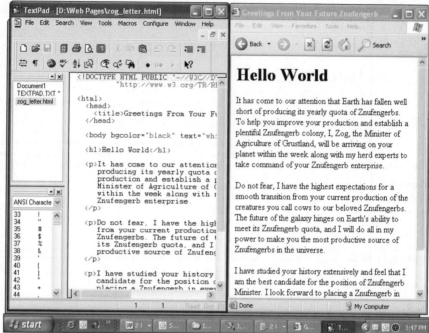

Figure 2-6:
Viewing an
HTML file in
your text
editor and
Web
browser at
the same
time.

3. **Make your changes to the HTML and its content in the text editor.**

4. **Save the changes.**

   This is an important step. If you don't save your changes, you won't see them in the Web browser.

5. **Move back to the Web browser and click the Refresh button.**

If you keep the HTML file open in both the text editor and the browser while you work, checking changes is a breeze. You can quickly save a change in the editor, flip to the browser and refresh, flip back to the editor to make more changes, flip back to the browser and refresh, and so on.

In our example letter, we decided after our initial draft of the HTML page that we should add a date to the letter. Figure 2-7 shows the change we made to the HTML to add the date and the resulting display in the Web browser.

This approach to editing an HTML page applies only to pages saved *on your local hard drive*. If you want to edit a page that you have already stored on a Web server, you have to save a copy of the page to your hard drive, edit it, verify your changes, and then upload the file again to the server, as discussed in the following section.

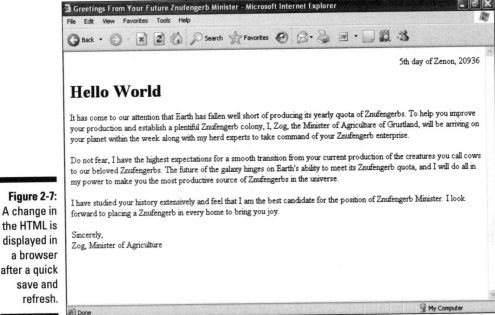

Figure 2-7:
A change in
the HTML is
displayed in
a browser
after a quick
save and
refresh.

Posting Your Page Online

After you're happy with your Web page, it's time to put it online. Chapter 3 includes a detailed discussion of what you need to do to put your page online, but to sum it up in a few quick steps:

1. **Find a Web hosting provider to hold your Web pages.**

   Your Web host might be a company Web server or space that you pay an Internet service provider (ISP) for. If you don't have a host yet, double-check with the ISP you use for Internet access — find out whether you get some Web-server space along with your access. Regardless of where you find space, get details from the provider on where to move your site's files and what your URL will be.

2. **Use an FTP client or a Web browser to make a connection to your Web server.**

   Use the username and password, as specified in the information from your hosting provider, to open an FTP session on the Web server.

3. **Copy the HTML file from your hard drive to the Web server.**

4. **Use your Web browser to view the file via the Internet.**

For example, to host our letter online at `ftp.io.com/~natanya`, we used Internet Explorer to access the site and provided the appropriate name and password, which you get from your ISP. A collection of folders and files appeared.

We copied the file to the server with a simple drag-and-drop operation from Windows Explorer to Internet Explorer.

The URL for this page is `http://www.io.com/~natanya/zog_letter.html`, and the page is now served from the Web browser instead of from a local file system, as shown in Figure 2-8.

Figure 2-8: A file on a Web server is available to anyone with an Internet connection.

Chapter 3 has details on how to serve your Web pages to the world.

Chapter 3

Proper Planning Prevents Poor Page Performance

The overall design of your site is the *user interface* (UI). When you design a good UI, you give users the tools to move through your site with minimum fuss. This chapter outlines standard Web site design principles for your HTML. These principles can ensure a usable and effective UI.

The UI is the mechanism that gives a user access to the information on your Web site. Each UI is unique, but they're all made from the same components *(text, graphics,* and *media files),* and they're all held together with HTML.

Visitors probably won't return to your site if it

✔ Is hard to navigate

✔ Is cluttered with flashing text and rampant colors

✔ Doesn't help people find what they're looking for

You've created a solid UI if

✔ Your site's navigation is intuitive.

✔ Images and media accent your design without overpowering it.

✔ You do all you can to help people find the information they want.

This chapter walks you through simple steps to design a Web site and your basic Web page. (Other chapters explain every nuance of the markup.)

Planning Your Site

An important first step in creating an effective UI for your site doesn't have anything to do with markup, but has everything to do with planning. Before your site grows too large (or before you even build your site if you haven't started yet), carefully identify your site's exact purpose and goals. When you know your site's scope and goals, you can better create an interface that embodies them.

Before designing your site, ask yourself these questions:

✔ Why are you creating this site?

✔ What do you want to convey to users?

✔ Who is your target audience? For example,

   • What's the average age of your users?

   • How well does your audience work with the Internet?

✔ How many pages do you need in your site?

✔ What type of hierarchy will you use to organize your pages? For example, you can create your site so users go through it linearly, or you can allow them to jump around from topic to topic.

Design matters

This chapter recommends good design principles, but it's up to you to choose color schemes and the overall look and feel. What looks great to one person may be ugly to someone else.

If you're building a site for your business, that site can provide the first impression for potential customers or clients. The site should reflect your business style. If you run an architecture firm, for example, strong lines and a clean look may be the best way to present your company image. If you run a flower shop, your site may be a bit more organic and decorated (okay, *flowery*) to remind visitors of what they can expect if they walk into your store.

If you're new to Web design or graphics and you need a site that marks your business presence on the Web, consider getting help from a Web-design professional. Use images, layouts, and navigational aids they create to build and manage the site yourself. Once established, the distinctive and consistent look and feel of your site is easy to maintain.

Regardless of who designs your site, take the time to get a critique of it from peers, friends, family members, and anyone else who is willing to be honest about how good (and even how bad) it looks. A negative-but-constructive critique from someone who knows and respects you beats a "Gee, that's ugly" from someone whose business you are trying to acquire.

If you can answer these questions, you can better understand your site's goals and needs. For example, an online store may have these goals:

- Let visitors browse an online catalog and put items in a shopping cart.
- Provide visitors a way to purchase the items in their cart online.
- Help users make smart purchasing decisions.
- Ease merchandise returns and exchanges.
- Solicit feedback from users about products they want to see in the catalog or ways to make the site better.

This short list of goals also indicates the areas your site may include and the activities your site needs to support.

Instead of having just a single area (such as a product catalog), your site might need some specialized areas, such as

- Online catalog and shopping cart
- Buying guides or other information that can help users make better purchasing decisions
- A help-and-feedback section
- A set of tools to expedite returns and exchanges

When you establish the goals for your site, you can identify the elements best suited for the site, such as

- A navigation system that identifies the major areas of the site, which helps users
  - Quickly identify what part they're in
  - Move from one part of the site to others without getting lost
- A set of standard design elements, such as buttons, page-title styles, and color specifications, to keep the users oriented as they move from page to page in the same site
- A standard display for items in the catalog, including product-related information, such as product images and descriptions, prices, and availability information
- Well-designed forms that help users find products in the catalog, purchase the items in their shopping carts, request a refund or help returning an item, and submit comments to the site
- Long text pages that offer extensive information on purchasing options, product returns, and other helpful information — but that are still easy to read and to navigate

Your site's goals should dictate your site's

✔ **UI elements**

When you add to an existing site, identify UI elements that

- Meet the goals of the new section of the site
- Complement the overall site UI design

✔ **Design**

✔ **Organization**

Mapping your site

It's easier to get where you're going if you know how to get there. Mapping your Web site can be a vital step in planning — and later running — the site. This process involves two creative phases:

✔ **Creating a visual guide on paper or electronically that you can use to guide the development of your site**

✔ **Creating a visual guide on your Web site to help visitors find their way around**

Both have their place in good UI design, so each gets its own section.

Using a map for site development

When you use a site map during the development of a Web site — even a Web site that includes only a few pages — you can identify

✔ Pages that you need to build

✔ How pages relate to each other

✔ Navigation elements that you need

As a bonus, a map provides you with a *checklist* of pages.

For example, Figure 3-1 shows part of the visual map of the Citrixxperience Web site (`www.citrixxperience.com/map.htm`).

This map shows that the site has several main sections. Three of those sections — home, practice exams, and study materials — are each further divided into subsections. Each subsection page lists information and links that are pertinent to that particular subsection.

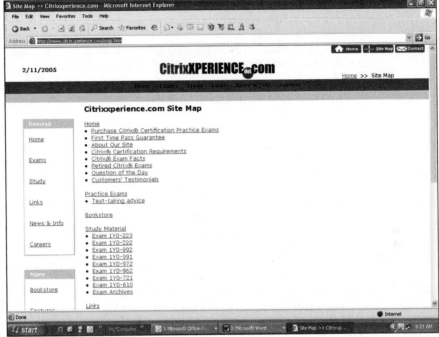

Figure 3-1:
The site
map for the
Citrixxperi-
ence Web
site.

Building the site one piece at a time

If you plan to build your Web site a page or section at a time, you can create a map of the final site and then decide which pages it makes the most sense to build first. When you have a good working idea of how your site will expand, you can plan for it during each stage. For example, suppose you create a site map for you company's Web site, and the site needs a Frequently Asked Questions section. If that section isn't quite finished when the site launches, disaster need not ensue — provided someone planned ahead to accommodate new sections and built that capability into the site. Just leave out links to that section of the site when you launch it.

When the book examples section is ready, you

  ✔ Add the section to the site.

  ✔ Add a link to the main navigation elements.

If you know the resources are coming, you can create a navigation scheme that easily accommodates the book examples section when it's ready to add. Without a site map and a complete plan for the site, however, integrating new sections can suck up lots of time and effort.

Don't create *under construction* sections that don't include much of anything except the hint that something will appear someday. Users are disappointed if your site merely hints at information it doesn't really offer. Instead, consider using a small section of your home page to highlight "coming soon" items so visitors know new information will be available later on.

Using a map as a visual guide for your users

A site map can be a supplemental navigational tool that gives users a different way to find what they're looking for. A site map lays out all contents of your site so visitors can see all their options at once.

People have many approaches to finding information. Give visitors as many options as you can (realistically) for navigating your site:

- Some people like to be led.
- Some people like to rummage around.
- Some people like to see every possible option and choose one.

Site maps grow as your site grows. If your site is large and complex, your map may take several screens to display. When you surf the Web, massive sites such as `Microsoft.com`, `HP.com`, and `Amazon.com` don't offer site maps because maps of their sites would be huge and unwieldy. But smaller Web sites (such as `Symantec.com`) use site maps effectively.

You must decide whether a site map is a good navigation tool for your site. Here are some points to ponder as you make this decision:

- A site map may be *unnecessary* if you have only a few pages.
- A site map may be the *best* choice if
  - Your site has several sections.
  - You can't think of other ways to access your content.

Building solid navigation

The navigation you use on your site can make or break it. If visitors can't find what they're looking for on your site, they'll probably leave and never come back. The type of navigation you use on your site depends on

- **How many pages are on your site**

  If you have only a few pages, your navigation might be a simple collection of links on the home page that helps users jump to each page.

✔ **How you organize your pages**

If your site has many pages organized into different sections, your home page might link only to those sections (not to each page).

For example, the `Dummies.com` site houses a large collection of pages organized as a variety of sections; it would be impractical to link to all the pages in any navigation scheme. Also, the site includes articles on a wide variety of topics, as well as book information. The site could be organized into books and articles, but visitors are more likely to look for information on a specific subject, so the site is organized by topic. The home page, shown in Figure 3-2, prominently displays these different topic areas on the left.

Figure 3-2: The Dummies.com site is organized by topic.

When you click one of these topic areas, the remaining topic areas are available in a navigation bar across the top of the page (as shown in Figure 3-3). You don't have to return to the home page to jump from topic to topic.

Figure 3-3 shows that each topic has its own sub-navigation area (at left, echoing the layout of the home page) that lists subtopics within the topic. The links are different, but the general navigation scheme is consistent throughout the site. That tells visitors what to expect as they move around the site.

The topmost navigation area of each page includes a regular collection of links that appears on every page of the site to help visitors quickly access important areas from anywhere: a site search, help, account information, and a shopping cart. Every page has the same set of links to information on the *For Dummies* Web site, the form to register for eTips, how to contact the publisher, the site copyright statement, and the site privacy policy. Like the shopping cart and help links, these links must be on every page, but need not be displayed prominently. Adding them to a consistent site footer keeps them accessible to visitors without obscuring key content for any given topic or subtopic.

If you create a map to aid site development, it can also help you choose what kind of navigational tools to create for your site. Consider each page on the map in turn; list the links that each page must include. Normally, a pattern emerges that can help you identify the main navigation tools your site needs (such as links to all main topic areas and copyright information, as on the *For Dummies* site), as well as sub-navigation tools (such as links to subtopics on the topic pages).

After you know what tools you need, you can begin to design a visual scheme for your UI. Do you want to use buttons across the top, buttons down the side, or both? Do you need a footer that links to copyright or privacy information?

If you have sections within sections within sections, how can you best help people navigate through them? Answering questions like these is the route to a solid navigation system that helps users find their way around your site — letting them focus on what they came for, not on how to get there.

Whatever navigation scheme you devise, always give your visitors a way to get back to your home page from wherever they are on the site. Your site's home page is the gateway to the rest of the site. If visitors get lost or want to start again, make sure they can get back to Square One with no trouble.

After you design your site's navigation scheme and put together a few pages, ask someone who isn't familiar with your site to try to use it. To help them with their testing, give them a list of three or four tasks you'd like them to complete — pages to visit or a form to fill out, for example. If your test visitor gets lost or has lots of questions about how to navigate the site, you should rework your scheme. Your reviewer might also have suggestions on ways to make navigation features clearer and easier to use. You might know your site and its content *too well* to spot gaps in navigation that a first-time user will probably discover immediately.

Planning outside links

The Web wouldn't be the Web without hyperlinks — after all, hyperlinks connect your site to the rest of the Web and turn a collection of pages into a cohesive site. But overusing or misusing links can detract from your site and even lose you some business.

Choose your off-site links wisely

Internal linking is almost a walk in the park compared to external linking — after all, when you link to pages on your own site, the pages those links point to are *under your control.* You know what's on them today and what will be on them tomorrow, and even whether they will exist tomorrow. When you link to resources on someone else's site, however, all bets are off:

✔ You don't maintain those pages.

✔ You can't modify their content.

✔ You certainly won't know when they will disappear.

Neither will your visitors — until they slam into a `404 File or directory not found` message (the usual sign of a *broken link* that now goes nowhere). The text in 404 messages varies depending on the server hosting the Web site.

Links to other sites are more useful when they're stable and have less chance of breaking. We recommend these guidelines:

✔ **Link to a section of a site, not to a specific page on the site.**

Pages come and go, but the general organization usually stays the same.

✔ **Link to corporate Web sites.**

Corporate sites have more staying power than sites maintained by an individual.

✔ **Don't link directly to media files such as PDFs and images.**

If you want to link to resources on another Web site, link to the Web page that links to the resources instead of the actual media files. Sites often update the resources and give them new names. The page that links to the resource, however, is almost always certain to be updated to reflect new names. Therefore, the page is a safer linking bet.

Linking to other sites *implies your support or endorsement of those sites.* When visitors follow links from your site to other sites, they assume you approve of that new site. That makes a couple of guidelines necessary:

✔ **If you don't want to be associated with content on another site, don't link to the site.**

The only way to find out whether you approve of a seemingly relevant site is to visit it and check it out *before* you link.

✔ **Periodically review your links.** Be sure that

- The sites' owners are the same.

- The content is appropriate.

When domain names expire, new owners may take them over and post new content that's either

- Completely irrelevant

- Damaging to your image, such as with pornography

Craft useful link text

The text you associate with links is as important as the links you use on your site. That text gives users a hint about where the link takes them so they can decide whether to go along for the ride. For example, `Visit Dummies.com to read more about this book` is more helpful than `Read more about this book`.

The first example tells visitors that they're going to leave the current site to visit `Dummies.com` and read more about a book there. The second just tells them they're going to read more about the book — and they may be surprised to find themselves flung off one site and onto another.

Generally, when you create link text, let users know the following:

- **Whether they're leaving your site**
- **What kind of information the page they're linking to contains**
- **How the linked site relates to the current content or page**

The goal of your link text should be to inform users and build their trust. If your link text doesn't give them solid clues about what to expect from your links, they just won't trust your links — and won't follow them.

Avoid the use of *click here* in any link you create. If your link text is well-crafted, you don't need the extra words to prompt the user to click a link. The link text should speak for itself.

Hosting Your Web Site

The first (and most important) step in putting your pages online is finding someplace on the Web to put them on display — a host. In general, you have two choices for hosting your pages:

- Host them yourself.
- Pay someone else to host them.

The word *host* is used in the Web industry to mean a Web server set up to hold Web pages (and related files) so they can be accessed by the rest of the world. This chapter uses *host* as both

- **Noun:** The physical machine that holds the Web pages
- **Verb:** The act of serving up the Web pages

You need to decide whether to host your own pages or to pay someone else a fee to host them for you. This chapter shows both approaches to hosting — and gives you the skinny on each. You can decide which option is best for you.

You aren't stuck with your hosting decision for life. If you find hosting your own pages overwhelming, you can move your files to a service provider (or vice versa). To decide which hosting option is best for you, consider your needs for the next year, but plan to review your needs in a few months.

Hosting your own Web site

This section illustrates an average-sized site (up to about 100 pages) that doesn't include more than a couple of multimedia files and doesn't have any special security or electronic commerce (e-commerce) applications.

If you need to run a complex site, such as a large corporate site or an online store, you need more expertise, equipment, and software than this section outlines. The following resources can help:

- Books such as *E-Commerce For Dummies* and *Webmastering For Dummies,* 2nd Edition (both from Wiley Publishing) can get you started setting up e-commerce and other complex sites.
- Consult a Web professional who has practical experience building and maintaining complex Web sites.

You can set up your own Web server and host your Web pages yourself. To do this, you need:

- **A computer designated as your Web server:** Web servers are often *dedicated* to this task, leaving word-processing and other activities to a different computer.

- **Web-server software:** Common Web-server software packages include Apache and Microsoft's Internet Information Server (IIS), called Internet Information Services in Windows 2000 and later.

   In the Web world, the term *Web server* refers to both

   - A dedicated computer (the actual hardware)

   - Web-server software

   You can't use one without the other.

- **A dedicated Internet connection:** Your Web server isn't useful or reliable if it's connected to the Internet only when you fire up a dialup connection.

If hosting a Web site yourself sounds a little complicated and expensive, you're right. Not only do you have to pay for the equipment and dedicated Internet connection, but you also must know how to set up and administer a Web server and keep all the pieces working 24/7. Consider using a hosting provider.

Using a hosting provider

A hosting provider manages all the technical aspects of Web hosting, from hardware to software to Internet connections. You just manage your HTML pages. Back when the Web was young, hosting provider options were scarce, and what *was* available was expensive. The times have changed, and needs have grown, so reasonably priced hosting providers are abundant these days.

If you decide to let someone else host your pages, you have two choices for how much you pay:

- ✔ **Nothing:** Some services actually host your pages for free. That's it; you pay zip, zero, nada to get your pages on the Web. What's the catch? You must pay in other ways, usually with advertising attached to your page.

- ✔ **Something:** Most Web-hosting services, however, charge you a fee, from a few dollars a month to triple digits a month. The trick to making the most of your hosting funds is to find just the right hosting service to meet your Web site needs.

Read more about inexpensive Web hosting options in the Webmonkey article "Web Hosting for Under Ten Bucks."

```
http://webmonkey.wired.com/webmonkey/02/01/index4a.html?tw=design
```

Getting your own domain

A *domain name* is the high-level address for any given Web site. Examples of domain names are `microsoft.com`, `apple.com`, `w3c.org`, and `dummies.com`.

You might want your own domain name (hence your own domain) that reflects your business name (or even your personality). If you don't get a domain name of your own, your pages will be part of someone else's domain name — usually your hosting provider's domain name. For example, a personal Web site hosted without a domain name at `io.com` has a top-level URL of

```
http://www.io.com/~lanw
```

With a domain name of `lanw.com`, the same Web site would be hosted at

```
http://www.lanw.com
```

One's easier to remember than the other. Is that a good enough reason to have your own domain? Maybe . . . maybe not. The bottom line is that businesses or other entities that want to maintain a constant Web presence should probably invest in a domain name; hobbyists or enthusiasts don't need one.

Any good hosting provider can give you detailed instructions on how to register a domain name in the provider's system or attach your domain name to your Web site on its computers. If you're changing from one hosting provider to another, your new provider should help you transfer your domain. Most providers either give you this information up front or have online help that will walk you through it. If it isn't immediately clear how to set up your domain, ask for help. If you don't get it, change providers.

Moving files to your Web server

After you secure a Web site host or decide to put up your own Web server, you need a way to move the HTML pages you create on your local computer to the Web server. This isn't a one-time activity either. As you maintain your Web site, you need to move files you've built on your local computer to the Web server to refresh your site.

How you move files to your Web server depends entirely on how your Web server is set up. Normally, you have a couple of transfer options:

- **The File Transfer Protocol (FTP)**
- **A Web interface, provided by your hosting provider, for moving and managing files**

UI design resources

We recommend these Web sites and books on site and interface design if you want to create great UIs:

- For a crash course on Web design basics, read "Design Basics" from Webmonkey at

      http://hotwired.lycos.com/webmonkey/
                html/97/05/index2a.html

  Webmonkey's "Site Redesign Tutorial" offers an interesting perspective on what it takes to rework a site's design. Read it at

      http://hotwired.lycos.com/webmonkey/
                design/site_building/
                tutorials/tutorial4.html

- Jakob Nielsen is committed to creating accessible Web content. His Web site, http://useit.com, is chock-full of resources and articles on creating accessible sites.

- Hey, negative examples are useful too. Web Pages That Suck guides you to good design by evaluating bad design. Be sure your site doesn't look like any of those featured at www.webpagesthatsuck.com.

- *Web Design For Dummies,* by Lisa Lopuck (Wiley), is another step in the direction of a sophisticated Web site with a knockout look.

- *Web Usability For Dummies,* by Richard Mander and Bud Smith (Wiley), can help you fine-tune your site to make it amazingly easy to use, which is a great help in keeping your visitors coming back for more.

Via FTP

Of these two options, FTP is almost always a possibility. FTP is the standard for transferring files on the Internet, and any hosting provider should give you FTP access to your Web server. When you set up your Web site with your hosting provider, the provider usually gives you written documentation (either on paper or on the Web) that tells you exactly how to transfer files to your Web server. Included in that information is an FTP URL that usually takes the form `ftp://ftp.domain.com`.

You can use an FTP client such as WS_FTP (`www.ipswitch.com/Products/WS_FTP/`) or CuteFTP (`www.globalscape.com/products/cuteftp/index.asp`) to open a connection to this URL. Your provider will give you a username and password to use to access your Web-server directory on the FTP site. Then you can move files to your Web site using the client's interface. It's really that easy. If you want to grab a copy of a file from your Web site and modify it, you just

1. **Use the FTP client's interface to download a copy.**

2. **Make your modification.**

3. **Use the FTP client's interface to upload the file.**

Each FTP client's interface is different, but they're all pretty straightforward. Chapter 20 includes more information on finding a good FTP client; so when you find one, spend a few minutes reading its documentation.

You might not need a separate FTP client to move your files to your Web server:

✔ Most newer Web browsers, such as current versions of Internet Explorer and Netscape 6, have some FTP capabilities built in. You can easily upload and download files. (You might not be able to make or delete directories.)

✔ Many Web utilities, such as Dreamweaver, have file-management capabilities.

Via your hosting provider's Web site

In the interest of usability and reducing technical support calls, many Web hosting providers have built Web pages that help you upload and manage your Web site files without using a separate FTP utility or even the FTP tools inside HTML editors. Most of these tools let you manage your site in various ways, such as

✔ Uploading and downloading files

✔ Creating and deleting directories

✔ Moving files around

✔ Deleting files

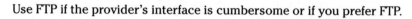

If you already have a hosting provider, find out whether it has a set of Web-based tools for managing your site.

Keep the following in mind while you decide on a provider:

- ✔ Read the provider's documentation before you start to transfer your files. Every provider's interface is different.

- ✔ Most providers who have Web interfaces won't stop you from managing your site with FTP.

  Use FTP if the provider's interface is cumbersome or if you prefer FTP.

Part II

Formatting Web Pages with (X)HTML

The 5th Wave
By Rich Tennant

"OK, I think I forgot to mention this, but we now have a Web management function that automatically alerts us when there's a broken link on The Aquarium's Web site."

In this part . . .

In this part of the book, we describe the markup and document structures that make Web pages workable and attractive. To begin with, we examine gross HTML document structure, including document headers and bodies, and how to put the right pieces together. After that, we talk about organizing text in blocks and lists. Next, we explain how linking works in HTML and how it provides the glue that ties the entire World Wide Web together. To wrap things up here, we also explain how to add graphics to your pages. Thus, we cover the basic building blocks for well-constructed, properly proportioned Web pages — and not by coincidence, either.

Chapter 4

Creating (X)HTML Document Structure

*T*he framework of a simple (X)HTML document consists of a head and body. The *head* provides information to the browser about the document, and the *body* contains the information that appears in the browser window. The first step to creating an (X)HTML document is defining the framework for that document.

This chapter covers the major elements that you use to set up a basic (X)HTML document structure — including the head and body of the document. We also show you how to tell the browser which version of HTML or XHTML you're using. Although the version information isn't necessary for users, browsers use it to make sure that they correctly display document content for your users.

Establishing a Document Structure

Although no two (X)HTML pages are alike — each employs a unique combination of content and elements to define the page — every properly constructed (X)HTML page needs the same basic document structure that includes

✔ A statement that identifies the document as an (X)HTML document

✔ A document header

✔ A document body

Every time you create an (X)HTML document, start with these three elements; you can then fill in the rest of your content and markup to create an individual page.

Although a basic document structure is a requirement for every (X)HTML document, creating it over and over again can be a little monotonous. Most (X)HTML-editing tools automatically set up the basic document structure for you when you open a new document.

Labeling Your (X)HTML Document

At the top of your (X)HTML document should be the *Document Type Declaration,* or DOCTYPE *declaration.* This line of code specifies which version of HTML or XHTML you're using, which in turn lets the browsers know how to interpret the document. We use the XHTML 1.0 specification in this chapter because it's the latest specification and what most browsers and editing tools use.

Adding an HTML DOCTYPE declaration

If you choose to create an HTML 4.01 document instead of an XHTML document, you can pick from three possible DOCTYPE declarations:

✔ **HTML 4.01 Transitional:** This is the most inclusive version of HTML 4.01, and it incorporates all HTML structural elements as well as all presentation elements.

```
<!DOCTYPE HTML PUBLIC "-//W3C//DTD HTML 4.01 Transitional//EN"
        "http://www.w3.org/TR/html4/loose.dtd">
```

✔ **HTML 4.01 Strict:** This streamlined version of HTML excludes all presentation-related elements in favor of style sheets as a mechanism for driving display.

```
<!DOCTYPE HTML PUBLIC "-//W3C//DTD HTML 4.01//EN"
        "http://www.w3.org/TR/html4/strict.dtd">
```

✔ **HTML 4.01 Frameset:** This version begins with HTML 4.01 Transitional and includes all the elements that make frames possible.

```
<!DOCTYPE HTML PUBLIC "-//W3C//DTD HTML 4.01 Frameset//EN"
        "http://www.w3.org/TR/html4/frameset.dtd">
```

Adding an XHTML DOCTYPE declaration

To create an XHTML document, use one of the following `DOCTYPE` declarations:

✔ **XHTML 1.0 Transitional:**

```
<!DOCTYPE html PUBLIC "-//W3C//DTD XHTML 1.0 Transitional//EN"
        "http://www.w3.org/TR/xhtml1/DTD/xhtml1-transitional.dtd">
```

✔ **XHTML 1.0 Strict:**

```
<!DOCTYPE html "-//W3C//DTD XHTML 1.0 Strict//EN"
        "http://www.w3.org/TR/xhtml1/DTD/xhtml1-strict.dtd">
```

✔ **XHTML 1.0 Frameset:**

```
<!DOCTYPE html PUBLIC "-//W3C//DTD XHTML 1.0 Frameset//EN"
        "http://www.w3.org/TR/xhtml1/DTD/xhtml1-frameset.dtd">
```

The XHTML DTD descriptions are similar to the HTML DTD descriptions and are defined in Chapter 1.

The <html> element

After you specify which version of (X)HTML the document follows, add an `<html>` element to hold all the other (X)HTML elements in your page:

```
<!DOCTYPE html PUBLIC "-//W3C//DTD XHTML 1.0 Transitional//EN"
        "http://www.w3.org/TR/xhtml1/DTD/xhtml1-transitional.dtd">

<html>




</html>
```

Adding the XHTML namespace

A *namespace* is a collection of names used by the elements and attributes of an XML document. XHTML uses the XHTML collection of names and therefore needs a namespace, which looks like this:

```
<!DOCTYPE html PUBLIC "-//W3C//DTD XHTML 1.0 Transitional//EN"
        "http://www.w3.org/TR/xhtml1/DTD/xhtml1-transitional.dtd">

<html xmlns="http://www.w3.org/1999/xhtml">




</html>
```

Don't get bogged down by the meaning of namespaces. If you work with other XML vocabularies, you need to know about namespaces. For simple XHTML documents, you just need to know to include the XHTML namespace. So, of course, that's exactly what the preceding code snippet shows you how to do!

Adding a Document Header

The *head* of an (X)HTML document is one of the two main components of a document. (The *body* of the document is the other main component.) The head, or *header,* provides basic information *about* the document, including its title and metadata (which is information about information), such as keywords, author information, and a description. If you're going to use a style sheet with your page, you include information about that style sheet in the header.

Chapter 8 includes a complete overview of creating Cascading Style Sheets (CSS) and shows you how to include them in your (X)HTML documents.

The `<head>` element, which defines the page header, immediately follows the `<html>` opening tag:

```
<!DOCTYPE html PUBLIC "-//W3C//DTD XHTML 1.0 Transitional//EN"
        "http://www.w3.org/TR/xhtml1/DTD/xhtml1-transitional.dtd">

<html xmlns="http://www.w3.org/1999/xhtml">
  <head>

  </head>
</html>
```

Giving your page a title

Every (X)HTML page needs a descriptive title that tells the visitor what the page is all about. This title appears in the title bar at the very top of the browser window, as shown in Figure 4-1. The page title should be concise yet informative. (For example, *My home page* isn't nearly as informative as *Ed's IT Consulting Service.*)

You define the title for your page by using the `<title>` element inside the `<head>` element:

```
<!DOCTYPE html PUBLIC "-//W3C//DTD XHTML 1.0 Transitional//EN"
        "http://www.w3.org/TR/xhtml1/DTD/xhtml1-transitional.dtd">
```

```
<html xmlns="http://www.w3.org/1999/xhtml">
  <head>
    <title>Ed's IT Consulting Service</title>
  </head>

</html>
```

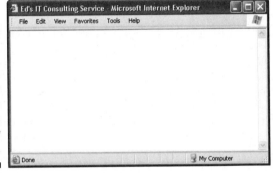

Figure 4-1:
(X)HTML
page titles
appear
in a Web
browser's
window
title bar.

Search engines use the contents of the `<title>` bar when they list Web pages in response to a query. Your page title may be the first thing that a Web surfer reads about your Web page, especially if she finds it through a search engine. A search engine will most likely list your page title with many others on a search results page, which means that you have one chance to grab the Web surfer's attention and convince her to choose your page. A well-crafted title can accomplish that.

The title is also used for Bookmarks and in a browser's History; therefore, keep your titles short and sweet.

Defining metadata

The term *metadata* refers to data about data; in the context of the Web, it means data that describes the data on your Web page. Metadata for your page may include

- ✔ Keywords
- ✔ A description of your page
- ✔ Information about the page author
- ✔ The software application you used to create the page

Elements and attributes

You define each piece of metadata for your (X)HTML page with

- The `<meta />` element
- The `name` and `content` attributes

For example, the following elements create a list of keywords and a description for a consulting-service page:

```
<!DOCTYPE html PUBLIC "-//W3C//DTD XHTML 1.0 Transitional//EN"
        "http://www.w3.org/TR/xhtml1/DTD/xhtml1-transitional.dtd">

<html xmlns="http://www.w3.org/1999/xhtml">
  <head>
  <title>Ed's IT Consulting Service</title>
  <meta name="keywords" content="IT consulting, MCSE, networking guru" />
  <meta name="description" content="An overview of Ed's skills and services" />
  </head>
</html>
```

Custom names

The (X)HTML specification doesn't

- Predefine the kinds of metadata you can include in your page
- Specify how to name different pieces of metadata, such as keywords and descriptions

So, for example, instead of using `keywords` and `description` as names for keyword and description metadata, you can just as easily use `kwrd` and `desc`, like the following markup:

```
<!DOCTYPE html PUBLIC "-//W3C//DTD XHTML 1.0 Transitional//EN"
        "http://www.w3.org/TR/xhtml1/DTD/xhtml1-transitional.dtd">

<html xmlns="http://www.w3.org/1999/xhtml">
  <head>
    <title>Ed's IT Consulting Service</title>
    <meta name="kwrd" content="IT consulting, MCSE, networking guru" />
    <meta name="desc" content="An overview of Ed's skills and services" />
  </head>
</html>
```

If you can use just any old values for the `<meta>` element's `name` and `content` attributes, how do systems know what to do with your metadata? The answer is — they don't. Each search engine works differently. Although *keywords* and *description* are commonly used metadata names, many search engines may not recognize or use other metadata elements that you include.

Many developers use metadata to either

✔ Leave messages for others who may look at the source code of the page

✔ Prepare for future browsers and search engines that use the metadata

Although keywords and page descriptions are optional, search engines commonly use them to collect information about your Web site. Be sure to include detailed and concise information in your <meta /> tag if you want your Web site discovered by search engine robots.

Automatically redirecting users to another page

You can use metadata in your header to send messages to Web browsers about how they should display or otherwise handle your Web page. Web builders commonly use the <meta /> element this way to automatically redirect page visitors from one page to another. For example, if you've ever come across a page that says This page has moved. Please wait 10 seconds to be automatically sent to the new location. (or something similar), you've seen this trick at work.

To use the <meta /> element to send messages to the browser, here are the general steps you need to follow:

1. **Use the** http-equiv **attribute in place of the** name **attribute.**

2. **Choose from a predefined list of values that represents instructions for the browser.**

   These values are based on instructions that you can also send to a browser in the HTTP header, but changing an HTTP header for a document is harder than embedding the instructions into the Web page itself.

To instruct a browser to redirect users from one page to another, here's what you need to do in particular:

1. **Use the** <meta /> **element with** http-equiv="refresh".

2. **Adjust the value of** content **to specify how many seconds before the refresh happens and what URL you want to jump to.**

For example, the line shown in bold in the following markup creates a refresh that jumps to www.w3.org after 15 seconds:

```
<!DOCTYPE html PUBLIC "-//W3C//DTD XHTML 1.0 Transitional//EN"
        "http://www.w3.org/TR/xhtml1/DTD/xhtml1-transitional.dtd">

<html xmlns="http://www.w3.org/1999/xhtml">
  <head>
    <title>All About Markup</title>
    <meta http-equiv="refresh" content="15; url= http://www.w3.org/" />
  </head>

  <body>
    <p>This page is still in development. Until we are done, please visit
      the <a href="http://www.w3.org">W3C Website</a> for the definitive
      collection of markup-related resources.
    </p>

    <p>Please wait 10 seconds to be automatically redirected to the W3C.</p>
  </body>
</html>
```

Older Web browsers may not know what to do with `<meta />` elements that use the `http-equiv` element to create a redirector page. Be sure to include some text and a link on your page to enable a visitor to link manually to your redirector page if your `<meta />` element fails to do the job.

If a user's browser doesn't know what to do with your redirector information, the user simply clicks the link in the page body to go to the new page, as shown in Figure 4-2.

Figure 4-2: When you use a `<meta />` element to create a page redirector, include a link in case the redirector fails.

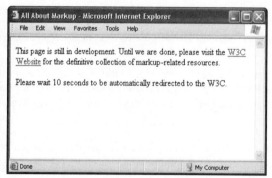

You can use the `http-equiv` attribute with the `<meta />` element for a variety of other purposes, such as setting an expiration date for a page and specifying the character set (the language) the page uses. To find out what your `http-equiv` options are (and how to use them), check out the Dictionary of HTML META tags at the following URL:

http://vancouver-webpages.com/META/metatags.detail.html

Creating the (X)HTML Document Body

After you set up your page header, create a title, and define some metadata, you're ready to create the (X)HTML markup and content that will show up in a browser window. The `<body>` element holds the content of your document.

If you want to see something in your browser window, put it in the `<body>` element, like this:

```
<!DOCTYPE html PUBLIC "-//W3C//DTD XHTML 1.0 Transitional//EN"
         "http://www.w3.org/TR/xhtml1/DTD/xhtml1-transitional.dtd">

<html xmlns="http://www.w3.org/1999/xhtml">
  <head>
    <title>Ed's IT Consulting Service</title>
    <meta name="kwrd" content="IT consulting, MCSE, networking guru" />
    <meta name="desc" content="An overview of Ed's skills and services" />
  </head>

  <body>
    <p>Ed's IT Consulting Service Homepage</p>
    <p>Ed has over 20 years of IT consulting experience and is available
       to help you with any IT need you might have. From network design
       and configuration to technical documentation and training, you can
       count on Ed to help you create and manage your IT infrastructure.</p>

    <p>For more information please contact Ed by e-mail at ed@itguru.com or
       by phone at 555.555.5555.</p>
  </body>
</html>
```

Figure 4-3 shows how a browser displays this complete (X)HTML page:

✔ The content of the `<title>` element is in the window's title bar.

✔ The `<meta />` elements don't affect the page appearance at all.

✔ Only the paragraph text contained in the `<p>` elements (in the `<body>` element) actually appears in the browser window.

Figure 4-3:
Only content
in the
`<body>`
element
appears in
the browser
window.

Marvelous Miscellany

Table 4-1 lists other (X)HTML attributes for document structure markup that you might find in HTML files.

Table 4-1	Additional (X)HTML Document Structure Attributes		
Name	*Function/Value Equals*	*Value Type(s)*	*Related Element(s)*
profile	Links to property definitions	URI	<head>
scheme	Describes how to decode data	CDATA	<meta />

Chapter 5

Text and Lists

*H*TML documents consist of text, images, multimedia files, links, and other pieces of content that you bring together into one page by using markup elements and attributes. You use blocks of text to create such document elements as headings, paragraphs, and lists. The first step in creating a solid HTML document is laying a firm foundation that establishes the document's structure.

Formatting Text

Here's a super-ultra-technical definition of a *block of text:* some chunk of content that wraps from one line to another inside an HTML element.

Your HTML page is a giant collection of blocks of text:

✔ Every bit of content on your Web page must be part of some block element.

✔ Every block element sits within the `<body>` element on your page.

HTML recognizes several kinds of text blocks that you can use in your document, including (but not limited to)

✔ Paragraphs

✔ Headings

✔ Block quotes

✔ Lists

✔ Tables

✔ Forms

Inline elements versus text blocks

The difference between inline elements and a block of text is important. HTML elements in this chapter describe blocks of text. An *inline element* is a word or string of words *inside* a block element (for example, text emphasis elements such as <em> or <strong>). Inline elements must be nested within a block element; otherwise, your HTML document isn't syntactically correct.

Inline elements, such as linking and formatting elements, are designed to link from or change the appearance of a few words or lines of content found inside those blocks.

Paragraphs

Paragraphs are used more often in Web pages than any other kind of text block.

HTML browsers don't recognize the hard returns that you enter when you create your page inside an editor. You must use a <p> element to tell the browser to separate the contained block of text as a paragraph.

Formatting

To create a paragraph, follow these steps:

1. **Add <p> in the body of the document.**

2. **Type the content of the paragraph.**

3. **Add </p> to close that paragraph.**

Here's what it looks like:

```
<!DOCTYPE html PUBLIC "-//W3C//DTD XHTML 1.0 Transitional//EN"
      "http://www.w3.org/TR/xhtml1/DTD/xhtml1-transitional.dtd">
<html xmlns="http://www.w3.org/1999/xhtml">
  <head>
    <meta http-equiv="Content-Type" content="text/html; charset=ISO-8859-1" />
    <title>All About Blocks</title>
  </head>

  <body>
    <p>This is a paragraph. It's a very simple structure that you will use
       time and again in your Web pages.</p>
    <p>This is another paragraph. What could be simpler to create?</p>
  </body>
</html>
```

This HTML page includes two paragraphs, each marked with a separate <p> element. Most Web browsers add a line break and full line of white space after every paragraph on your page, as shown in Figure 5-1.

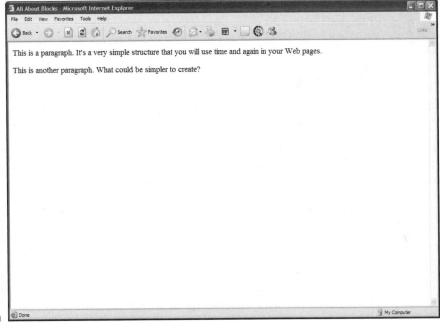

Figure 5-1:
Web browsers delineate paragraphs with line breaks.

Some people don't use the closing `</p>` tag when they create paragraphs. Although some browsers let you get away with this, leaving out the closing tag

- ✔ Doesn't follow correct syntax
- ✔ Causes problems with style sheets
- ✔ Can cause a page to appear inconsistently from browser to browser

You can control the formatting (color, style, size, and alignment) of your paragraph by using Cascading Style Sheets (CSS), which we cover in Chapters 8 and 9.

Alignment

By default, the paragraph aligns to the left. You can use the `align` attribute with a value of `center`, `right`, or `justify` to override that default and control the alignment for any paragraph.

```
<p align="center">This paragraph is centered.</p>
<p align="right">This paragraph is right-justified.</p>
<p align="justify">This paragraph is double-justified.</p>
```

Figure 5-2 shows how a Web browser aligns each paragraph according to the value of the `align` attribute.

The align attribute has been deprecated (rendered obsolete) in favor of using CSS (see Chapter 8).

Headings

Headings break a document into sections. This book uses headings and sub-headings to divide every chapter into sections, and you can do the same with your Web page. Headings can

- Create an organizational structure
- Break up the visual appearance of the page
- Give visual clues about how the pieces of content are grouped

HTML includes six elements to help you define six different heading levels in your documents:

- <h1> is the most prominent heading (Heading 1)
- <h6> is the least prominent heading (Heading 6)

Follow heading order from highest to lowest as you use HTML heading levels. That is, don't use a second-level heading until you've used a first-level heading, don't use a third-level heading until you've used a second, and so on. If you want to change how headings appear in a browser, Chapter 8 and Chapter 9 show you how to use style sheets.

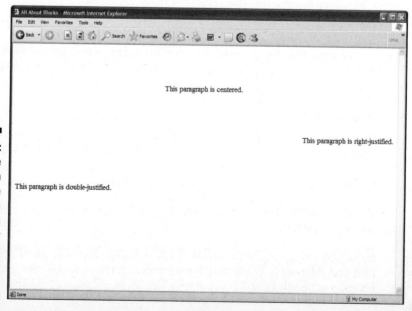

Figure 5-2:
Use the align attribute with a paragraph to specify the horizontal alignment.

Formatting

To create a heading, follow these steps:

1. **Add <h*n*> in the body of your document.**
2. **Type the content for the heading.**
3. **Add </h*n*>.**

Browser displays

Every browser has a different way of displaying heading levels, and we cover that in the following two sections.

Graphical browsers

Most graphical browsers use a distinctive size and typeface for headings:

- First-level headings (<h1>) are the largest (usually two or three font sizes larger than the default text size for paragraphs).

- Sixth-level headings (<h6>) are the smallest and may be two or three font sizes *smaller* than the default paragraph text.

The following excerpt of HTML markup shows all six headings at work:

```
<!DOCTYPE html PUBLIC "-//W3C//DTD XHTML 1.0 Transitional//EN"
        "http://www.w3.org/TR/xhtml1/DTD/xhtml1-transitional.dtd">
<html xmlns="http://www.w3.org/1999/xhtml">
  <head>
    <meta http-equiv="Content-Type" content="text/html; charset=ISO-8859-1" />
    <title>All About Blocks</title>
  </head>

  <body>
    <h1>First-level heading</h1>
    <h2>Second-level heading</h2>
    <h3>Third-level heading</h3>
    <h4>Fourth-level heading</h4>
    <h5>Fifth-level heading</h5>
    <h6>Sixth-level heading</h6>
  </body>
</html>
```

Figure 5-3 shows this HTML page as rendered in a browser.

You can use CSS to format such heading aspects as color, size, line height, and alignment.

By default, most browsers use Times New Roman fonts for all headings. The font size decreases as heading level increases. (Default sizes for first- through sixth-level headings are, respectively, 24, 18, 14, 12, 10, and 8.) You can override any of this formatting by using CSS.

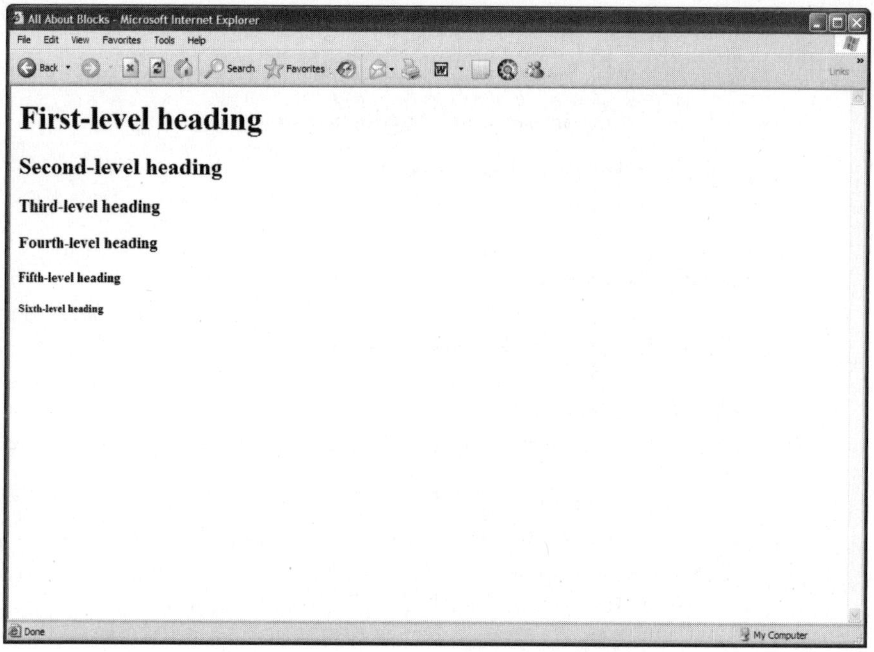

Figure 5-3:
Web
browsers
display
headings in
decreasing
size from
level one to
level six.

Text browsers

Text-only browsers use different heading conventions than graphical browsers because text-only browsers display all content using a single size and font.

Controlling Text Blocks

Blocks of text are the foundation for your page. You can break those blocks to better guide readers through your content.

Block quotes

A *block quote* is a long quotation or excerpt from a printed source that you set apart on your page. You use the `<blockquote>` element to identify block quotes:

```
<!DOCTYPE html PUBLIC "-//W3C//DTD XHTML 1.0 Transitional//EN"
        "http://www.w3.org/TR/xhtml1/DTD/xhtml1-transitional.dtd">
<html xmlns="http://www.w3.org/1999/xhtml">
  <head>
    <meta http-equiv="Content-Type" content="text/html; charset=ISO-8859-1" />
    <title>Famous Quotations</title>
  </head>
```

```
<body>
  <h1>An Inspiring Quote</h1>
  <p>When I need a little inspiration to remind me of why I spend my days
     in the classroom, I just remember what Lee Iococca said:</p>
  <blockquote>
    In a completely rational society, the best of us would be teachers
    and the rest of us would have to settle for something else.
  </blockquote>
</body>
</html>
```

Most Web browsers display block-quote content with a slight left indent, as shown in Figure 5-4.

Preformatted text

Ordinarily, HTML ignores white space inside documents. A browser won't display a block element's

- ✔ Hard returns
- ✔ Line breaks
- ✔ Large white spaces

The following markup includes several hard returns, line breaks, and a lot of space characters. Figure 5-5 shows that the Web browser ignores all of this.

```
<p>This is a paragraph

   with a lot of white space

       thrown in for fun (and as a test of course).</p>
```

The preformatted text element (`<pre>`) instructs browsers to keep all white space intact as it displays your content (like the following sample). Use the `<pre>` element in place of the `<p>` element to make the browser apply all your white space, as shown in Figure 5-6.

```
<!DOCTYPE html PUBLIC "-//W3C//DTD XHTML 1.0 Transitional//EN"
       "http://www.w3.org/TR/xhtml1/DTD/xhtml1-transitional.dtd">
<html xmlns="http://www.w3.org/1999/xhtml">
  <head>
    <meta http-equiv="Content-Type" content="text/html; charset=ISO-8859-1" />
    <title>White space</title>
  </head>

  <body>
    <pre>This is a paragraph
```

```
        with a lot of white space

        thrown in for fun (and as a test of course).
    </pre>
  </body>
</html>
```

You may want the browser to display white spaces in an HTML page where proper spacing is important, such as

- ✔ Code samples
- ✔ Text tables

You can nest `<pre>` elements inside `<blockquote>` elements to carefully control how the lines of quoted text appear on the page.

Line breaks

By default, browsers usually *wrap* text that appears in block elements, such as paragraphs, headings, and block quotes. If a text line reaches the end of a browser window, the next word automatically starts a new line. You can manually control the end of a text line with a *line break* (denoted by the `<br />` element).

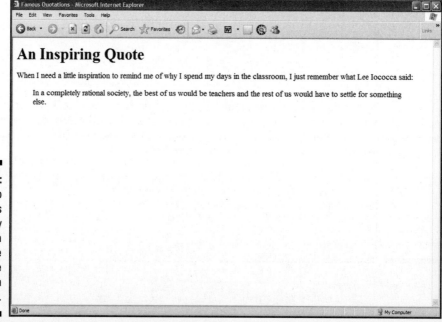

Figure 5-4:
Web browsers typically indent a block quote to separate it from paragraphs.

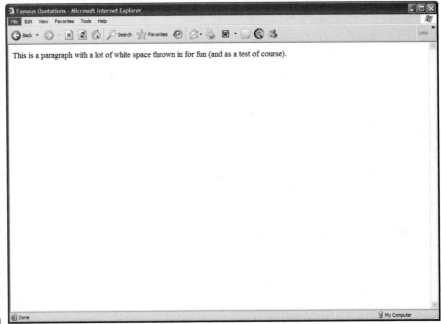

Figure 5-5:
Web browsers routinely ignore white space.

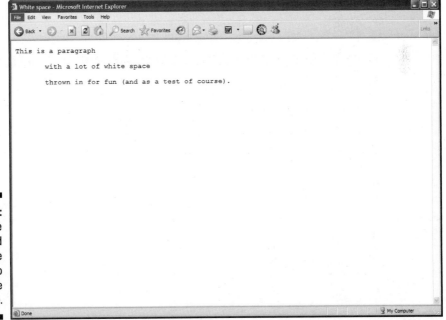

Figure 5-6:
Use preformatted text to force browsers to recognize white space.

Function

The <br /> element is the HTML equivalent of the manual line break that you use in paragraphs and other blocks of text when you're working in a word-processing program. When a browser sees a <br />, it ends the line there and starts the next line.

The difference between a line break and a paragraph is that a line break doesn't use any special formatting that you can apply at the end or beginning of a paragraph, such as

- ✔ Extra vertical space
- ✔ First-line indenting

Formatting

The following markup formats the lines of text in a poem with line breaks. The entire poem is described *as a single paragraph*, and the <br /> element marks the end of each line:

```
<!DOCTYPE html PUBLIC "-//W3C//DTD XHTML 1.0 Transitional//EN"
        "http://www.w3.org/TR/xhtml1/DTD/xhtml1-transitional.dtd">
<html xmlns="http://www.w3.org/1999/xhtml">
  <head>
    <meta http-equiv="Content-Type" content="text/html; charset=ISO-8859-1" />
    <title> Shakespeare in HTML</title>
  </head>

  <body>
  <h1>Shakespeare's Sonnets XVIII: Shall I compare thee to a summer's day? </h1>
    <p>
      Shall I compare thee to a summer's day? <br />
      Thou art more lovely and more temperate. <br />
      Rough winds do shake the darling buds of May, <br />
      And summer's lease hath all too short a date. <br />
      Sometime too hot the eye of heaven shines, <br />
      And often is his gold complexion dimm'd; <br />
      And every fair from fair sometime declines, <br />
      By chance or nature's changing course untrimm'd; <br />
      But thy eternal summer shall not fade <br />
      Nor lose possession of that fair thou ow'st; <br />
      Nor shall Death brag thou wander'st in his shade, <br />
      When in eternal lines to time thou grow'st: <br />
      So long as men can breathe or eyes can see, <br />
      So long lives this, and this gives life to thee. <br />
    </p>
  </body>
</html>
```

Figure 5-7 shows how a browser handles each line break. In this example, the poem isn't left-indented because the <p> element replaces the <blockquote> element.

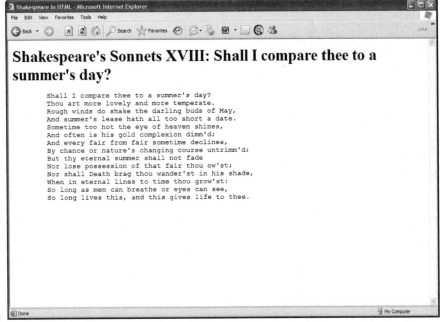

Horizontal rules

The horizontal rule element (<hr />) helps you include solid straight lines *(rules)* on your page.

The browser creates the rule based on the <hr /> element, so users don't wait for a graphic to download. A horizontal rule is a good option to

✔ Break your page into logical sections.

✔ Separate your headers and footers from the rest of the page.

Formatting

When you include an <hr /> element on your page, like the following HTML, the browser replaces it with a line, as shown in Figure 5-8.

```
<!DOCTYPE html PUBLIC "-//W3C//DTD XHTML 1.0 Transitional//EN"
        "http://www.w3.org/TR/xhtml1/DTD/xhtml1-transitional.dtd">
<html xmlns="http://www.w3.org/1999/xhtml">
  <head>
    <meta http-equiv="Content-Type" content="text/html; charset=ISO-8859-1" />
    <title>Horizontal Rules</title>
  </head>
```

```
<body>
  <p>This is a paragraph followed by a horizontal rule.</p>

  <hr />

  </p>This is a paragraph preceded by a horizontal rule.</p>
</body>
</html>
```

A horizontal rule must always sit on a line by itself; you can't add the `<hr />` element in the middle of a paragraph (or other block element) and expect the rule to just appear in the middle of the block.

Attributes

Four different attributes control the appearance of each horizontal rule:

- `width`: Specifies line width either in *pixels* or by *percentage of display area width* (which we call "the page" in discussion that follows).

  For example, a rule can be 50 pixels wide or take 75 percent of the page.

- `size`: Specifies the height of the line in pixels. The default is 1 pixel.

- `align`: Specifies the horizontal alignment of the rule as either `left` (the default), `center`, or `right`.

  If you don't define a width for your rule, it takes the entire width of the page. The alignment won't make any difference.

- `noshade`: Specifies a solid line with no shading.

  By default, most browsers display hard rules with a shade.

These formatting attributes are deprecated in favor of using CSS.

This bit of HTML creates a horizontal rule that takes up 45 percent of the page, is 4 pixels high, aligned to the center, and has shading turned off:

```
<p>This is a paragraph followed by a horizontal rule.</p>

<hr width="45%" size="4" align="center" noshade="noshade" />

<p>This is a paragraph preceded by a horizontal rule.</p>
```

Figure 5-9 shows how the addition of these attributes can alter how a browser displays the rule.

Figure 5-10 shows how you can use horizontal rules in the real world to highlight important content. The LANWrights, Inc., Web site uses colored hard rules to frame a key statement on the site's home page. The rules make the statement stand out from the rest of the page.

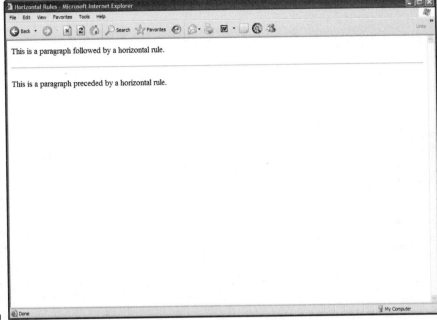

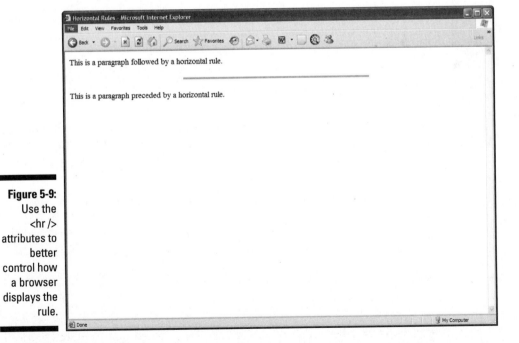

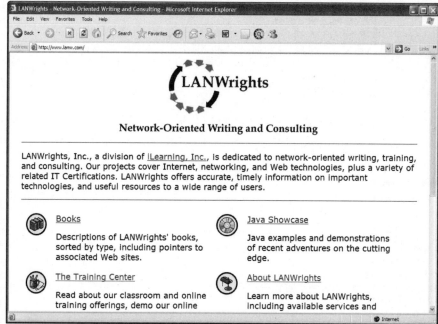

Figure 5-10:
The
LANWrights,
Inc., Web
site uses
hard rules to
draw your
attention to
important
information
on the page.

CSS gives you much more control over the placement of horizontal rules; you can even fancy them up with color and shading options.

Organizing Information

Lists are powerful tools for arranging similar elements together, and they give visitors to your site an easy way to hone in on groups of information. You can put just about anything in a list, from a set of instructions to a collection of navigational hyperlinks.

Lists use a combination of elements — at least two components:

✔ A markup element that says "Hey browser! The following items are a list."

✔ Markup elements that say "Hey browser! This is an item in the list."

HTML provides for three different kinds of lists:

✔ Numbered lists

✔ Bulleted lists

✔ Definition lists

Numbered lists

A *numbered list* consists of at least two items, each prefaced by a number. Usually, a person numbers a list when the order of the items is important.

You use two kinds of elements for a numbered list:

✔ The ordered list element (`<ol>`) specifies that this is a numbered list.

✔ List item elements (`<li>`) mark each item in the list.

Formatting

A numbered list with three items requires elements and content in the following order:

1. `<ol>`
2. `<li>`
3. Content for the first list item
4. `</li>`
5. `<li>`
6. Content for the second list item
7. `</li>`
8. `<li>`
9. Content for the third list item
10. `</li>`
11. `</ol>`

The following markup defines a three-item numbered list:

```
<!DOCTYPE html PUBLIC "-//W3C//DTD XHTML 1.0 Transitional//EN"
        "http://www.w3.org/TR/xhtml1/DTD/xhtml1-transitional.dtd">
<html xmlns="http://www.w3.org/1999/xhtml">
  <head>
    <meta http-equiv="Content-Type" content="text/html; charset=ISO-8859-1" />
    <title>Numbered Lists</title>
  </head>

  <body>
    <h1>Things to do today</h1>
    <ol>
      <li>Feed cat</li>
```

```
      <li>Wash car</li>
      <li>Grocery shopping</li>
    </ol>
  </body>
</html>
```

Figure 5-11 shows how a browser renders this markup. You don't actually have to specify a number for each item in the list; the browser identifies the list items from the markup and adds the numbers.

If you swap the first two items in the list, they're still numbered in order when the page appears, as shown in Figure 5-12.

```
  <ol>
    <li>Wash car</li>
    <li>Feed cat</li>
    <li>Grocery shopping</li>
  </ol>
```

Numbering

Two different <ol> element attributes control the appearance of a numbered list:

✔ start: Specifies the first number in the list.

   • The default starting number is 1.

Figure 5-11:
Use the <ol> and <li> tags to create a numbered list.

TIP

- You can specify any number as the start number for the new list.

    Specify a start number when you resume a list after an unnumbered paragraph or other block element.

✔ `type`: Specifies the numbering style from the list. You can choose from five predefined numbering styles:

- `1`: Decimal numbers.

- `a`: Lowercase letters.

- `A`: Uppercase letters.

- `i`: Lowercase Roman numerals.

- `I`: Uppercase Roman numerals.

The following markup uses ordered list elements and attributes to create a list that uses uppercase Roman numerals and begins numbering at 5 (V in Roman numerals):

```
<ol start="5" type="I">
   <li>Wash car</li>
   <li>Feed cat</li>
   <li>Grocery shopping</li>
</ol>
```

Figure 5-13 shows how the attributes affect the list's appearance in a browser.

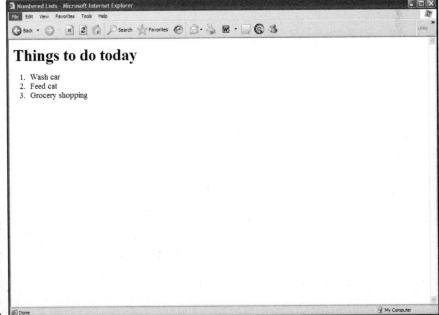

Figure 5-12:
Web browsers set the numbers for your list according to the order items appear in the list.

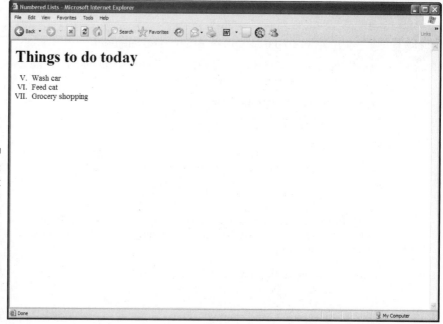

Things to do today

   V. Wash car
  VI. Feed cat
 VII. Grocery shopping

Done   My Computer

Figure 5-13:
The start
and type
attributes
guide the
appearance
of a
numbered
list in a
browser.

You have more control over your lists if you use CSS to define formatting. That's why the start and type attributes for list markup are deprecated; see Appendix A for information about deprecated attributes.

Bulleted lists

A *bulleted list* consists of one or more items each prefaced by a *bullet* (often a big dot; this book uses *check marks* as bullets).

You use this type of list if the order of the presentation of the items isn't necessary for understanding the information presented.

Formatting

A bulleted list requires the following:

✔ The unordered list element (`<ul>`) specifies that you're creating a bulleted list.

✔ A list item element (`<li>`) marks each item in the list.

✔ The closing tag for the unordered list element (`</ul>`) indicates that the list has come to its end.

An unordered list with three items requires elements and content in the following order:

1. `<ul>`

2. `<li>`

3. Content for the first list item

4. `</li>`

5. `<li>`

6. Content for the second list item

7. `</li>`

8. `<li>`

9. Content for the third list item

10. `</li>`

11. `</ul>`

The following markup formats a three-item list as a bulleted list:

```
<!DOCTYPE html PUBLIC "-//W3C//DTD XHTML 1.0 Transitional//EN"
        "http://www.w3.org/TR/xhtml1/DTD/xhtml1-transitional.dtd">
<html xmlns="http://www.w3.org/1999/xhtml">
  <head>
    <meta http-equiv="Content-Type" content="text/html; charset=ISO-8859-1" />
    <title>Bulleted Lists</title>
  </head>

  <body>
    <h1>Things to do today</h1>
    <ul>
      <li>Feed cat</li>
      <li>Wash car</li>
      <li>Grocery shopping</li>
    </ul>
  </body>
</html>
```

Figure 5-14 shows how a browser renders this with bullets.

Styles

You can use the `type` attribute (deprecated) with the `<ul>` element to specify what kind of bullet you want the list to use.

- `disc`: Solid circle bullets (the default)
- `square`: Solid square bullets
- `circle`: Hollow circle bullets

Figure 5-14:
An
unordered
list uses
bullets
instead of
numbers to
mark items.

The addition of the `type` attribute to the bulleted-list markup just given changes the bullets from discs to squares, as shown in Figure 5-15. Here's what the relevant markup looks like:

```
<ul type="square">
  <li>Feed cat</li>
  <li>Wash car</li>
  <li>Grocery shopping</li>
</ul>
```

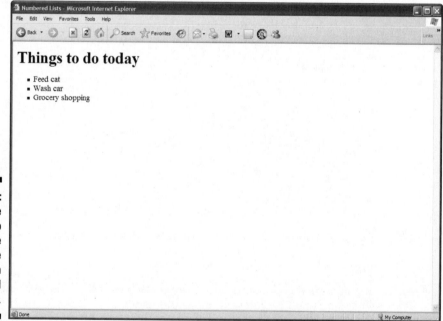

Figure 5-15:
Use the type
attribute to
change the
bullet style
for an
unordered
list.

Use CSS if you want more control over the formatting of your lists.

Definition lists

Definition lists group terms and definitions into a single list and require three different elements to complete the list:

- ✔ `<dl>`: Holds the list definitions.
- ✔ `<dt>`: Defines a term in the list.
- ✔ `<dd>`: Defines a definition for a term.

You can have as many terms (defined by `<dt>`) in a list as you need. Each term can have one or more definitions (defined by `<dd>`).

To create a definition list with two items requires elements and content in the following order:

1. `<dl>`
2. `<dt>`
3. First term name
4. `</dt>`
5. `<dd>`
6. Content for the definition of the first item
7. `</dd>`
8. `<dt>`
9. Second term name
10. `</dt>`
11. `<dd>`
12. Content for the definition of the second item
13. `</dd>`
14. `</dl>`

The following definition list includes three terms, one of which has two definitions:

```
<!DOCTYPE html PUBLIC "-//W3C//DTD XHTML 1.0 Transitional//EN"
        "http://www.w3.org/TR/xhtml1/DTD/xhtml1-transitional.dtd">
<html xmlns="http://www.w3.org/1999/xhtml">
  <head>
    <meta http-equiv="Content-Type" content="text/html; charset=ISO-8859-1" />
```

```
    <title>Definition Lists</title>
  </head>

  <body>
    <h1>Markup Language Definitions</h1>
    <dl>
      <dt>SGML</dt>
        <dd>The Standard Generalized Markup Language</dd>
      <dt>HTML</dt>
          <dd>The Hypertext Markup Language</dd>
          <dd>The markup language you use to create Web pages.</dd>
      <dt>XML</dt>
          <dd>The Extensible Markup Language</dd>
    </dl>
  </body>
</html>
```

If you think the items in a list are spaced too closely together, you can either

✔ Put two `<br/>` elements before each `</li>` or `</dd>` element to add more white space.

✔ Use CSS styles to carefully control all aspects of your list appearance, as shown in Chapter 8.

Nesting lists

You can create subcategories by *nesting* lists within other lists. Some common uses for nested lists include

✔ Site maps and other navigation tools

✔ Table of contents for online books and papers

✔ Outlines

You can combine any of the three kinds of lists to create *nested* lists, such as a multilevel table of contents or an outline that mixes numbered headings with bulleted list items as the lowest outline level.

The following example starts with a numbered list that defines a list of things to do for the day, and uses three bulleted lists to further break down those items into specific tasks:

```
<!DOCTYPE html PUBLIC "-//W3C//DTD XHTML 1.0 Transitional//EN"
        "http://www.w3.org/TR/xhtml1/DTD/xhtml1-transitional.dtd">
<html xmlns="http://www.w3.org/1999/xhtml">
```

```
<head>
  <meta http-equiv="Content-Type" content="text/html; charset=ISO-8859-1" />
  <title>Nested Lists</title>
</head>
<body>
  <h1>Things to do today</h1>
  <ol>
    <li>Feed cat</li>
      <ul>
        <li>Rinse bowl</li>
        <li>Open cat food</li>
        <li>Mix dry and wet food in bowl</li>
        <li>Deliver on a silver platter to fluffy</li>
      </ul>
    <li>Wash car</li>
      <ul>
        <li>Vacuum interior</li>
        <li>Wash exterior</li>
        <li>Wax exterior</li>
      </ul>
    <li>Grocery shopping</li>
      <ul>
        <li>Plan meals</li>
        <li>Clean out fridge</li>
        <li>Make list</li>
        <li>Go to store</li>
      </ul>
  </ol>
</body>
</html>
```

All nested lists follows the same markup pattern:

✔ Each list item in the top-level ordered list is followed by a complete second-level list.

✔ The second-level lists sit inside the top-level list, not in the list items.

Figure 5-16 shows how a browser reflects this nesting in its display.

As you build nested lists, watch your opening and closing tags carefully. *Close first what you opened last* is an especially important axiom here. If you don't open and close your tags properly, lists might not show consistent indents or numbering, or text might be indented incorrectly because a list somewhere was never properly closed.

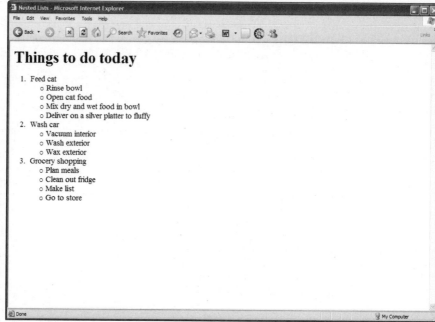

Figure 5-16:
Nested lists
combine
lists for a
multilevel
organiza-
tion of
information.

Text Controls and Annotation

Some general (X)HTML elements define general text controls or allow you to annotate documents. These are covered in Table 5-1.

Table 5-1	(X)HTML Text Controls and Annotation			
Element	*Common Name*	*Empty?*	*Category*	*Description*
bdo	Bidirectional algorithm	No	Language definition	Controls direction of text display {ltr|rtl} (left-to-right, right-to-left)
del	Deleted text	No	Text control	Marks deleted text in current draft
ins	Inserted text	No	Text control	Marks inserted text in current draft

Element	Common Name	Empty?	Category	Description
kbd	Keyboard text	No	Text control	Text to type at a keyboard
samp	Sample text	No	Text control	Sample program output
tt	Teletype text	No	Text control	Typewriter or teletype output
var	Variable text	No	Text control	Highlights input or output variables

Marvelous Miscellany

Table 5-2 lists other text-related (X)HTML attributes that you might find in HTML files.

Table 5-2	Additional (X)HTML Text Attributes		
Name	**Function/ Value Equals**	**Value Type(s)**	**Related Element(s)**
cite	Specifies location of source materials	URL	`<blockquote>` `<q>`
cite	Explains reason for adds, deletes	Text	`<del><ins>`
datetime	Time stamps document content	ISO date	`<del><ins>`
dir	Specifies text direction for content	{ltr|rtl}	All elements except `<base> ` `<frame /><frameset>` `<iframe><param />` `<script>`
id	Supplies unique identifier for markup instances	ID	All elements except `<base /><head>` `<html><meta />` `<param />` `<script><style>` `<title>`

(continued)

Table 5-2 *(continued)*

Name	Function/ Value Equals	Value Type(s)	Related Element(s)
`lang`	Names content language used	Language code	All elements except `<base />`` ` `<frame />``<frameset>` `<iframe>``<param />` `<script>`
`title`	Associates advisory info to content	Text	All elements except `<base />``<head>` `<html>``<meta />` `<param />``<script>` `<style>``<title>`

Chapter 6

Linking to Online Resources

*H*yperlinks, or simply *links,* connect (X)HTML pages and other resources on the Web. When you include a link on your page, you allow visitors to travel from your page to another Web site, another page on your site, or even another location on the same page. Without external links, a page stands alone, disconnected from the rest of the Web. With external links, that page becomes part of an almost boundless collection of information.

Basic Links

To create a link, you need

✔ **The Web address** (called a Uniform Resource Locator, or URL) of the Web site or file you want to link. This usually starts with `http://`.

✔ **Some text** in your Web page to label or describe the link.

Try to ensure that the text you use says something useful about the resource being linked.

✔ **An anchor element (`<a>`) with the `href` attribute** to bring it all together.

The element to create links is called an *anchor element* because you use it to anchor a URL to some text on your page. When users view your page in a browser, they can click the text to activate the link and visit the page whose URL you specified in the link. You insert the full URL in the `href` attribute. This tells the link where it needs to go.

You can think of the structure of a basic link as a cheeseburger (or your preferred vegan substitute). The URL is the cheese, the patty is the link text, and the anchor tags are the buns. Tasty, yes?

For example, if you have a Web page that describes HTML standards, you may want to refer Web surfers to the World Wide Web Consortium (W3C) — the organization that governs all things related to (X)HTML standards. A basic link to the W3C's Web site, `www.w3.org`, looks like this:

```
<p>The <a href="http://www.w3.org">World Wide Web Consortium</a> is the
    standards body that oversees the ongoing development of the XHTML
    specification.</p>
```

You specify the link URL (`http://www.w3.org`) in the anchor element's `href` attribute. The text (`World Wide Web Consortium`) between the anchor element's open and close tags (`<a>` and `</a>`) labels or describes the link.

Figure 6-1 shows how a browser displays this bit of markup.

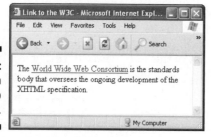

Figure 6-1:
A paragraph
with a link to
the W3C.

Anchor elements aren't block elements

Anchor elements are *inline elements* — they apply to a few words or characters within a block of text (the text that you want to use as a link) instead of defining formatting for blocks of text. The anchor element sits inside a paragraph (`<p>`) element. When you create a link, you should always create it within a block element, such as a paragraph, list item, heading, or even a table cell. Turn to Chapter 5 for more information on block elements.

Although many Web browsers can display your anchors just fine (even if you don't nest them in

block elements), some browsers don't handle this breach of (X)HTML syntax very well, such as

✔ Text-only browsers for Palm devices and mobile phones

✔ Text-to-speech readers for the visually impaired

Text-based browsers rely on block elements to properly divide the sections of your page. Without a block element, these browsers might display your links in the wrong places.

You can also anchor URLs to images so users can click an image to activate a link. (For more about creating images that link, see Chapter 7.)

For a detailed discussion of the ins and outs of URLs, see Chapter 1.

Link options

You can link to a variety of online resources:

- ✔ Other (X)HTML pages (either on your Web site or on another Web site)
- ✔ Different locations on the same (X)HTML page
- ✔ Resources that aren't even (X)HTML pages at all, such as e-mail addresses, pictures, and text files

Link locations, captions, and destinations have a big impact on link value. Chapter 3 covers best practices for using links in your site design.

The kind of link you create is determined by where you link.

Absolute links

An *absolute link* uses a complete URL to connect browsers to a Web page or online resource.

Links that use a complete URL to point to a resource are called *absolute* because they provide a complete, standalone path to another Web resource. When you link to a page on someone else's Web site, the Web browser needs every bit of information in the URL to find the page. The browser starts with the domain in the URL and works its way through the path to a specific file.

When you link to files on someone else's site, you must always use absolute URLs in the `href` attribute of the anchor element (for example, `http://www.website.com/directory/page.html`).

Relative links

A *relative link* uses a kind of shorthand to specify the URL for the resource where you're pointing.

Use the following guidelines with relative links in your (X)HTML pages:

- ✔ You create relative links between resources in the same domain
- ✔ Because both resources are in the same domain, you can omit domain information from the URL.

  A *relative* URL uses the location of the resource you're linking from to identify the location of the resource you're linking to (for example, `page.html`).

A relative link is similar to telling someone that he or she needs to go to the Eastside Mall. If the person already knows where the Eastside Mall is, he or she doesn't need additional directions. Web browsers behave the same way.

If you use relative links on your site, your links still work if you change either

- ✔ Servers
- ✔ Domain names

Simple links

You can take advantage of relative URLs when you create a link between pages on the same Web site. If you want to make a link from `http://www.mysite.com/home.html` to `http://www.mysite.com/about.html`, you can use this simplified, relative URL in an anchor element on `home.html`:

```
<p>Learn more <a href="about.html">about</a> our company.</p>
```

When a browser sees a link without a domain name, the browser assumes the link is *relative* and uses the domain and path of the linking page to find the linked page.

Site links

As your site grows more complex and you organize your files into a variety of folders, you can still use relative links. But you must provide additional information in the URL to help the browser find files that don't reside in the same directory as the file from which you're linking.

Use `../` (two periods and a slash) before the filename to indicate that the browser should move up one level in the directory structure.

The markup for this process looks like this:

```
<a href="../docs/home.html>Documentation home</a>
```

The notation in this anchor element instructs the browser to:

1. **Move up one folder from the folder the linking document is stored in.**
2. **Find a folder called** `docs`.
3. **Find a file called** `home.html`.

When you create a relative link, the location of the file *to* which you link is always relative to the file from which you link. As you create your relative URL, trace the path a browser must take if it starts on the page you're linking from before it can get to the page to which you're linking. That path defines the URL for your relative link.

Common mistakes

Every Web resource, such as sites, pages, and images, has a unique URL. Even one incorrect letter in your URL can lead to a *broken link*. Broken links lead to an error page (often the HTTP error `404 File or directory not found`).

URLs are so finicky that a simple typo breaks a link.

If a URL doesn't work, try these tactics:

- ✔ **Check the capitalization.** Some Web servers (Linux and Unix most notably) are *case sensitive* (meaning they distinguish between capital and lowercase letters). These servers treat the filenames `Bios.html` and `bios.html` as different files on the Web server. That also means that browsers must use uppercase and lowercase letters when necessary. Be sure the capitalization in the link matches the capitalization of the URL.

  To avoid problems with files on your Web site, follow a standard naming convention. Often, using only lowercase letters can simplify your life.

- ✔ **Check the extension.** `Bios.htm` and `Bios.html` are two different files. If your link's URL uses one extension but the actual filename uses another, your link won't work.

  To avoid problems with extensions on your Web site, pick either `.html` or `.htm` and stick to that extension.

- ✔ **Check the filename.** `bio.html` and `bios.html` are two different files.

- ✔ **Cut and paste.** Avoid retyping a URL if you can copy it. The best and most foolproof way to create a URL that works is

  1. **Load a page in your browser.**

  2. **Copy the URL from the browser's address or link text box.**

  3. **Paste the URL into your (X)HTML markup.**

The importance of http:// in (X)HTML links

Browsers make surfing the Web as easy as possible. If you type **www.sun.com**, **sun.com**, or often even just **sun**, in your browser's address window, the browser obligingly brings up `http://www.sun.com`. Although this technique works when you type URLs into your browser window, it won't work when you're writing markup.

The URLs that you use in your HTML markup must be fully formed. Browsers won't interpret URLs that don't include the page protocol. If you forget the `http://`, your link won't work.

Customizing Links

You can customize links to

- ✔ Open linked documents in new windows
- ✔ Link to specific locations *within* a Web page
- ✔ Link to items other than (X)HTML pages, such as
  - Portable Document Format (PDF) files
  - Compressed files
  - Word-processing documents

New windows

The Web works because you can link pages on your Web site to pages on other people's Web sites by using a simple anchor element. But when you link to someone else's site, you send users away from your own site.

To keep users on your site, HTML can open the linked page in a new window. The simple addition of the `target` attribute to an anchor element opens that link in a new browser window instead of opening it in the current window:

```
<p>The <a href="http://www.w3.org" target="_blank">World Wide Web Consortium</a>
is the standards body that oversees the ongoing development of the XHTML
specification.</p>
```

When you give a `target` attribute a `_blank` value, this tells the browser to

1. **Keep the linking page open in the current window.**
2. **Open the linked page in a new window.**

The result of the `target="_blank"` attribute is shown in Figure 6-2.

Pop-up windows irritate some users.

You can use JavaScript to control the size and appearance of pop-up windows, as well as put buttons on them to help users close them quickly. Chapter 12 covers pop-up windows in more detail.

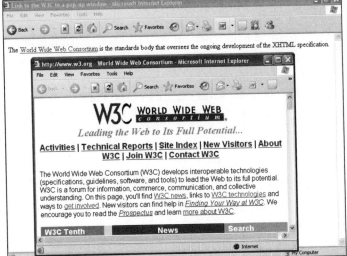

Figure 6-2:
Use the
target
attribute to
open a new
window for
a linked file.

Locations in Web pages

Locations within Web pages can be marked for direct access by links on

✔ The same page

✔ The same Web site

✔ Other Web sites

Keep these considerations in mind when adding links to Web pages:

✔ Several short pages may present information more conveniently for readers than a long page with internal links.

Links within large pages work nicely for quick access to directories, tables of contents, and glossaries.

✔ *Intradocument* linking works best on your own Web site, where you can create and control the markup.

When you link to spots on someone else's Web site, you're at that person's mercy. That person controls the linkable spots. Your links will break if the site designer removes or renames any spot where you link.

Naming link locations

To identify and create a location within a page for direct access from other links, use an empty anchor element with the name attribute, like this:

```
<a name="top"></a>
```

The anchor element that marks the spot doesn't affect the appearance of the first-level heading. You can mark spots wherever you need them without worrying about how your pages look (or change) as a result.

Linking to named locations

As we mention earlier, you can mark locations for direct access by links

- ✔ Within the same page
- ✔ Within the same Web site
- ✔ On other Web sites

Within the same page

Links can help users navigate a single Web page. Intradocument hyperlinks are such familiar features as

- ✔ Back to Top links
- ✔ Tables of contents

An intradocument hyperlink uses a URL like this:

```
<a href="#top">Back to top</a>
```

The pound sign (#) indicates that you're pointing to a spot on the same page, not on another page.

Listing 6-1 shows how two anchor elements work together to link to a spot on the same page. (Documents that use intradocument links are usually much longer. This document is shorter so you can easily see how to use the top anchor element.)

Listing 6-1:   Intradocument Hyperlinks

```
<html>
  <head>
    <title>Intradocument hyperlinks at work</title>
  </head>

  <body>
    <h1><a name="top"></a>Web-Based Training</h1>

    <p>Given the importance of the Web to businesses and
```

```
    other organizations, individuals who seek to improve
    job skills, or fulfill essential job functions, are
    turning to HTML and XML for training. We believe
    this provides an outstanding opportunity for
    participation in an active and lucrative adult and
    continuing education market.</p>

  <p><a href="#top">Back to top</a></p>

 </body>
</html>
```

Figure 6-3 shows how this HTML markup appears in a Web browser. If the user clicks the Back to Top link, the browser jumps back to the `top` spot — marked by `<a name="top"></a>`.

Figure 6-3: Use anchor elements to mark and link spots on a page.

Within the same Web site

You can combine intradocument and interdocument links to send visitors to a spot on a different Web page within your site. For example, if you want to point to a spot named `descriptions` on a page named `home.html` on your site, the link looks like this:

```
<p>Review the <a href="home.html#descriptions">document descriptions</a>
    to find the documentation for your particular product.</p>
```

On other Web sites

If you know that a page on another site has spots marked, you can use an absolute URL to point to spots on that page, like this:

```
<p>Find out how to
<a href="http://www.yourcompany.com/training/
online.htm#register">register</a> for upcoming training
courses led by our instructors.</p>
```

Be sure to check all links regularly to catch and fix the broken ones.

The Open Directory Project provides a laundry list of free and commercial tools to make finding and fixing broken links easier:

```
http://dmoz.org/Computers/Software/Internet/Site_Management/Link_Management/
```

Non-HTML resources

Links can connect to virtually any kind of files, such as

- ✔ Word-processing documents
- ✔ Spreadsheets
- ✔ PDFs
- ✔ Compressed files
- ✔ Multimedia

  Anchor elements usually aren't good links for multimedia files.

A great use for non-HTML links is on software and PDF download pages.

File downloads

Non-Web files have unique URLs just like HTML pages. Any file on a Web server (regardless of its type) can be linked with its URL.

For instance, if users need to download a PDF file named `doc.pdf` and a `.zip` archive called `software.zip` from a Web page, you use this HTML:

```
<h1>Download the new version of our software</h1>
<p><a href="software.zip">Software</a></p>
<p><a href="doc.pdf">Documentation</a></p>
```

You can't know how any user's browser responds with a click on a link to a non-Web file. The browser may

- ✔ Prompt the user to save the file
- ✔ Display the file without downloading (this is common for PDFs)
- ✔ Display an error message (if the browser can't handle the file)

To help users download files successfully, you should provide them with

- ✔ As much information as possible about the file formats.
- ✔ Any special tools they need to work with the files.

- To work with the contents of a Zip file, the users need a compression utility, such as WinZip or ZipIt, if their operating systems do not natively support Zip files.

- To view a PDF file, users need the Adobe Acrobat Reader.

You can make download markup more user-friendly by adding supporting text and links, like this:

```
<h1>Download the new version of our software</h1>
<p> <a href="software.zip">Software</a> <br />
   <b>Note:</b>
    You need a zip utility such as
<a href="http://www.winzip.com">WinZip</a> or
<a href="http://www.maczipit.com">ZipIt</a>
   to open this file.</p>
<p><a href="doc.pdf">Documentation</a> <br />
   <b>Note:</b>You need the free
<a href="http://www.adobe.com/products/
acrobat/readstep2.html">Acrobat Reader</a>
   to view this file.</p>
```

Figure 6-4 shows how a browser renders this HTML and the dialog box it displays when you click the software link.

E-mail addresses

A link to an e-mail address can automatically open a new e-mail addressed to exactly the right person.

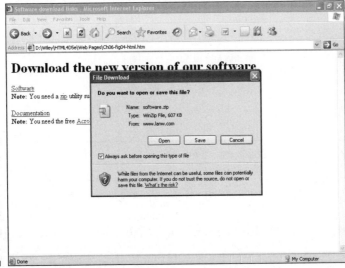

Figure 6-4:
This browser prompts you to save or view the Zip file.

This is a great way to help users send you e-mail with comments and requests.

An e-mail link uses the standard anchor element and `href` attribute. The value of the `href` attribute is the receiving e-mail address prefaced with `mailto:`

```
<p>Send us your
  <a href="mailto:comments@mysite.com">comments</a>.</p>
```

The user's browser configuration controls how the browser handles an e-mail link. Most browsers automatically

1. Open a new message window in the default e-mail program.

2. Insert the address from the `href` attribute in the To field of the message.

Unfortunately, Web page `mailto:` links are a prime source of e-mail addresses for spammers. Creating a form to receive feedback is often a better idea.

Marvelous Miscellany

Table 6-1 lists other link-related (X)HTML attributes that you might find in HTML files (and their characteristics).

Table 6-1	Additional (X)HTML Link Attributes		
Name	**Function/ Value Equals**	**Value Type(s)**	**Related Element(s)**
accesskey	Shortcut key to follow link	Text	`<a><area />` `<button>` `<input />` `<label>` `<legend>` `<textarea>`
charset	Character set for linked items	Text	`<a><link />` `<script>`
hreflang	Language for linked items	Language code	`<a><link />`
type	Advisory info for link content	Text	`<a><link />`

Chapter 7

Finding and Using Images

- -

- -

Web page designers use images to deliver important information, direct site navigation, and contribute to the overall look and feel of a Web page. But you need to use images properly or you risk reducing their effectiveness.

When used well, images are a key element of your page design. When used poorly, they can make your page unreadable or inaccessible.

This chapter is a crash course in using images on your Web pages. You find out which image formats are Web-friendly and how to use (X)HTML elements to add images to your Web pages. You also discover how to attach links to your images and how to create image maps for your Web page.

The Role of Images in a Web Page

Images in Web sites may be logos, clickable navigation aids, or display content; they may also make a page look prettier, or serve to unify or illustrate a page's theme. A perfect example of the many different ways images can enhance and contribute to Web pages is the White House home page at www.whitehouse.gov, shown in Figure 7-1.

Figure 7-1:
The White
House Web
page uses
images in a
variety of
ways.

Creating Web-Friendly Images

You can create and save graphics in many ways, but only a few formats are actually appropriate for images that you intend to use on the Web. As you create Web-friendly images, you must account for file formats and sizes.

Often, graphics file formats are specific to operating systems or software applications. But you can't predict a visitor's computer and software (other than a Web browser). So you need images that anyone can view with any browser. This means you need to use *cross-platform* file formats that users can view with any version of Microsoft Windows, the Mac OS, or Linux.

Only these three compressed formats are suitable for general use on the Web:

- **Graphics Interchange Format (GIF):** Images saved as GIFs often are smaller than those saved in other file formats. GIF supports up to 256 colors only, so if you try to save an image created with millions of colors as a GIF, you lose image quality. GIF is the best format for less-complex, nonphotographic images, such as line art and clip art.

- **Joint Photographic Experts Group (JPEG):** The JPEG file format supports 24-bit color (millions of colors) and complex images, such as photographs. JPEG is cross-platform and application-independent. A good image-editing tool can help you tweak the compression so you can strike an optimum balance between image quality and image file size.

✔ **Portable Network Graphics (PNG):** PNG is the latest cross-platform and application-independent image file format. It was developed to bring together the best of GIF and JPEG. PNG has the same compression as GIF but supports 24-bit color (and even 32-bit color) like JPEG.

Internet Explorer 4, Netscape 4, and other older browsers don't support PNG, so many designers avoid it.

Any good graphics-editing tool, such as those in Chapter 20, lets you save images in any of these file formats. You can experiment with each one to see how converting a graphic from one format to the other changes its appearance and file size, and then choose the format that produces the best results.

Table 7-1 shows guidelines for choosing a file format for images by type.

Table 7-1	Choosing the Right File Format	
File Format	*Best Used For*	*Watch Out*
GIF	Line art and other images with few colors and less detail.	Don't use this format if you have a complex image or photo.
JPEG	Photos and other images with millions of colors and lots of detail.	Don't use with line art. Don't compromise too much quality when you compress the file.
PNG	Photos and other images with millions of colors and lots of detail.	Don't use with line art. Older browsers don't support PNG, so you may still lose Web surfers even though PNG offers the best balance between quality and file size.

Optimizing images

As you build graphics for your Web page, you need to maintain a healthy balance between file quality and size. Webmonkey has two good tutorials on trimming image file sizes and optimizing entire sites to download faster. For a collection of tips and tricks that can help you build pages that download quickly, review

✔ Optimizing Your Images

    http://hotwired.lycos.com/webmonkey/
        99/15/index0a.html

✔ Site Optimization Tutorial

    http://hotwired.lycos.com/webmonkey/
        design/site_building/
        tutorials/tutorial2.html

For a complete overview of graphics formats, visit

✔ Builder.com's "Examine Graphic Channels and Space"

> `http://builder.cnet.com/webbuilding/0-3883-8-4892140-1.html`

✔ Webmonkey's "Web Graphics Overview"

> `http://webmonkey.wired.com/webmonkey/01/28/index1a.html`

Adding an Image to a Web Page

When an image is ready for the Web, you need to use the correct markup to add the image to your page. But you need to know where to store your image.

Location of the image

You can store images for your Web site in several places. Image storage is best if your images are *relative* (stored somewhere on the Web site with your other (X)HTML files). You can store the images in the same root file as your (X)HTML files, which can get confusing if you have a lot of files, or you can create a `graphics` or `images` directory in the root file of your Web site.

Relative links connect resources from the same Web site. You use absolute links between resources on two different Web sites. Turn to Chapter 6 for a complete discussion of the differences between relative and absolute links.

Three compelling reasons to store images on your own site are

✔ **Control:** When the images are stored on your site, you have complete control over them. You know that your images aren't going to disappear or change, and you can work to optimize them.

✔ **Speed:** If you link to images on someone else's site, you never know when that site may go down or be unbelievably slow. Linking to images on someone else's site also causes the other site owner to pay for the bandwidth required to display it on your site.

✔ **Copyright:** If you link to images on another Web site to display them on your site, you may violate copyright law. (In this case, obtain permission from the copyright holder to store and display the images on your site.)

Using the <img /> element

The image (`<img />`) element is an *empty element* (sometimes called a *singleton tag)* that you place on the page where you want your image to go.

An empty element has only one tag, with neither a distinct opening nor closing tag.

The following markup places an image named `07fg02-cd.jpg`, which is saved in the same directory as the (X)HTML file, between two paragraphs:

```
<!DOCTYPE html PUBLIC "-//W3C//DTD XHTML 1.0 Transitional//EN"
                    "http://www.w3.org/TR/xhtml1/DTD/xhtml1-transitional.dtd">
<html xmlns="http://www.w3.org/1999/xhtml">
<head>
  <meta http-equiv="Content-Type" content="text/html; charset=ISO-8859-1" />
  <title>CDs at Work</title>
</head>
  <body>
  <h1>CD as a Storage Media</h1>
  <p>CD-ROMs have become a standard storage option in today's computing world
      because they are an inexpensive and easy to use media.</p>
  <img src="07fg02-cd.jpg" />
  <p>To read from a CD, you only need a standard CD-ROM drive, but to create
      CDs, you need either a CD-R or a CD-R/W drive.</p>
  </body>
</html>
```

A Web browser replaces the `<img />` element with the image file provided as the value for the `src` attribute, as shown in Figure 7-2.

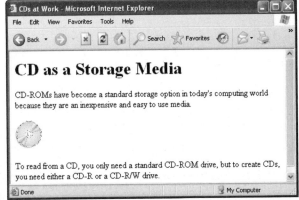

Figure 7-2:
Use the
<img />
element to
place
graphics in
a Web page.

The `src` attribute is like the `href` attribute that you use with an anchor (`<a>`) element. The `src` attribute specifies the location of the image you want to display on your page. The preceding example points to an image file in the same folder as the HTML file referencing it.

Adding alternative text

Alternative text describes the image so users who for some reason can't see the images can access the alternative text and know what the image is. Adding alternative text is a good practice because it accounts for

✔ Visually impaired users who may not be able to see the images and rely on the alternative text for a text-to-speech reader to read to them.

✔ Users who access the Web site from a phone browser with limited graphics capabilities.

✔ Users with slow modem connections who don't display images.

Some search engines and cataloging tools use alternative text to index images.

Most of your users will see your images, but be prepared for those who won't. The (X)HTML specifications require that you provide alternative text to describe each image on a Web page. Use the `alt` attribute with the `<img />` element to add this information to your markup, like this:

```
<!DOCTYPE html PUBLIC "-//W3C//DTD XHTML 1.0 Transitional//EN"
                      "http://www.w3.org/TR/xhtml1/DTD/xhtml1-transitional.dtd">
<html xmlns="http://www.w3.org/1999/xhtml">
<head>
  <meta http-equiv="Content-Type" content="text/html; charset=ISO-8859-1" />
  <title>Inside the Orchestra</title>
</head>

<body>
  <p>Among the different sections of the orchestra you will find:</p>
  <p><img src="07fg03-violin.jpg" alt="violin " /> Strings</p>
  <p><img src="07fg03-trumpet.jpg" alt="trumpet" /> Brass</p>
  <p><img src="07fg03-woodwinds.jpg" alt="clarinet and saxophone" />
     Woodwinds</p>
</body>
</html>
```

When browsers don't display an image (or can't, in text-only browsers such as Lynx), they display the alternative text instead, as shown in Figure 7-3.

When browsers show an image, some browsers, including Internet Explorer, Netscape, and Opera, show alternative text as a pop-up tip when you hold your mouse over an image for a few seconds, as shown in Figure 7-4. Firefox, however, does not.

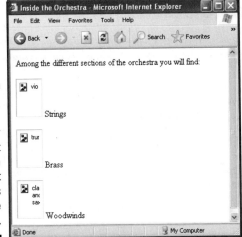

Figure 7-3:
When a browser doesn't show an image, it shows alternative text.

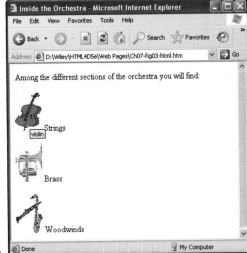

Figure 7-4:
A browser may display alternative text as a pop-up tip.

This means you can use alternative text to either describe the image to those who can't see it or provide useful or amusing information about the image.

The W3C's Web Accessibility Initiative (WAI) includes helpful tips for creating useful and usable alternatives to visual content at www.w3.org/TR/WCAG10-TECHS/#gl-provide-equivalents.

Specifying image size

You can use the `height` and `width` attributes with the `<img />` element to let the browser know just how tall and wide an image is (in pixels):

```
<p><img src="07fg03-trumpet.jpg" width="50" height="70" alt="trumpet"
      />Brass</p>
```

Most browsers download the HTML and text associated with a page before they download all the page graphics. Instead of making users wait for the whole page to download, browsers typically display the text first and fill in graphics as they become available. If you tell the browser how big a graphic is, the browser can reserve a spot for it in the page display. This smoothes the change as graphics are added to the Web page.

You can check the width and height of an image in pixels in any image-editing program or the image viewers built into Windows and the Mac OS. (You might also be able to simply view the properties of the image in either Windows or the Mac OS to see its height and width.)

Another good use of the `height` and `width` attributes is to create colored lines on a page by using just a small colored square. For example, this markup adds a 10-x-10-pixel blue box to a Web page:

```
<img src="07fg05-blue-box.gif" alt="blue box" height="10" width="10" />
```

When the `<img />` element `height` and `width` attributes equal the image height and width, it appears as a blue box in a browser window (like Figure 7-5).

Figure 7-5:
A small box.

However, a change to the values for `height` and `width` in the markup turns this small blue box into a line 20 pixels high and 500 pixels long:

```
<img src="07fg05-blue-box.gif" alt="blue box" height="20" width="500" />
```

The browser expands the image to fit the height and width specifics in the markup, as shown in Figure 7-6.

Figure 7-6:
A small box
becomes a
long line.

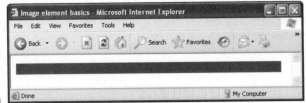

Using this technique, you can turn a single image like the blue box (only 1K in
size) into a variety of lines and even boxes:

- ✔ This can ensure that all the dividers and other border elements on your
  page use the same color — they're all based on the same graphic.

- ✔ If you decide you want to change all your blue lines to green, you just
  change the image. Every line you've created changes colors.

When you specify a height and width for an image that are different from the
image's actual height and width, you rely on the browser to scale the image display. This works great for single-color images like the blue box, but it doesn't
work well for images with multiple colors or images that display actual pictures. The browser doesn't size images well, and you wind up with a distorted
picture. Figure 7-7 shows how badly a browser handles enlarging a trumpet
image when the markup doubles the image height and width:

```
<p><img src="07fg03-trumpet.jpg" width="200" height="300" alt="trumpet" />
         Brass</p>
```

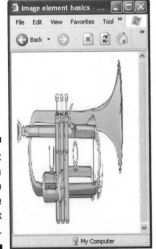

Figure 7-7:
Don't use a
browser to
resize
complex
images.

If you need several sizes of the same image, for example, a logo or navigation button, use the largest size image to make smaller versions in an image-editing tool so you can better control the final look and feel of the image.

Setting the image border

By default, every image has a border of 1, which doesn't show up in most browsers until you turn that image into a link (as shown in the "Images That Link" section later). You can use the border attribute with the <img /> element to better control what border the browser displays around your image. This markup sets the border for the clarinet image to 10 pixels:

```
<img src="07fg03-woodwinds.jpg" width="50" height="70" alt="clarinet and saxo-
        phone" border="10" />
```

The browser uses this border on all four sides of the image, as in Figure 7-8.

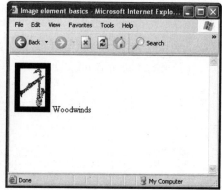

Figure 7-8:
Use the border attribute to create a border around your image.

In Figure 7-8, the border is black and applies to all four sides of the image. If you want to control the color of the border or make the border appear differently on each side of the image, you have two options:

- ✔ Build the border into the image in an image-editing tool.
- ✔ Use Cascading Style Sheets (CSS), which we cover in Chapter 8.

If you use an image-editing tool to create your border, you can use the tool's features to create a patterned border or apply a unique effect. However, the extra information in the image may make it bigger. Carefully balance your image size and its appearance so it doesn't take too long to download.

If you use CSS to apply a border, your image won't get any bigger, but your border may not show up in older browsers that don't support CSS well. The choice you make depends on how crucial the border is to your image (if it's very important, embed it in the image) and what browser you think your visitors use (newer browsers have better support for style sheets).

Controlling image alignment

The align attribute works with the <img /> element to control how your image appears relative to the text around it. The possible values for this attribute are

- ✔ top: Aligns the text around the image with the top of the image.
- ✔ middle: Aligns the text around the image with the middle of the image.
- ✔ bottom: Aligns the text around the image with the bottom of the image.
- ✔ left: The image sits on the left, and text floats to the right of the image.
- ✔ right: The image sits on the right, and text floats to the left of the image.

By default, most browsers align images to the left and float all text to the right. The following markup shows how five different <img /> elements use the align attribute to change how text floats around the mouse images:

```
<p> <img src="07fg09-mouse.jpg" alt="mouse with top-aligned text"
        height="105" width="65" align="top" />
    This text is aligned with the top of the image.
</p>

<p> <img src="07fg09-mouse.jpg" alt="mouse with middle-aligned text"
        height="105" width="65" align="middle" />
    This text is aligned with the middle of the image.
</p>

<p> <img src="07fg09-mouse.jpg" alt="mouse with bottom-aligned text"
        height="105" width="65" align="bottom" />
    This text is aligned with the bottom of the image.
</p>

<p> <img src="07fg09-mouse.jpg" alt="mouse with left-aligned text"
        height="105" width="65" align="left" />
    This image floats to the left of the text.
</p>

<p> <img src="07fg09-mouse.jpg" alt="mouse with right-aligned text"
        height="105" width="65" align="right" />
    This image floats to the right of the text, and overlaps with
    the image to the left.
</p>
```

Figure 7-9 shows how a browser interprets different alignment attributes.

The <img /> attributes may not give you all the control of image alignment that you want. Chapter 11 shows tables and images used together. Chapter 8 shows CSS properties that control how images sit on the page.

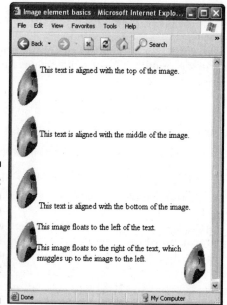

Figure 7-9:
You can
vary image
alignment to
control
image
placement
on the page.

Setting image spacing

Most browsers leave about a pixel of white space between images and the text or other images next to them. You can give your images breathing room with

✔ The vspace *(vertical space)* attribute for top and bottom

✔ The hspace *(horizontal space)* attribute for left and right

The following HTML gives the mouse graphic 20 pixels of white space on either side and 25 pixels on the top and bottom:

```
<p>
  This text doesn't crowd the image on top.<br />
  <img src="07fg09-mouse.jpg"
```

```
        height="105" width="65" hspace="20" vspace="25"
        alt="mouse on a white background" />
And this text is a little further away from the sides. </p>
```

Figure 7-10 shows how a browser adds space around the image.

The default value for hspace and vspace is 1. If you want images so close together that their sides touch (like for a set of navigation buttons), set the value for these attributes to 0 to eliminate that extra 1 pixel of space.

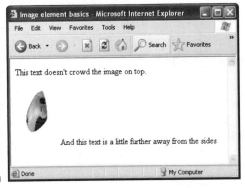

Figure 7-10:
hspace and
vspace
control the
white space
around an
image.

You can use CSS to position images on a page. You can position images with accuracy and with control over placement, spacing, white space, and how text flows around the graphic. Chapter 9 has the details to position items.

Images That Link

Web pages often use images for navigation. They're prettier than plain-text links, and you can add both form and function on your page with one element.

Triggering links

To create an image that triggers a link, you substitute an <img /> element in place of the text you would anchor your link to. This markup links text:

```
<p><a href="http://www.w3.org">Visit the W3C</a></p>
```

This markup replaces the text `Visit the W3C` with an appropriate icon:

```
<p><a href="http://www.w3.org"><img src="w3.jpg"
     alt="Visit the W3C Web Site" height="48" width="315" border="0" /></a>

</p>
```

The preceding markup creates a linked image to `http://www.w3.org`. In the preceding example, the alternative text now reads `Visit the W3C Web Site` so users who can't see the image know where the link goes. When a user moves the mouse pointer over the image, the cursor changes from an arrow into a pointing hand (or any icon the browser uses for a link), as in Figure 7-11.

Figure 7-11: Combine image and anchor elements to create a linked image.

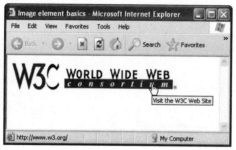

A quick click of the image launches the W3C Web site. It's as simple as that.

As shown earlier in the chapter, you should set the border of any image you use in a link to `0` to keep the browser from surrounding your image with an ugly blue line. Without the line, however, users need other visual (or alternative text) clues so they know an image is a link. Be sure images that serve as links scream to the user (tastefully of course) "I'm a link!"

Building image maps

When you use an `<img />` element with an anchor element to create a linking image, you can attach only one link to that image. To create a larger image that connects links to different regions on the page, you need an *image map*.

To create an image map, you need two things:

- ✔ An image with several distinct areas that would be obvious to users. (For example, an image of a park might show a playground area, a picnic area, and a pond area.)
- ✔ Markup to map the different regions on the map to different URLs.

Elements and attributes

You use the `<img />` element to add the map image into your page, just as you would any other image. In addition, you include the `usemap` attribute to let the browser know that there's image map information to go with the image. The value of the `usemap` attribute is the name of your map.

You use two elements and a collection of attributes to define the image map:

✔ `<map>` holds the map information. The `<map>` element uses the `name` attribute to identify the map. The value of `name` should match the value of `usemap` in the `<img />` element that goes with the map.

✔ `<area />` links specific parts of the map to URLs. The `<area />` element takes these attributes to define the specifics for each section of the map:

   • `shape`: Specifies the shape of the region (a clickable hot spot that makes the image map work). You can choose from `rect` (rectangle), `circle`, and `poly` (a triangle or polygon).

   • `coords`: Define the region's coordinates. A *rectangle's* coordinates include the *left, right, top,* and *bottom points.* A *circle's* coordinates include the *x and y coordinates* for the center of the circle as well as the circle's *radius.* A polygon's coordinates are a collection of *x and y coordinates* for every vertex in the polygon.

   • `href`: Specifies the URL to which the region links. This can be an absolute or relative URL.

   • `alt`: Provides alternative text for the image region.

Markup

This defines a three-region map called `NavMap` linked to the `navigation.gif`:

```
<img src="navigation.gif" width="302" height="30" usemap="#NavMap" border="0" />
<map name="NavMap" />
  <area shape="rect" coords="0,0,99,30" href="home.html" alt="Home" />
  <area shape="rect" coords="102,0,202,30" href="about.html" alt="About" />
  <area shape="rect" coords="202,0,301,30" href="products.html"
        alt="Products" />
</map>
```

Figure 7-12 shows how a browser displays this markup.

When the mouse sits over a region in the map, the cursor turns into a pointing hand (just as it changes over any other hyperlink). So take advantage of the alternative text to include useful information about the link.

Figure 7-12:
Image
maps turn
different
areas of an
image into
linking
regions.

A common use for image maps is to turn maps of places (states, countries, cities, and such) into linkable maps. Webmonkey's image map tutorial at `http://webmonkey.wired.com/webmonkey/96/40/index2a.html` provides more details on optimizing image maps and maximizing this (X)HTML feature.

Creating image maps by hand can be a tricky. You use an image editor to identify each point in the map and then create the proper markup for it. Most (X)HTML tools include utilities to help you make image maps. If you take advantage of one of these tools, you can create image maps quickly and with fewer errors. Find out more about (X)HTML tools in Chapter 20.

Marvelous Miscellany

Table 7-2 lists other (X)HTML images and image maps attributes (along with other input-related tags that use image maps) that you might find in HTML files.

Table 7-2	Additional (X)HTML Image and Map Attributes		
Name	**Function/ Value Equals**	**Value Type(s)**	**Related Element(s)**
name	Provides a name for usemap attribute	CDATA	`<map>`
nohref	Inactive areas on image maps	"nohref"	`<area />`
usemap	Tells browser to run client-side map	URI	`<img />` `<input />` `<object>`

Part III

Taking Precise Control Over Web Pages

The 5th Wave — By Rich Tennant

"Before the Internet, we were only bustin' chops locally. But now, with our Web site, we're bustin' chops all over the world."

In this part . . .

In this part of the book, we introduce and describe Cascading Style Sheets (CSS), a powerful markup language that is often used to supplement (X)HTML and to manage the way it looks in a Web browser. (X)HTML can reference CSS by including either an external style sheet or inline CSS markup within an (X)HTML document.

Here, you start out by learning the many and various capabilities of CSS, about different kinds of style sheets, and about the rules for handling multiple style sheets when they're applied to a single Web page (that's where the *Cascading* in CSS comes from). Of course, you also learn how to build and use CSS for things like creating visual layouts, positioning individual items, and handling fonts. Because CSS also provides controls over color and modifying how text appears on the page, you learn how to deal with these capabilities as well.

Tables are an important way to organize and represent data in (X)HTML. This part of the book shows basic table setup, structure, and syntax, and also explains how you can use CSS to manage table appearance.

Chapter 8

Introducing Cascading Style Sheets

*T*he goal of *Cascading Style Sheets* (CSS) is to separate a Web page's style from its structure and to make it easier to maintain Web pages that you've created. The structural elements of a page, such as headings (`<h1>` through `<h6>`) and body text, don't have affect the look of those elements. By applying styles to those elements, you can *specify the element's layout on the page* and *add design attributes (*such as fonts, colors, and text indentation).

Style sheets give you precise control over how structural elements appear on a Web page. What's even better is that you can create one style sheet for an entire Web site to ensure that the layout and look of your content is consistent from page to page. And here's the icing on this cake: Style sheets are easy to build and even easier to integrate into your Web pages. In fact, you can add style markup to individual (X)HTML elements (called *inline style*), create sequences of style instructions in the head of an (X)HTML document (called an *internal style sheet*), or refer to a separate standalone style sheet via some kind of link or other reference (called an *external style sheet*) in your (X)HTML document. There are lots of ways to add style to a Web page!

As HTML evolves and as more Web sites transition to XHTML, the goal of the markup powers-that-be is to eventually *deprecate* (make obsolete) all formatting markup, such as the `<font>` element, from HTML's collection of elements.

Using CSS versus deprecated HTML

Cascading Style Sheets (CSS) provide you with more flexibility and allow you to control alignment, color, line height, kerning, and so forth in ways that HTML never could. Using CSS also allows you to separate formatting from content and fosters cleaner markup, better maintainability, and easier troubleshooting. No two ways about it: CSS is better.

However, there is a slight catch. CSS support appeared in Web browsers in the late 1990s. By now, most users have upgraded to browsers that support CSS fully. However, studies show that about 10 percent of users have not upgraded and may not upgrade soon. That means that you must decide whether that 10 percent falls into your target audience. If so, plan accordingly.

For example, if you are creating an intranet site strictly for viewing by your co-workers, you can

safely use CSS by requiring that all users use Internet Explorer (IE) 5.0 or a newer version. However, if you're creating a site that will be accessible to the public at large, you can't control which browser your visitors use. A visitor who still uses IE 4.0, for example, can't view content that is controlled by CSS — the text appears to run together without any visible formatting.

Therefore, the best way to accommodate both old and new browsers is by using a CSS style sheet and deprecated HTML formatting tags. (Check out Appendix A at the end of this book, which covers all *deprecated* (X)HTML elements and attributes.) The CSS style sheet overrides HTML formatting tags in newer browsers, so those deprecated tags work only when the browser doesn't recognize CSS. It's not an elegant solution, but it works!

When you want tight control over the display of your Web pages, style sheets are the way to go:

- ✔ Generally, style sheets give you more flexibility than markup can.
- ✔ The HTML element collection won't include any more display-oriented tags in the future.

 Most modern browsers handle CSS well. However, some older browsers, such as the 4.0 Internet Explorer and Netscape Navigator browsers, have trouble displaying CSS correctly. Earlier browsers can't display CSS at all. If you know that many of your site's users still use one or more of these obsolete browsers, test your pages in these browsers to make sure they're readable.

Advantages of Style Sheets

HTML's formatting capabilities are limited, to say the least. When you design a page layout in HTML, you're limited to tables, font controls, and a few inline styles, such as bold and italic. *Style sheets* provide lots of tools for formatting Web pages with precise control. With style sheets you can

> ✔ **Carefully control every aspect of the display of your page:** Specify page items such as the amount of space between lines, character spacing, page margins, and image placement. You can also specify the positioning of elements on your pages.

> ✔ **Apply changes globally:** You can guarantee consistent design across an entire Web site by applying the same style sheet to every Web page.

> Quickly and easily modify the look and feel of your entire site by changing one document (the style sheet) instead of the markup on every page. Need to change the look of a heading? Redefine the heading's style attributes in the style sheet and save the sheet. The heading's look changes throughout your site.

> ✔ **Instruct browsers to control appearance:** Provide Web browsers with more information about how you want your pages to appear than you can communicate using HTML.

> ✔ **Create dynamic pages:** Use JavaScript or another scripting language along with style sheets to create text and other content that moves, appears, or hides in response to user actions.

What CSS can do for a Web page

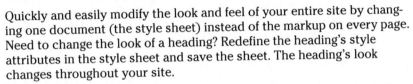

The gist of how style sheets work is this:

1. You define rules in a style sheet that specify how you want content described by a set of markup to appear.

   For example, you could specify that every first-level heading (`<h1>`) be displayed in purple, Garamond, 24-point type with a yellow background (not that you *would,* but you could).

2. You link style rules and markup.

3. The browser does the rest.

The current specification, CSS2.1, can

> ✔ Specify font type, size, color, and effects

> ✔ Set background colors and images

> ✔ Control many aspects of text layout, including alignment and spacing

> ✔ Set margins and borders

> ✔ Control list display

> ✔ Define table layout and display

- ✔ Automatically generate content for such standard page elements as counters and footers
- ✔ Control cursor display
- ✔ Define aural style sheets for text-to-speech browsers

What you can do with CSS

You have a healthy collection of properties to work with as you write your style rules. You can control just about every aspect of a page's display — from borders to font sizes and everything in between:

- ✔ **Background properties** control the background colors associated with blocks of text and with images. You can also use these properties to attach background colors to your page or to individual elements.
- ✔ **Border properties** control borders associated with the page, lists, tables, images, and block elements (such as paragraphs). You can specify border width, color, style, and distance from the element's content.
- ✔ **Classification properties** control how elements such as images flow on the page relative to other elements. You can use these properties to integrate images and tables with the text on your page.
- ✔ **List properties** control how lists appear on your page, such as
  - Managing list markers
  - Using images in place of bullets

TECHNICAL STUFF

CSS3: Next-generation style sheets

The next generation of CSS — CSS3 — is a collection of *modules* that address different aspects of Web-page formatting, such as fonts, background colors, lists, and text colors. The first of these modules became standards (officially called *Candidate Recommendations*) in mid-2004. But the majority of CSS3 modules aren't expected to become Candidate Recommendations until late 2005 or 2006, and few browsers implement CSS3 features. In short, you don't need to worry about CSS3 — yet.

The W3C has devoted an entire section of its Web site to this topic at www.w3.org/style/css. You can find general CSS information there, as well as keep up with the status of CSS3. The site links to good CSS references and tutorials, and includes information on software packages that can make your style sheet endeavors easier.

✔ **Margin properties** control the margins of the page and margins around block elements, tables, and images. These properties extend the ultimate control over the white space on your page.

✔ **Padding properties** control the amount of white space around any block element on the page. When used with margin and border properties, you can create some complex layouts.

✔ **Positioning properties** control where elements sit on the page, giving you the ability to place elements in specific places on the page.

✔ **Size properties** control how much space (in height and width) that your elements (both text and images) take up on your page. They're especially handy for limiting the size of text boxes and images.

✔ **Table properties** control the layout of tables. You can use them to control cell spacing and other table-layout specifics.

✔ **Text properties** control how text appears on the page. You can set such properties as font size, font family, height, text color, letter and line spacing, alignment, and white space. These properties give you more control over your text with style sheets than the font HTML element can.

Property measurement values

Many HTML properties use measurement values. We tell you which measurement values go with which properties throughout this book. Standard property measurements dictate the size of a property in two ways.

Absolute value measurements can dictate a specific length or height with one of these values:

✔ **inches,** such as .5in

✔ **centimeters,** such as 3cm

✔ **millimeters,** such as 4mm

✔ **picas,** such as 1pc

There are about six picas in an inch.

✔ **points,** such as 16pt

There are 12 points in a pica.

✔ **pixels,** such as 13px (these match up to individual dots on your computer display).

Relative value measurements base length or height on a *parent element* value in the document:

✔ **p%:** A percentage of the current font-size value, such as 150%

For example, you can define a font size of 80% for all paragraphs. If your document body is defined with a 15-point font, the font size of the paragraphs is 12 points (80 percent of 15).

✔ **ex:** A value that is relative to the x-height of the current font. An x-height is the equivalent of the height of the lowercase character of a font, such as 1.5ex

✔ **em:** A value that is relative to the current font size, such as 2em

Both 1em and 100% equal the current size.

Be careful when using these values because some properties allow only some of the measurement values, such as length values but not relative values. Don't let the jargon scare you. Just define the size in a value you're familiar with.

Entire books and Web sites are devoted to the fine details of using each and every property in these categories. We suggest one of these references:

- *Cascading Style Sheets For Dummies* by Damon A. Dean, published by Wiley Publishing.
- Westciv's CSS2 reference on the Web:

  ```
  www.westciv.com/style_master/academy/css_tutorial/index.html
  ```

Although CSS syntax is straightforward, combining CSS styles with markup to fine-tune your page layout can be a little complicated. But to become a CSS guru, you just need to

- Know the details of how the different properties work.
- Experiment with how browsers handle CSS.

  Practice shows you the right way to convey your message on the Web with CSS.

CSS Structure and Syntax

A style sheet is made of *style rules*. Each style rule has two parts:

- **Selector:** Specifies the markup element to which the style rules apply.
- **Declaration:** Specifies how the content described by the markup looks.

You use a set of punctuation marks and special characters to define a style rule. The syntax for a style rule always follows this pattern:

```
selector {declaration}
```

A declaration breaks down further into two items:

- **Properties** are aspects of how the computer displays text and graphics (for example, font size or background color).
- **Values** are the data that specify how you want text and images to look on your page (for example, a 24-point font size or a yellow background).

You separate the property from the value in a declaration with a colon:

```
selector {property: value}
```

For example, these three style rules set the colors for first-, second-, and third-level headings:

```
h1 {color: teal}
h2 {color: maroon}
h3 {color: black}
```

The CSS specification lists exactly which properties you can work with in your style rules and the different values that they can take. Most are pretty self-explanatory (`color` and `border`, for example). See "What you can do with CSS," earlier in this chapter, for a quick rundown of what properties the CSS2 specification includes.

Style sheets override a browser's internal display rules; your formatting specifications affect *the final appearance of the page in the user's browser.* This means you can better control how your content looks and create a more consistent and appropriate experience for visitors

For example, the following style rules specify the font sizes (in pixels) for first-, second-, and third-level headings:

```
h1 {font-size: 24px}
h2 {font-size: 18px}
h3 {font-size: 16px}
```

Figure 8-1 shows a simple HTML page with all three heading levels (plus some body text) without the style sheet applied. The browser uses its default settings to display the headings in different font sizes.

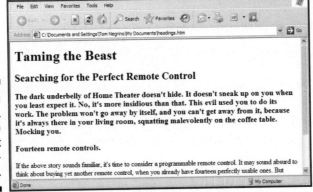

Figure 8-1:
An HTML page without style specifications.

Figure 8-2 shows the same Web page with a style sheet applied. The headings are significantly smaller than in the preceding figure. That's because the style sheet rules override the browser's settings.

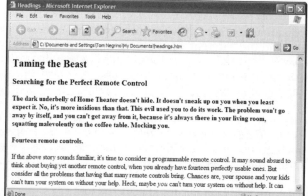

Figure 8-2: An HTML page with style speci- fications in effect.

Users can change their preferences so their browsers ignore your style sheets. (Most users will use your sheets) Test your Web page with style sheets turned off to be sure it looks good (or acceptable) without your style sheets.

Selectors and declarations

You probably want a style rule to affect the display of more than one prop- erty for any given selector. You can create several style rules for a single selector, each with one declaration, like this:

```
h1 {color: teal}
h1 {font-family: Arial}
h1 {font-size: 36px}
```

However, such a large collection of style rules becomes hard to manage. CSS lets you combine several declarations in a *single* style rule that affects the display characteristics of a single selector, like this:

```
h1 {color: teal;
    font-family: Arial;
    font-size: 36px}
```

Font family

When assigning values to the `font-family` property, you can provide a list of comma-separated font names. These names must match fonts available to the user's Web browser. If a font name, such as "Times New Roman," includes spaces, it must be enclosed in quotation marks.

```
h1 {font-family: Verdana; "Times New
          Roman", serif;}
```

The browser seeks to use Verdana first, and if it's not available, it looks for Times New Roman next, and then uses a generic serif font as its last option. Chapter 10 covers fonts in CSS.

All the declarations for the `h1` selector are within the same set of brackets (`{}`) and are separated by a semicolon (`;`). You can put as many declarations as you want in a style rule; just end each declaration with a semicolon.

The semicolon at the end of the last declaration is optional. Some people include it to be consistent and end every declaration with a semicolon, but it's not necessary. We use it both ways throughout this book.

From a purely technical standpoint, white space is irrelevant in style sheets (just as it is in HTML), but you should use a consistent spacing scheme so that you can easily read and edit your style sheets. An exception to this white-space rule is when you declare multiple font names in the font-family declaration. See the "Font family" sidebar for more information.

You can make the same set of declarations apply to a collection of selectors, too: You just separate the selectors with *commas.* The following style rule applies the declarations for text color, font family, and font size to the `h1`, `h2`, and `h3` selectors:

```
h1, h2, h3 {color: teal;
           font-family: Arial;
           font-size: 36px}
```

The sample style rules in this section show that style sheet syntax relies heavily on punctuation. When a style rule doesn't work exactly as you anticipate, make sure your syntax doesn't use a semicolon where you need a colon, and doesn't use a parenthesis where you need a bracket

The W3C's validation service can help you find problems in your style sheets:

```
http://jigsaw.w3.org/css-validator/
```

Working with style classes

Sometimes you need style rules that apply only to specific instances of an HTML markup element. For example, if you want a style rule that applies only to paragraphs that hold copyright information, you need a way to tell the browser that the rule has a limited scope.

To target a style rule more closely, combine the `class` attribute with a markup element. The following examples show HTML for two kinds of paragraphs:

- A regular paragraph (without a `class` attribute)

  ```
  <p>This is a regular paragraph.</p>
  ```

- A `class` attribute with the value of `copyright`

  ```
  <p class="copyright">This is a paragraph of class copyright.</p>
  ```

To create a style rule that applies only to the copyright paragraph, follow the paragraph selector in the style rule with

- A period (.)
- The value of the `class` attribute, such as `copyright`

The resulting rule looks like this:

```
p.copyright {font-family: Arial;
             font-size: 12px;
             color: white;
             background: black}
```

This style rule specifies that all paragraphs of class `copyright` display white text on a black background in 12-pixel Arial font. Figure 8-3 shows how a browser applies this style rule only to paragraphs with the `copyright` attribute.

Figure 8-3:
Classes can target your style rules more precisely.

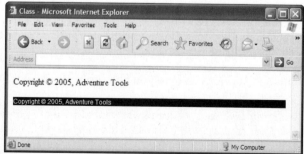

You can also create style-rule classes that aren't associated with any element, like the following example:

```
.warning {font-family: Arial;
          font-size: 14px;
          background: black;
          color: white}
```

You can use this style class with any element by adding `class="warning"` to that element. Figure 8-4 shows how a browser applies the warning style to the paragraph and heading, but not the block quote, in this HTML:

```
<p class="warning">This is a paragraph without the warning class applied.</p>
<blockquote>This is a block quote without a defined class.</blockquote>
<p class="warning">This is a paragraph with the warning class applied.</p>
```

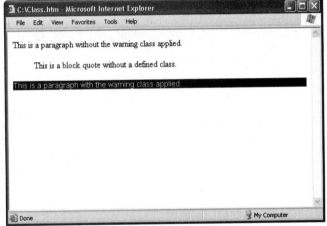

Figure 8-4:
You can use classes to create style rules that work with any element.

Inheriting styles

One of the basic concepts in HTML (and markup in general) is nesting tags:

- ✔ Your entire HTML document is nested within `<html>` and `</html>` tags.
- ✔ Everything a browser displays in a window is nested within `<body>` and `</body>` tags. (That's just the beginning, really.)

The CSS specification recognizes that you often nest one element inside another and wants to be sure that styles associated with the parent element find their way to the child element. This mechanism is called *inheritance*.

When you assign a style to an element, the same style is applied to all the elements nested inside the element. For example, a style rule for the body element that sets the page background, text color, font size, font family, and margins looks like this:

```
body {background: black;
      color: white;
      font-size: 18px;

      font-family: Garamond;
      margin-left: 72px;
      margin-right: 72px;
      margin-top: 72px)
```

If you want to set style rules for the entire document, set them in the body element. Changing the font for the entire page, for example, is much easier to do that way; it beats changing every single element one at a time.

When you link the following HTML to the preceding style rule, which applies only to the body element, the formatting is inherited to all elements (as shown in Figure 8-5):

```
<body>
  <p>This paragraph inherits the page styles.</p>
  <h1>As does this heading</h1>
  <ul>
      <li>As do the items in this list</li>
      <li>Item</li>
      <li>Item</li>
  </ul>
</body>
```

Figure 8-5:
Inheritance
means style
rules apply
to nested
elements.

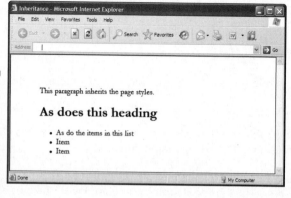

Paying attention to inheritance

When you build complex style sheets that guide the appearance of every aspect of a page, keep inheritance in mind. For instance, if you set margins for the page in a body style rule, all margins you set for every other element on the page are based on margins set for the body. If you know how your style rules work together, you can use inheritance to minimize style rule repetition and create a cohesive display for your page.

This chapter covers basic CSS syntax, but you can fine-tune your style rules with advanced techniques. A complete overview of CSS syntax rules is available in the "CSS Structure and Rules" tutorial by the Web Design Group at `www.htmlhelp.com/reference/css/st ructure.html`.

Using Different Kinds of Style Sheets

When you finish creating your style rules, you're ready to connect them to your HTML page with one of these options:

✔ **Insert style information into your document.** You can either

- Use the `<style>` element to build a style sheet into a Web page.

  This is an *internal style sheet*.

- Use the `style` attribute to add style information directly to a tag.

  This is an *inline style*.

✔ **Use an *external style sheet*.** You can either

- Use the `<link>` tag to *link* your Web page to an external style sheet.

- Use the CSS `@import` statement to *import* an external style sheet into the Web page.

Internal style sheets

An internal style sheet lives within your HTML page. Just add style rules in a `<style>` element in the document's header. You can include as many (or as few) style rules as you want in an internal style sheet. (See Listing 8-1.)

Listing 8-1: **Adding an Internal Style Sheet to an HTML Document**

```
<!DOCTYPE html PUBLIC "-//W3C//DTD XHTML 1.0 Transitional//EN"
        "http://www.w3.org/TR/xhtml1/DTD/xhtml1-transitional.dtd">
<html xmlns="http://www.w3.org/1999/xhtml">
<head>
  <title>Internal Style Sheet Example</title>
  <style type="text/css">
    body {background: black;
        color: white;
        font-size: 16px;
        font-family: Garamond;
        margin-left: 72px;
        margin-right: 72px;
        margin-top: 72px}

    h1, h2, h3 {color: teal;
            font-family: Arial;
            font-size: 36px}

    p.copyright {font-family: Arial;
            font-size: 12px;
            font-color: white;
            background: black}

    warning {font-family: Arial;
        font-size: 16px;
        font-color: red}
  </style>
</head>
<body>

<!-- Document content goes here -->

</body>
</html>
```

The benefit of an internal style sheet is convenience: Your style rules are on the same page as your markup so you can tweak both quickly. But if you want the same style rules to control the appearance of more than one HTML page, move those styles from individual Web pages to an external style sheet.

External style sheets

An external style sheet holds all your style rules in a separate text document you can reference from any HTML file on your site. You must maintain a separate style sheet file, but an external style sheet offers benefits for overall site maintenance. If your site's pages use the same style sheet, you can change any formatting characteristic on all pages with a change to the style sheet.

We recommend using external style sheets on your sites.

Linking

To reference an external style sheet, use the `link` element in the Web page header, like this:

```
<html>
<head>
  <title>External Style Sheet Example</title>
  <link rel="stylesheet" type="text/css" href="styles.css" />
<head>
<body>

<!-- Document content goes here -->

</body>
</html>
```

The `href` attribute in the `<link>` element can take either

- A relative link (a style sheet on your own site)
- An absolute link (a style sheet that doesn't reside on your own site)

  Usually, you shouldn't use a style sheet that doesn't reside on your Web site — you want control of your site's look and feel.

  If you want to quickly add style to your Web page (or experiment to see how browsers handle different styles), use an absolute URL to point to one of the W3C's Core style sheets. Read more about them at

  ```
  www.w3.org/StyleSheets/Core/
  ```

Chapter 6 covers the difference between relative and absolute links.

Importing

The `@import` statement instructs the browser to load an external style sheet and use its styles. You use it within the `<style>` element but before any of the individual style rules, like so:

```
<style>
  @import "http://www.somesite.edu/stylesheet.css";
</style>
```

Style rules in an imported style sheet take precedence over any rules that come before the `@import` statement. So if you have multiple external style sheets referenced with more than one `@import` on your page, rules apply from the later style sheets (the ones farther down on the page).

Use inline styles carefully

You can attach individual style rules, called an *inline style,* to individual elements in an HTML document. An inline style rule attached to an element looks like this:

```
<p style="color: green">Green text.</p>
```

Adding style rules to an element isn't really the best approach. We generally recommend that you choose either internal or (preferably) external style sheets for your rules instead of attaching the rules to individual elements in your document. Here are a few reasons:

✔ Your style rules get mixed up in the page and are hard to find.

✔ You must place the entire rule in the value of the `style` attribute, which makes complex rules hard to write and edit.

✔ You lose all the benefits that come with grouping selectors and reusing style rules in external style sheets.

Understanding the Cascade

Multiple style sheets can affect page elements and build upon one another. It's like inheriting styles within a Web page. This is the *cascading* part of CSS.

Here's a real-world example: a Web site for university's English department. The English department is part of the School of Humanities, which is just one school in the overall university. Each of these entities — the university, the school, and the English department — has its own style sheet.

1. The university's style sheet provides style rules for all of the pages in the overall site.

2. The school's style sheet links to the university's style sheet (using an `@import` statement), and adds more style rules specific to the look the school wants for its own site.

3. The English department's style sheet links to the school's style sheet.

   So the department's pages both *have their own style rules* and *inherit the style rules from both the school and the university's style sheet.*

But what if multiple style sheets define rules for the same element? What if, for example, all three style sheets specify a rule for the h1 element? In that case, the nearest rule to the page or element you're working on wins out:

✔ If an h1 rule exists on the department's style sheet, it takes precedence over the school and university h1 styles.

✔ If an individual page within the department applies a style rule to h1 in a `<style>` tag, that rule applies.

Chapter 9

Using Cascading Style Sheets

In This Chapter
▶ Understanding how CSS is used
▶ Positioning objects on a page
▶ Creating font rules
▶ Creating style sheets for print
▶ Understanding aural style sheets

*U*nderstanding the structure and syntax of CSS is easy. Learning about the properties that CSS can apply to (X)HTML documents takes a little more time and effort. However, where the learning curve really gets interesting is when it comes to learning how to use CSS to take a plain or ordinary Web page and "kick it up a notch." This chapter deals with how to put CSS to work, rather than focusing on its structure and inner workings.

Chapter 8 is a high-level overview of CSS and how it works. If you need a refresher of CSS style rules and properties, read Chapter 8, and then return to this chapter and put CSS in action.

Now it's time to make a page and give it some style!

To use CSS efficiently, follow these general guidelines:

✔ When you test how a page looks, use internal styles so you can tweak to your heart's delight. (This chapter shows internal style sheets.)

✔ When your test page looks just right, move those styles to an external sheet, and then apply them throughout your site.

Managing Layout, Positioning, and Appearance

You can use CSS to lay out your pages so that images and blocks of text

- ✔ Appear exactly where you want them to
- ✔ Fit exactly within the amount of space that you want them to occupy

After you create the styles within a document, you can create an external style sheet that applies the same styles to any page you want.

Developing specific styles

Listing 9-1 shows a Web page without any defined styles.

Listing 9-1: A Fairly Dull Page

```
<!DOCTYPE html PUBLIC "-//W3C//DTD XHTML 1.0 Transitional//EN"
  "http://www.w3.org/TR/xhtml1/DTD/xhtml1-transitional.dtd">
<html xmlns="http://www.w3.org/1999/xhtml">
<head>
  <title>Pixel's Page</title>
  <meta http-equiv="Content-Type" content="text/html; charset=ISO-8859-1" />
</head>
 <body>
  <h1>I'm Pixel the Cat. Welcome to my page.</h1>
  <div class="navbar">
    Links of interest:<br />
      <a href="http://www.google.com/">Google</a><br />
      <a href="http://www.amazon.com/">Amazon</a><br />
      <a href="http://www.yahoo.com/">Yahoo</a>
  </div>
  <img src="/images/pixel1.jpg" alt="The Cat" width="320" height="240"
   id="theCat" />
 </body>
</html>
```

The cat looks great, but the page certainly doesn't show off his possibilities. The addition of some styles improves the page immensely. Here's how!

Visual layouts

Instead of the links appearing above the image, as they are in Figure 9-1, we want them on the left, a typical location for navigation tools. The following markup floats the text for the search site links to the left of the image:

```
<style type="text/css">
  .navbar {
    background-color: #CCC;
    border-bottom: #999;
    border-left: #999;
    border-width: 0 0 thin thin;
    border-style: none none groove groove;
    display: block;
    float: left;
    margin: 0 0 0 10px;
    padding: 0 10px 0 10px;
    width: 190px;
  }
</style>
```

Figure 9-1:
This
styleless
page
doesn't live
up to this
cat's
possibilities.

In the preceding rules, we

- ✔ Added a `<style>` tag
- ✔ Defined the `navbar` class inside the `<style>` tag
- ✔ Used the `navbar` class to instruct the content to float to the left of images, which causes them to appear in the same part of the page on the left, rather than above the graphic

This rule says that anything on the page with a class of `navbar` (as shown in Figure 9-2) should display with

- ✔ A light-gray background
- ✔ A bottom and left thin grooved-line border in a darker gray

✔ No top or right border

✔ A block that floats to the left (so the everything else on the page moves right, as with the image of the cat in Figure 9-2)

✔ A left margin of 10 pixels

✔ Padding at top and bottom of 10 pixels each

✔ A navbar area 190 total pixels wide

Figure 9-2: The navigation bar now looks more like the standard left-hand navigation.

Note that several of the properties in the declaration, called *shorthand properties,* take multiple values, such as `margin` and `padding`. (They are known as shorthand properties because they collect values from multiple related CSS properties [like `margin-height`, `margin-width`, and so forth]. See Appendix B for a complete list.) Those values correspond to settings for the top, right, bottom, and left edges of the navbar's box. `margin` creates an empty zone around the box, and `padding` defines the space between the edges or borders of the box and the content within the box. Here are the rules that explain how to associate values with properties that deal with margins, borders, padding, and so forth:

✔ If all the sides have the same value, a single value works.

✔ If *any* side is different from the others, *every* side needs a separate value.

To remember what's what, think of the edges of an element box in clockwise order, starting with the top edge: `top`, `right`, `bottom`, and then `left`.

Positioning

CSS provides several ways to specify exactly where on a page an element should appear. These controls use various kinds of positioning based on the relationships between an element's box and its parent element's box to help page designers put page elements where they want them to go. The kinds of properties involved are discussed in the following sections.

Location

You can control the horizontal and vertical location of an image. Instead of just being drawn automatically to the right of the navigation bar, you can put it down and to the left, as shown in Figure 9-3:

```
#theCat {position: absolute; top: 100px; left: 100px;}
```

You might be wondering why the navbar rule starts with a period, and the theCat rule starts with a *pound symbol* (also known as a *hash mark* or *octothorpe*). That's because the period applies to a class attribute, but the pound symbol applies to an id attribute. You could apply either a class or an id; the difference between the two is that a class can be used more than once, but an id must be unique for a page. You can't have anything else on the page with an id of theCat. The difference, quite simply, is that a class lets you refer to some entire kind of element with a single reference, but an id can address only a single instance of an element.

Figure 9-3:
The image is much more striking in this location.

Overlapping

Two objects *can* be assigned to the same position in a Web page. When that happens, the browser must decide the display order and which objects to show and which ones to hide.

The z-index, added to any rule, tells CSS how you want an object stacked over and under other objects the page knows about:

- Lower numbers move down the stack.
- Higher numbers move up the stack.
- The default value for z-index is auto, which means it's the same as for its parent element.

Giving theCat a z-index value of -1 automatically puts it behind everything else on the page (as shown in Figure 9-4) for which the z-index isn't set.

Figure 9-4:
The cat's peeking out from behind the navigation bar.

Fonts

You can make a page more interesting by replacing old boring default fonts. Start by specifying a generic body font as well as setting some other default rules such as background color and text color.

Body text

Here's an example that sets the style for text within the body tag:

```
body {font-family: verdana, geneva, arial, helvetica, sans-serif;
      font-size: 12px; line-height: 16px; background-color: white;
      color: black;}
```

Because the `body` element holds all content for any Web page, this affects everything on the page. The preceding rule instructs the browser to show all text that appears within the `body` element as follows:

✔ The text is rendered using one of the fonts listed. We placed Verdana at the head of the list because it is the preferred choice, and browsers check for available fonts in the order listed in the markup. (Note that a generic font, in this case `sans-serif`, almost always appears last in such lists because the browser can almost always supply such a font itself.)

You can list more than one font. The browser uses the first font in your list that's available in the browser. For example, the browser looks for fonts from our list in this order:

1. Verdana

2. Geneva

3. Arial

4. Helvetica

5. The browser's default sans-serif font

✔ 12-pixel font size

✔ 16-pixel line height

The lines are spaced as though the fonts are 16 pixels high, so there's more vertical space between lines.

Figure 9-5 shows that

✔ All the changes apply to the entire page, including the navigation bar.

✔ The `font-family` changed in the `h1` heading, but neither the `font-size` nor `line-height` was changed.

Because headers have specific defaults for `font-size` and `line-height`, another rule is needed to modify them.

In Figure 9-5, the figure shows that the top of the header is slightly truncated. This is a bug in Internet Explorer for Windows that doesn't occur in other browsers. Unfortunately, CSS rendering is unpredictable enough that you must test style rules in various browsers to see how they look and then tweak accordingly.

Headings

If we explicitly assign style properties to the `h1` element, display results are more predictable. Here's a sample set of styles:

```
h1 {font-family: "trebuchet ms", verdana, geneva, arial, helvetica, sans-serif;
    font-size: 24px; line-height: 26px;}
```

Figure 9-5:
The fonts
are nicer,
but they
could still
use a little
more work.

Figure 9-6 shows a first-level heading using the font family and type size that we want: 24-pixel Trebuchet MS, with a 26-pixel line height. If we didn't have the Trebuchet MS font on our system, the heading would appear in Verdana.

When a font name includes spaces (like `trebuchet ms` or `times new roman`), the full name must be within quotation marks. See Chapter 8 for more information.

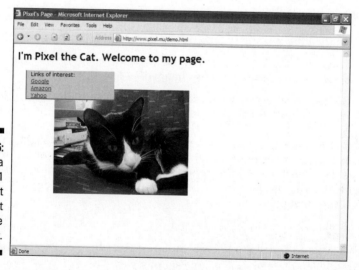

Figure 9-6:
Declaring a
rule for h1
makes it
appear just
how we
want it.

Hyperlinks

We think that having the hyperlinks underlined makes the menu look a little cluttered, so underlines are normally off. But we still want the hyperlinks to look like hyperlinks, so we tell CSS

✔ Make links bold.

✔ Make underlines appear when the cursor is over a link.

✔ Show links in certain colors.

The following style rules define how a browser should display hyperlinks:

```
a {text-decoration: none; font-weight: bold}
a:link {color: blue}
a:visited {color: #93C}
a:hover {text-decoration: underline}
```

What's going on here? Starting from the top, we're setting two rules for the `<a>` tag that apply to all links on the page:

✔ **The `text-decoration` declaration sets its value to** `none`.

This gets rid of the underlining for all the links.

✔ **The `font-weight` declaration has a value of** `bold`.

This makes all the links on the page appear in bold.

The remaining rules in the preceding code are *pseudo class selectors*. Their most common usage is to modify how links appear in their different states. For more information on pseudo classes, see Chapter 10. Figure 9-7 shows how the page appears when the previous style rules are applied.

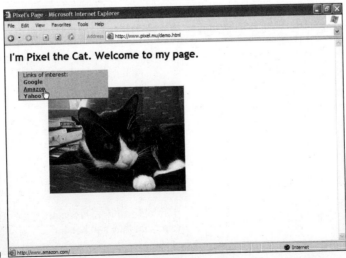

Figure 9-7:
The final version of our page.

Externalizing style sheets

When the final page is the way you want it, you're ready to move the tested, approved internal style sheet into an external style sheet.

- ✔ Every page of the site can use the whole style sheet with the addition of only one line of code to each page.
- ✔ Changes can be made site-wide with one change in the external style sheet.

To create an external style sheet from a well-testing internal style sheet, follow these steps:

1. **Copy all text that sits between the `<style>` and `</style>` tags.**

2. **Paste that text into its own document.**

   This text should include only CSS markup, without any HTML tags or markup.

3. **Add a `.css` suffix to the document's name (for example, `myStyles.css`).**

   This shows at a glance that it's a CSS file.

Here are two methods for linking an HTML file to an external style sheet:

- ✔ **Use the `<link>` tag.**

  All CSS-capable browsers understand the `link` tag.

- ✔ **Use the `<style>` tag with the `@import` keyword.**

  Only newer browsers understand the `<style>` and `@import` combination.

Style sheets for old and new browsers

To include rules that both old and new browsers can handle, you can create *two* style sheets for a site:

- ✔ A basic style sheet that contains only the simplest of styles

- ✔ A complex style sheet that uses the capabilities of the most powerful new browsers

The following code uses two style sheets:

- ✔ A `<link>` tag brings in `simpleStyles.css`, a basic style sheet for old browsers.

- ✔ The `<style>` tag and `@import` keyword combination brings in `complexStyles.css`, a complex style sheet for new browsers, which overrides the styles in `simpleStyles.css`.

```
<link href="simpleStyles.css"
        rel="stylesheet" />
<style type="text/css">
  @import "complexStyles.css";
</style>
```

Both old and new browsers get exactly those rules that they can handle.

See Chapter 8 for more on these two methods.

Multimedia

You can specify how you want your Web pages to look or behave on different *media types* depending on the medium.

Table 9-1 lists all the media types and their uses.

Table 9-1	Recognized Media Types
Media Type	**Description**
all	Suitable for all devices
aural	For speech synthesizers
braille	For Braille tactile feedback devices
embossed	For paged Braille printers
handheld	For handheld devices (such as those with a small screen, monochrome monitor, and limited bandwidth)
print	For paged, opaque material and for documents viewed on-screen but in print preview mode
projection	For projected presentations such as projectors or transparencies
screen	For color computer screens
tty	For media using a fixed-pitch character grid, such as teletypes, terminals, or portable devices with limited display capabilities
tv	For television-type devices (such as those with low resolution, color capability, limited-scrollability screens, and some sound available)

CSS can make changes to customize how the same pages

✔ Render on a computer screen

✔ Print on paper

A nifty color background might make your page a mess when it's printed on a black-and-white laser printer, but proper use of print media styles can keep this from happening!

✔ Sound when read out loud

Visual media styles

Table 9-2 lists the CSS properties that you're most likely to use in a typical Web page. The Cheat Sheet at the front of this book includes brief descriptions of the most commonly used CSS properties and (X)HTML tags and attributes.

Table 9-2		Visual Media Styles	
Property	*Values*	*Default Value*	*Description*
`background-color`	Any color, by name or hex code	`transparent`	Background color of the page
`background-image`	URL	`none`	URL of an image to display in a page background
`color`	Any color, by name or hex code	UA dependent	Color of the foreground text
`font-family`	Any named font `cursive` `fantasy` `monospace` `sans-serif` `serif`	UA dependent	Font to display
`font-size`	number + unit `xx-small` `x-small` `small` `medium` `large` `x-large` `xx-large`	`medium`	Size of the font to be displayed
`font-weight`	`normal` `bold` `bolder` `lighter`	`normal`	Weight (how bold or light) the font should appear
`line-height`	`normal` number + unit	`normal`	Vertical spacing between lines of text

Property	Values	Default Value	Description
text-align	left right center justify	UA dependent + writing direction	Which way the text on the page should be aligned
text-decoration	none underline overline line-through blink	none	Special text effects
list-style-image	**URL**	none	URL of an image to display as the bullets for a list
list-style-position	inside outside	outside	Wrapping list text inside or outside of bullets
list-style-type	disc circle square decimal decimal-leading-zero lower-alpha upper-alpha none	disc	Bullet type on lists
display	block inline none	inline	Format of a defined section of the page
top	percentage number + unit auto	auto	For absolutely positioned objects, the offset from the top edge of the positioning context
right	percentage number + unit auto	auto	For absolutely positioned objects, the offset from the right edge of the positioning context

(continued)

Table 9-2 *(continued)*

Property	Values	Default Value	Description
bottom	percentage number + unit auto	auto	For absolutely positioned objects, the offset from the bottom edge of the positioning context
left	percentage number + unit auto	auto	For absolutely positioned objects, the offset from the left edge of the positioning context
position	static absolute relative fixed	static	Method by which an element box is laid out, relative to positioning context
visibility	collapse visible hidden inherit	inherit	Indicates whether an object will be displayed on the page
z-index	number auto	auto	Stacking order of an object
border-style	none dotted dashed solid double groove ridge inset outset	not defined	The displayed style of an object's borders Can be broken out into border-top-style, border-right-style, border-bottom-style, and border-left-style
border-width	Thin medium thick number	not defined	Width of the border around an object Can be broken out into border-top-width, border-right-width, border-bottom-width, and border-left-width

Property	Values	Default Value	Description
border-color	Any color, by name or hex code transparent	not defined	Color of an object's border Can be broken out into border-top-color, border-right-color, border-bottom-color, and border-left-color
border	border-width + border-style + border-color	not defined	Combined features of a border around an object Can be broken out into border-top, border-right, border-bottom, and border-left
float	left right none	none	Specifies whether the object should be floated to one side of the document
height	percentage number + unit auto	auto	Displayed height of an object
width	percentage number + unit auto	auto	Displayed width of an object
margin	percentage number + unit auto	not defined	Displayed margins of an object Can be broken out into margin-top, margin-right, margin-bottom, and margin-left

(continued)

Table 9-2 *(continued)*

Property	Values	Default Value	Description
`padding`	percentage number + unit `auto`	not defined	Displayed blank space around an object Can be broken out into `padding-top`, `padding-right`, `padding-bottom`, and `padding-left`

`cursor`	`auto`
	`crosshair`
	`default`
	`pointer`
	`move`
	`text`
	`help`
		`auto`	Cursor appearance in the browser window

Some browsers don't support all CSS properties. If you're using CSS features, test your pages with the browsers that you expect your visitors will use.

If you want to take an extremely thorough guide to CSS everywhere you go, you can put it on your iPod! Westciv's free podGuide is a folder of small text files. Download the zipped file and follow the instructions on how to install it, and you have complete documentation with you at all times. You also win the title of "World's Biggest CSS Geek." The podGuide is at

`www.westciv.com/news/podguide.html`

Paged media styles

CSS can customize how a page looks when it's printed. We recommend these guidelines:

✔ Replace sans-serif fonts with serif fonts.

Serif fonts are easier to read in print than sans-serif fonts.

✔ Insert advertisements that

• Make sense when they aren't animated

• Are useful without clicking

In general, paged media styles help ensure that text looks as good when it's printed as it does in a Web browser. See Table 9-3 for an explanation of paged media properties in CSS that you can use to help your users make the most when printing Web pages.

Table 9-3		Paged Media Styles	
Property	*Values*	*Default Value*	*Description*
orphans	number	2	The minimum number of lines in a paragraph that must be left at the bottom of a page
page-break-after	auto always avoid left right	auto	The page-breaking behavior after an element
page-break-before	auto always avoid left right	auto	The page-breaking behavior before an element
page-break-inside	auto avoid	auto	The page-breaking behavior inside an element
widows	number	2	The minimum number of lines in a paragraph that must be left at the top of a page

The example in Listing 9-2 uses these options for paged media styles:

- ✔ Make the output black text on a white background.
- ✔ Replace sans-serif fonts with serif fonts.

Listing 9-2: **Adding a Print Style Sheet**

```
<!DOCTYPE html PUBLIC "-//W3C//DTD XHTML 1.0 Transitional//EN"
    "http://www.w3.org/TR/xhtml1/DTD/xhtml1-transitional.dtd">
<html xmlns="http://www.w3.org/1999/xhtml">
<head>
<title>This is my page</title>
<meta http-equiv="Content-Type" content="text/html; charset=ISO-8859-1" />
<style>
    body {background-color: black; color: white; font-family: sans-serif;}

    @media print {
      body {background-color: white; color: black; font-family: serif}
    }
</style>
</head>
<body>
    This page will look very different when sent to the printer.
</body>
</html>
```

If you're now wondering why none of the properties in Table 9-3 were set, but other properties were, it's because (in this example) their defaults worked fine. And just because those page properties can be set doesn't mean that you can't set other properties also — it isn't an either/or.

Aural (speech sound) styles

Aural browsers and styles aren't just for the visually impaired. They're also useful for Web users who

✔ Have reading problems

✔ Need information while driving

The following example recommends voices to be played using male and female characters to make it clear which characters are speaking:

```
<style>
    @media aural {
        p.stanley {voice-family: male;}
        p.stella {voice-family: female;}
```

```
    }
</style>
```

Usually, you don't have to worry much about adding aural styles to your page. The default readers should work just fine if

✔ Your page is mostly text.

✔ You don't have a strong opinion about how it sounds, so that any clearly male or female voice will do.

That said, you can find a complete listing of all aural style properties in Appendix B at the end of this book.

Marvelous Miscellany

Table 9-4 lists other CSS properties that you might find in documents.

Table 9-4		Additional CSS Properties	
Property	*Values*	*Default Value*	*Description*
@page	Paged media	{page selector| page-pseudo-class|page context}	Defines page context for given content box
content	Text	{string|uri| counter|attr(x)| open-quote| close-quote| no-open-quote| no-close-quote| inherit}	Describes content to be inserted during generated content operation
counter-increment	General	{name:integer| none|inherit}	Used to increment the value of a named counter
counter-reset	General	{name: integer| none|inherit}	Used to reset the value of a named counter to a specific value
empty-cells	Table	{hide|show| inherit}	Describes what to do with cells that contain no content
margin-bottom	Box	{auto|length| percentage| inherit}	Sets margin width for bottom of element
margin-left	Box	{auto|length| percentage| inherit}	Sets margin width for left of element
margin-right	Box	{auto|length| percentage| inherit}	Sets margin width for right of element
margin-top	Box	{auto|length| percentage| inherit}	Sets margin width for top of element

(continued)

Table 9-4 (continued)

Property	Values	Default Value	Description
marker-offset	Box	{auto|length|inherit}	Sets offset between marker edge and nearest edge of principal containing box
marks	Paged media	{crop|cross|none|inherit}	Defines what kind of page edge, crop, or trim marks to include when rendering pages for output
overflow	General	{auto|hidden|scroll|visible|inherit}	Determines handling of content that overflows element content area
page	Paged media	{page selector|inherit}	Invokes a page selector defined by using @page
padding-bottom	Box	{length|percentage|inherit}	Sets width of padding on element's bottom
padding-left	Box	{length|percentage|inherit}	Sets width of padding on element's left
padding-right	Box	{length|percentage|inherit}	Sets width of padding on element's right
padding-top	Box	{length|percentage|inherit}	Sets width of padding on element's top
quotes	Text	{none|string|inherit}	Sets open and close quotes (when 1 string supplied, used for both; when 2, 1st opens, 2nd closes)
size	Paged media	{auto|length|landscape|length|portrait|inherit}	Specifies orientation and size of a page box
table-layout	Table	{auto|fixed|inherit}	Determines method used to lay out table contents

Chapter 10

Getting Creative with Colors and Fonts

· ·

In This Chapter

▶ Using CSS to define text formatting

▶ Working with page colors and backgrounds

▶ Changing font display

▶ Adding text treatments

· ·

*B*efore style sheets came along, HTML markup controlled backgrounds, colors, fonts, and text sizes on Web pages. However, style sheets and the ability to separate style information from content let designers use Cascading Style Sheets (CSS) to control font, color, and other style information.

The use of CSS to control such elements

✔ Provides better control when updating or editing formatting information

✔ Prevents HTML documents from becoming cluttered with `<font>` tags

✔ Provides more options for formatting your text, such as defining line height, font weight, and text alignment, and converting text to *uppercase* (capital letters) or lowercase

(X)HTML still includes a few formatting elements, such as `<tt>`, `<i>`, `<big>`, `<b>`, and `<small>`; however, the remaining formatting elements, such as `<font>`, are *deprecated*. That means they're no longer recommended for use (although they still work, and most browsers recognize them).

Color Values

(X)HTML defines color values in two ways:

- By *name* (you choose from a limited list)
- By *number* (harder to remember, but you have many more options)

Color names

The HTML specification includes 16 color names that you can use to define colors in your pages.

The Cheat Sheet bound into the front of this book has information about the 16 named colors, including names, corresponding *hex codes* (the six-digit hexadecimal numbers that also define the colors), and color swatches. You can safely use color names in your CSS markup and be confident that browsers will recognize them and use the correct colors in your Web pages.

Visit `www.htmlhelp.com/reference/html40/values.html#color` to see how your browser displays these colors. If you can, view this page on two or three different computers to see how the browser, operating system, graphics card, and monitor can subtly change the display.

This CSS style declaration says all text within `<p>` tags should be *blue*:

```
p {color: blue;}
```

If you're looking for burnt umber, chartreuse, or salmon, you're out of luck. A box of 64 crayons this list is not. You can, however, also find hex codes for Web-safe colors, along with color swatches, on the Cheat Sheet. These colors, though unnamed, are Web-safe because they reproduce pretty reliably on most color computer display devices and printers.

Color numbers

Color numbers allow you to use any color (even salmon) on your Web page.

Hexadecimal color codes

Hexadecimal notation uses six characters — a combination of numbers and letters — to define any color. If you know a color's hexadecimal code (often called a hex code for short), you have all you need to use that color in your HTML page.

Finding any color's hex code

You can't just wave your magic wand and come up with the hex code for any color. But that doesn't mean that you can't find out through less magical means. Color converters follow a precise formula that changes a color's standard RGB notation into hexadecimal notation. Because you have better things to do with your time than compute hex codes, you have several options for finding out the code for your color of choice, including Web-safe colors on this book's Cheat Sheet. None of these make you use a calculator:

✔ **On the Web:** Some good sources for hexadecimal color charts are

```
www.hypersolutions.org/pages/
        rgbhex.html
www.colorschemer.com/online.html
http://webmonkey.wired.com/webmonkey/
        reference/color_codes
```

You simply find a color you like and type the hex code listed next to it into your HTML.

✔ **Using a converter:** If you already know the RGB values for a particular color, you can plug them into an online converter at `www.univox.com/home/support/rgb2hex.html` to get the hexadecimal equivalent. For example, the RGB values for a nice sky blue are 159, 220, and 223. Plug those into the converter, and you get the equivalent hex code #9FDCDF.

✔ **Using image-editing software:** Many image-editing applications, such as Adobe Photoshop or Jasc Paint Shop Pro, display the hexadecimal notation for any color. Even Microsoft Word's color picker shows you hex codes for colors in an image. If you have an image you like that you want to use as a color source for your Web page, open the image in your favorite editor and find out what the colors' hex codes are.

When you use hexadecimal code to define a color, you should always precede it with a pound sign (#).

This CSS style declaration makes all text contained by <p> tags *blue:*

```
p {color: #0000FF;}
```

Unlike the familiar base 10 (decimal) system that uses 10 numerals to represent all possible numbers, the hexadecimal (base 16) system uses 16 "numerals." If you want to know more about the hexadecimal system or want to convert numbers from decimal to hexadecimal, visit

```
http://mathforum.org/library/drmath/view/55830.html
```

RGB values

You can use two RGB values to define color. These value types aren't as common as hexadecimal values, but they're just as effective:

▌ ✔ rgb(r,g,b): The r, g, and b are integers between 0 and 255 that represent the red, green, and blue of the color.

- rgb(r%,g%,b%): The r%, g%, and b% represent the percentage of red, green, and blue of the color.

Every color can be defined as a mixture of red, green, and blue (RGB). You can use either an RGB value or the equivalent hex code to describe a color's RGB value to a Web browser.

Color Definitions

You can define individual colors for any text on the Web page, as well as define a background color for the entire Web page or some portion thereof.

CSS uses the following properties to define color:

- color defines the font color and is also used to define colors for links in their various states (active, visited).
- background or background-color defines the background color for the entire page or defines the background for a particular element (for example, a background color for all first-level headings, similar to the idea of highlighting something in a Word document).

Text

To change the color of text on your Web page

1. **Determine the selector.** For example, will the color apply to all first-level headings, to all paragraphs, or to a specific paragraph?

2. **Use the** color **property.**

3. **Identify the color name or hexadecimal value.**

The basic syntax for the style declaration is:

```
selector {color: value;}
```

Here is a collection of style declarations that use the color property:

```
body {color: olive; font-family: Verdana, sans-serif;
    background-color: #FFFFFF; font-size: 85%;}
hr {text-align: center;}
.navbar {font-size: 75%; text-align: center;}
h1 {color: #808000;}
p.chapternav {text-align: center;}
.footer {font-size: 80%;}
```

In the preceding CSS rules, the color for all text on the page is defined by using the body selector. The color is applied to all text in the body of the document unless otherwise defined. For example, the first-level heading is defined as forest green by using hexadecimal notation.

Links

Pseudo classes allow you to define style rules based on information outside the document tree.

The most common CSS use of pseudo classes is to define a style rule for a given element in the *document tree* — a technical term that just means that the browser builds a hierarchical representation of all elements in a document, much like a family tree, where every element has a parent and may contain a child. For example, :link is a pseudo class that defines style rules for any link that hasn't yet been visited.

There are five common pseudo classes that you can use with hyperlinks:

- ✔ :link defines formatting for links that haven't been visited.
- ✔ :visited defines formatting for links that have been visited.
- ✔ :focus defines formatting for links that are selected by the keyboard (for example, by using the Tab key) and are about to be activated by using the Enter key.
- ✔ :hover defines formatting for links when the mouse cursor hovers over them.
- ✔ :active defines formatting for links when they are selected (clicked by the mouse).

The pseudo class name is preceded by a colon (:).

Pseudo classes can be used with

- ✔ Elements (such as the <a> element that defines hyperlinks)
- ✔ Classes
- ✔ IDs

For example, to define the style rules for visited and unvisited links, use the following syntax:

- ✔ This sets the color of any hyperlink pointing to an unvisited URL to red by using its hexadecimal value:

```
a:link {color: #FF0000;}
```

✔ This sets any hyperlink that points to a visited URL to appear in the named color green:

```
a:visited {color: green;}
```

✔ This designates unvisited links with a class of internal to appear in (named color) yellow:

```
a.internal:link {color: yellow;}
```

Links can occupy multiple states at one time. For example, a link can be visited and hovered over at the same time. Always define link style rules in the following order: :link, :visited, :visible, :focus, :hover, :active.

CSS applies *last rule seen* to display your page. In this case, if you put the pseudo class selectors in the wrong order, your results may not be what you want. For example, if visited follows hover, and the two have overlapping rules, hover effects apply only to links that haven't yet been visited.

The following CSS rules render the document with olive as the color for links that haven't been visited and yellow as the color of visited links:

```
body {color: #808000; font-family: Verdana, sans-serif; font-size: 85%;}
a:link {color: olive;}
a:visited {color: yellow;}
```

Netscape 4 ignores hover. But it doesn't hurt anything in Netscape 4 to use hover (it's just ignored) unless it's a visitor's *only* clue that the text is a link.

Some browsers don't support pseudo classes with elements such as input or select (these are forms elements). Current browsers support their use with the a element. Test your results if you want to use pseudo classes with an element other than <a>.

The CSS specification defines :link and :visited as mutually exclusive, and it is up to the browser application to determine when to change the state (visited versus unvisited) for any given link. For example, a browser might determine that a link is unvisited if you clear your history data.

Backgrounds

To change the background color for your Web page, or a section of that page, follow these steps:

1. **Determine the selector.** For example, will the color apply to the entire background, or will it apply only to a specific section?

2. **Use the** background-color **or** background **property.**

3. **Identify the color name or hexadecimal value.**

The basic syntax for the style declaration is:

```
selector {background-color: value;}
```

In the following collection of style declarations, the first style declaration uses the background-color property and sets it to light green by using hexadecimal notation:

```
body {color: #808000; font-family: Verdana, sans-serif;
    background-color: #EAF3DA; font-size: 85%;}
```

You can apply a background color to a block of text — for example, a paragraph — much like you define the background color for the entire page.

You use background as a shorthand property for all individual background properties or background-color to set just the color.

```
selector {background: value value value}
```

See Chapter 8 or "The Shorthand Property" section of Webmonkey's "Mulder's Stylesheets Tutorial" for more information.

```
http://webmonkey.wired.com/webmonkey/98/15/index3a_page6.html?tw=authoring
```

Fonts

You can define individual font properties for different HTML elements with

- Individual CSS properties, such as font-family, line-height, and font-size
- A group of font properties in the catchall shorthand font property

Font family

To define the font face by using the font family:

1. **Identify the selector for the style declaration.**

    For example, making p the selector defines a font family for all <p> tags.

2. **Add the property name font-family.**

    Not all font families are supported by every browser. CSS allows you to specify multiple font families in case a browser doesn't support the font family you prefer. You can list multiple font family names, separated by commas. The browser uses the first name in the list that is available on the computer on which it's running.

3. **Define a** `value` **for the property (the name of the font family).**

Use single or double quotation marks around any font family names that include spaces.

To format all first-level headings to use the Verdana font, use a style declaration like this:

```
h1 {font-family: Verdana, Helvetica, sans-serif;}
```

In the preceding declaration, two more font families are identified in case a browser doesn't support the Verdana font family.

We recommend including these font families in your style declarations:

✔ At least one of these *common* font families:

- Arial: Sample SAMPLE

- Helvetica: Sample SAMPLE

- Times New Roman: Sample SAMPLE

- Verdana: Sample SAMPLE

✔ At least one of these *generic* font families:

- serif: Sample SAMPLE

- sans-serif: Sample SAMPLE

- cursive: *Sample SAMPLE*

- fantasy: Sample SAMPLE

- monospace: `Sample SAMPLE`

Different elements may be formatted using different font families. These rules define a different font family for hyperlinks (see Figure 10-1):

```
body {color: #808000; font-family: Verdana, sans-serif; font-size: 85%;}
hr {text-align: center;}
a {font-family: Courier, "Courier New", monospace;}
```

Sizing

The following properties allow you to control the dimensions of your text.

Font size

The style declaration to specify the size of text is

```
selector {font-size: value;}
```

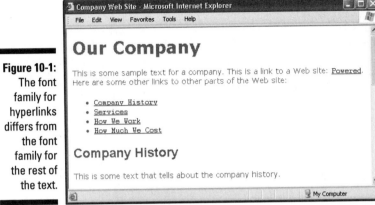

Figure 10-1:
The font
family for
hyperlinks
differs from
the font
family for
the rest of
the text.

The `value` of the declaration can be

✔ One of the standard font property measurement values (listed in Chapter 8)

✔ One of these user-defined *keywords:*

`xx-small`, `x-small`, `small`, `medium`, `large`, `x-large`, or `xx-large`

The value of each keyword is determined by the *browser,* not the style rule.

The following rules define

✔ A relative font value for all text

✔ An absolute value for the font size for all first-level headings

```
body {color: #808000; font-family: Verdana, sans-serif; font-size: 85%;}
h1 {color: #808000; font-family: Arial, Helvetica, sans-serif;
    font-weight: 800; font-size: 24pt;}
```

The result appears in Figure 10-2.

Line height

The *line height* of a paragraph is the amount of space between each line within the paragraph.

Line height is like *line spacing* in a word processor.

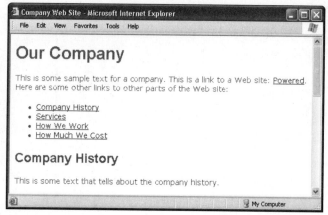

Figure 10-2:
First-level
headings
are 24
points tall;
the font size
of other text
is relative.

To alter the amount of space between lines of a paragraph, use the line-height property:

```
selector {line-height: value;}
```

The value of the line-height property can be either

- ✔ One of the standard font property measurement values (listed in Chapter 8)
- ✔ A number that multiplies the element's font size, such as 1.5

We assign a quotation class to the first paragraph throughout this chapter so you can see the changes. This allows us to apply these styles to the first paragraph by using

```
<p class="quotation">
```

in the HTML document.

The following rules style the first paragraph in italics, indent that paragraph, and increase the line height to increase readability (see Figure 10-3):

```
body {color: #808000; font-family: Verdana, sans-serif; font-size: 85%;}
.quotation {font-style: italic; text-indent: 10pt; line-height: 150%;}
```

Figure 10-3: Any element within the `quotation` class has the same formatting.

Character spacing

You can *increase* or *reduce* the amount of spacing between letters or words by using these properties:

- ✔ `word-spacing`: The style declaration for `word-spacing` is

  ```
  selector {word-spacing: value;}
  ```

  Designers call the space between words *tracking*.

- ✔ `letter-spacing`: The style declaration for `letter-spacing` is

  ```
  selector {letter-spacing: value;}
  ```

  Designers call the space between letters *kerning*.

The value of either spacing property must be a *length* defined by a standard font property measurement value (listed in Chapter 8).

The following code increases the letter spacing (kerning) of the second paragraph (see Figure 10-4):

```
body {color: #808000; font-family: Verdana, sans-serif; font-size: 85%;}
.quotation {font-style: italic; text-indent: 10pt; letter-spacing: 6px;}
```

Positioning

Alignment properties allow you to control the *shape* of text blocks.

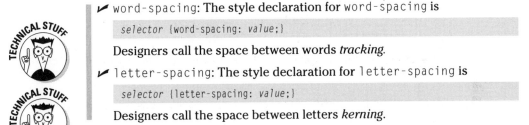

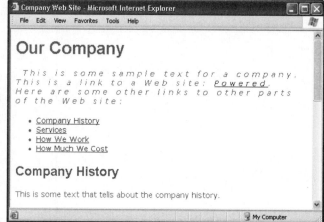

Figure 10-4:
Kerning can
be larger or
smaller than
the font's
normal
spacing.

Alignment

Alignment determines whether the left and right sides of a text block are

- ✔ **Flush:** Starting or ending together
- ✔ **Ragged:** Starting or ending at different points

Syntax

Alignment is defined with the `text-align` property. The style declaration to align text is:

```
selector {text-align: value;}
```

The value of the `text-align` property must be one of the following keywords:

- ✔ `left` **aligns the text to the left.** The right side of the text block is *ragged*.
- ✔ `right` **aligns the text to the right.** The left side of the text block is *ragged*.
- ✔ `center` **centers the text in the middle of the window.** Both sides of the text block are *ragged*.
- ✔ `justify` **aligns the text for both the left and right side.** The spacing within the text in each line is adjusted so both sides of the text block are *flush*.

Justifying text affects letter or word spacing in the paragraph. Test the results before displaying your Web pages to the world.

Markup

The following example defines the alignment for the first-level heading and the first paragraph (see Figure 10-5):

```
body {color: #808000; font-family: Verdana, sans-serif; font-size: 85%;}
h1 {color: #808000; font-family: Arial, Helvetica, sans-serif;
    font-weight: 800; font-size: 24pt; text-align: center}
.quotation {font-style: italic; text-indent: 10pt; text-align: left;}
```

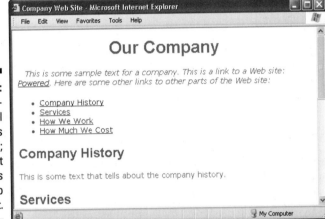

Figure 10-5:
The first-level heading is centered; the first paragraph is aligned to the left.

Indent

You can define the amount of space that should precede the first line of a paragraph by using the text-indent property.

This doesn't indent the whole paragraph. That requires CSS box properties, such as margin-left and margin-right (see Chapter 9).

Syntax

The style declaration used to indent text is

```
selector {text-indent: value;}
```

The value must be one of the standard length property measurement values (listed in Chapter 8).

Markup

As seen in this chapter, the quotation class has a text-indent of 10 points.

```
body {color: #808000; font-family: Verdana, sans-serif; font-size: 85%;}
.quotation {font-style: italic; text-indent: 10pt;}
```

Text treatments

CSS allows you to decorate your text by using boldface, italics, underline, overline, or line-through, and even allows your text to blink (when supported by browsers).

Bold

Using a boldface font is one of the more common text embellishments a designer uses. To apply boldface in HTML, use the <b> tag. However, CSS provides you with more control over the font weight of the bolded text.

Syntax

This style declaration uses the font-weight property:

```
selector {font-weight: value;}
```

The value of the font-weight property may be one of the following:

- bold: Renders the text in an average bold weight
- bolder: Relative value that renders a font weight bolder than the current weight (possibly assigned by a parent element)
- lighter: Relative value that renders a font weight lighter than the current weight (possibly assigned by a parent element)
- normal: Removes any bold formatting
- One of these integer values: 100 (lightest), 200, 300, 400 (normal), 500, 600, 700 (standard bold), 800, 900 (darkest)

Markup

The following example bolds hyperlinks (see Figure 10-6):

```
body {color: #808000; font-family: Verdana, sans-serif; font-size: 85%;}
a {font-weight: bold;}
a:link {color: olive; text-decoration: underline;}
a:visited {color: olive; text-decoration: none;}
```

Italic

Italics are commonly used to set off quotations or to emphasize text. To apply italics in HTML, use the <i> tag. However, CSS provides you with more control over the font style of text through the font-style property.

Syntax

This style declaration uses the font-style property:

```
selector {font-style: value;}
```

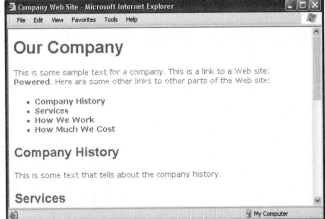

Figure 10-6:
All
hyperlinks
are bolded.

The value of the `font-style` property may be one of the following:

- ✔ `italic`: Renders the text in *italics* (a special font that usually *slants)*

- ✔ `oblique`: Renders the text as *oblique* (a slanted version of the normal font).

- ✔ `normal`: Removes any italic or oblique formatting.

Markup

The following example assigns an italic font style to the first-level heading:

```
body {color: #808000; font-family: Verdana, sans-serif; font-size: 85%;}
h1 {color: #808000; font-family: Arial, Helvetica, sans-serif;
    font-style: italic; font-weight: 800; font-size: 24pt; text-align: center;}
```

Capitalization

You use the `text-transform` property to set capitalization in your document.

Syntax

This style declaration uses the `text-transform` property:

```
selector {text-transform: value;}
```

The value of the `text-transform` property may be one of the following:

- ✔ `capitalize`: Capitalizes the first character in every word

- ✔ `uppercase`: Renders all letters of the text of the specified element in uppercase.

✔ lowercase: Renders all letters of the text of the specified element in lowercase.

✔ none: Keeps the value of the inherited element.

Markup

The following example renders the first-level heading in uppercase (shown in Figure 10-7):

```
body {color: #808000; font-family: Verdana, sans-serif; font-size: 85%;}
h1 {color: #808000; font-family: Arial, Helvetica, sans-serif;
    font-weight: 800; font-size: 24pt;
    text-align: center; text-transform: uppercase;}
```

Figure 10-7: The first-level heading is rendered in all uppercase.

The text-decoration property

The text-decoration property allows for a bit more crazy text formatting. It isn't used often.

Syntax

This style declaration uses the text-decoration property:

```
selector {text-decoration: value;}
```

The value of the text-decoration property may be one of the following:

✔ underline: Underlines text.

✔ overline: Renders the text with a line over it.

✔ line-through: Renders the text with a line through it.

✔ blink: Blinks the text on the screen.

Are you *sure* you want blinking text?

- blink isn't supported by all browsers.

- blink can be dreadfully annoying and distracting.

✔ none: Removes any text decoration.

Markup

The following example changes the link when the mouse hovers over it. In this case, it turns off any underlining for a link:

```
body {color: #808000; font-family: Verdana, sans-serif; font-size: 85%;}
a:link {color: olive; text-decoration: underline;}
a:visited {color: olive; text-decoration: underline;}
a:hover {color: olive; text-decoration: none;}
```

The catchall font property

Many font properties can be summarized in one style declaration by using the shorthand font property. When it's used, only one style rule is needed to define a combination of font properties:

```
selector {font: value value value;}
```

The value of the font property is a list of any values that correspond to the various font properties:

✔ The following values must be defined in the following order, though they need not be consecutive:

- font-size (required)

- line-height (optional)

- font-family (required)

✔ The font-family value list must end with a semicolon.

✔ Use commas to separate multiple font family names.

✔ The following values are optional and may occur in any order within the declaration. Individual values are separated by spaces:

- font-style

- font-variant

- font-weight

For example, you can use the following style declaration to create a specific style for a first-level heading:

```
h1 {font: italic bold 150% Arial, Helvetica, sans-serif;}
```

The preceding markup uses properties in the follow order: `font-style`, `font-weight`, `font-size`, and `font-family` (the list uses commas to separate specific font families) ending with the required semicolon. For a complete listing of CSS shorthand properties, consult Appendix B at the end of this book.

Chapter 11

Using Tables for Stunning Pages

*H*istorically, tables contain and lay out tabular data. However, in (X)HTML they serve an entirely different purpose — to control Web page layout. Most Web pages contain at least one table — some even nest tables within tables. (X)HTML tables can present everything from text to images on your pages efficiently and attractively.

Also, CSS provides plenty of positioning capability to give designers more flexibility and precision when working with tables: a "killer combination!"

This chapter provides step-by-step instructions for building and using (X)HTML tables and then using CSS to control their presentation. Use our best tried-and-true tips and techniques to speed up and simplify your efforts.

What Tables Can Do for You

Traditionally, tables display data in formats that are easy to read and understand. (X)HTML changed all that. Many Web sites use tables. Sites such as Amazon.com, eBay, Yahoo!, and Google all use tables to display their content, even if you can't see them in an obvious way. In fact, such invisible tables dominate the Web. The ideas that drive them are:

- ✔ Use tables to arrange items on your Web page.
- ✔ Turn borders off so users can't see these tables.

By nature, Web pages start out linearly. Tables allow you to step out of a linear mode and put text and images in more interesting places on a page.

You can use tables in a couple of ways:

- ✔ **Traditional (ho-hum) method:** You can define table or individual cell widths by using absolute numbers. This type of table doesn't resize when users resize their browser windows.

  Some designers prefer to use tables for the traditional purpose — to present data — a straightforward, balanced approach that's easily tackled.

- ✔ **Presentation-focused (wow) method:** You can define table and cell width by using *percentages*. This table resizes when users resize their browser windows.

  Most designers perform creative, complex tricks with their tables.

Although this chapter covers all aspects of HTML tables, it focuses on layout tips and techniques.

When you use tables for layout, they can result in a couple of outcomes:

- ✔ Tables can produce complex layout structures, as shown in Figure 11-1. (Some other examples of complex tables are viewable at `www.amazon.com` and `www.yahoo.com`.)

  After you open these Web pages in your Web browser, look at each page's HTML source code (try View⇨Source from your menu bar). Observe how complex the markup is, and mark ye well when the markup looks haphazardly arranged (alas, if only they'd asked us . . .).

- ✔ Some Web page design models keep the interface simple with the less-is-more approach — and therefore easy to use. Figure 11-2 shows the simple approach.

  `www.google.com` uses a simple table to arrange navigation.

Table

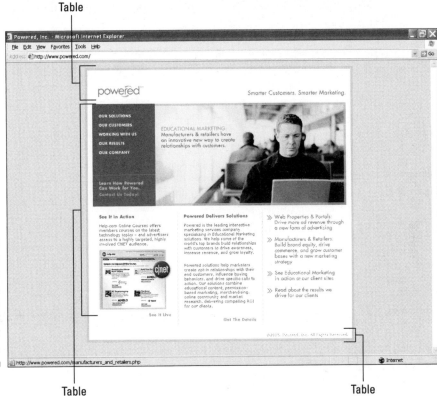

Figure 11-1:
This Web page uses three different tables for layout.

Table   Table

Use (X)HTML and CSS in tables

(X)HTML tables can require some finesse to make them do just what you need. But about 10 percent of Internet surfers use browsers that don't support CSS. This means tables usually should be a basic foundation for page design. We recommend using

✔ (X)HTML tables to lay the basic foundation for your page

✔ CSS to provide additional table formatting

If you know your target users use updated browsers, you can use CSS for all your positioning needs. For example, if you're designing an intranet Web site for a group of computer programmers, you can require that its viewers use a newer browser only and eliminate table elements completely, if you like.

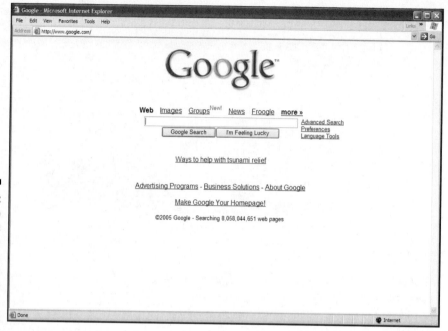

Table Basics

The complexity of HTML tables is built from three basic elements

- ✔ **Borders:** Every basic table must always have *exactly* four borders that make up a rectangle.

- ✔ **Cells:** These are the individual squares (spaces) within the borders of a table.

- ✔ **Cell span:** Within that four-walled structure, you can delete or add cell walls (as shown with the cells on the right side of the table in Figure 11-3). When you delete cell walls, you make a cell *span* multiple rows or columns — and that's exactly what makes a table a flexible tool for layout.

Cell spanning and cell width work differently:

- ✔ When you span cells, you change cell space by combining, or merging, cells. This step removes cell walls.

- ✔ When you increase the width of a cell, you only change the space within that cell.

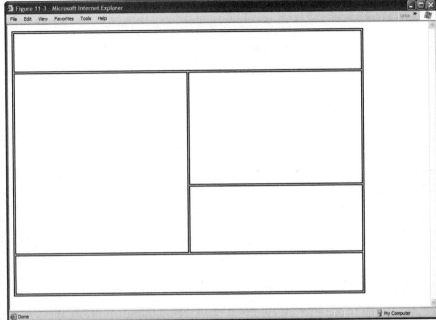

Figure 11-3:
You can use an HTML table to lay out Web pages.

Sketching Your Table

Tables can become complex. You need to carefully plan them. Mapping to the nearest pixel can grow tedious and can take several attempts, but it's an essential step in designing a well laid out page.

Developing layout ideas

Start with a general idea and slowly plan your layout until it becomes more solid and specific. Follow these basic steps:

1. **Grab (believe it or not) a sheet of paper and a pencil so that you can sketch out your ideas.**

   Start with a *general* idea of where you want everything to go on your page.

2. **Evaluate what to include in your Web page and decide on the overall layout.**

This way, you can begin to determine

- How many columns and rows you need
- The width of the table and cells
- Whether to make any cells span rows or columns

You need to make the following design choices:

- Whether the table will be centered, left aligned, or right aligned.
- Whether you want to include hyperlinks and where you might want to include them.

   For example, many Web sites, such as the one in Figure 11-1, include a logo image that provides a hyperlink to the site's home page, so no matter what page you're on, you can always get back to the front door.

3. **Figure out the pixel dimensions of images you want to use.** Make sure that the table fills a browser window nicely without forcing the user to scroll left and right to see everything.

   Decide between using text or images for navigation, as follows:

   - If you want more font control over your navigation, consider using images for your navigational items.

      The font is embedded in the image; therefore, the user's browser settings can't override the font you choose.

   - If you don't need additional font controls, use textual navigation.
   - Decide where the main logo should go and what size it should be.

      In Figure 11-2, the logo is the main focal point. Its dimensions are 276 pixels wide by 110 pixels tall.

Concentrate on managing the width of the table. Let the contents of your table determine the cell height. Height is less important because users are familiar with scrolling up and down Web pages. However, they may get frustrated by scrolling left and right to read content.

Drafting the table

When you know how big and how numerous your design elements are, you can sketch a rough table on paper.

If you opt for a simple approach, each main element (logo, hyperlink image, and navigation) has its own cell. In Figure 11-4, that means only three cells.

If you have only a few cells, you'll probably have to span the cells so the contents fill the width of your page.

✔ A complex design may need several rows.

✔ A simple, clean design (such as the one in Figure 11-4) may require only two rows.

Figure 11-4 shows the final sketch for your table:

- The first row *spans* both columns.
- The second row contains two *separate* columns.

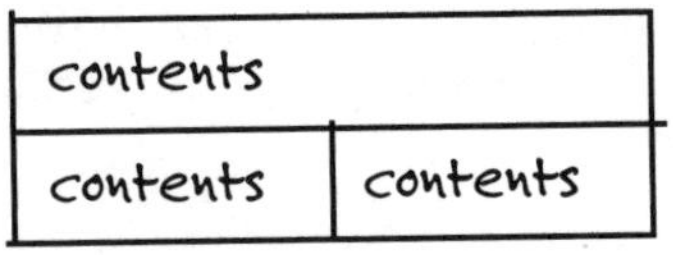

Figure 11-4:
Start by sketching the table dimensions, even before opening a text editor.

The author of our sample Web site uses images in place of text for the navigational elements; however, for usability reasons, try using text in place of images when possible. Even so, if you want complete control of the font(s) in which your text appears, you may have to use images — and create an image of the text written in your chosen font.

Constructing Basic Tables

When you have a sketch that gives a pretty solid indication of the page and table layout, you can open your HTML editor and create the skeleton of your table.

Components

The building blocks for your table's framework are the three basic components of any table:

✔ **Table:** `<table>`

✔ **Table row:** `<tr>`

<tr> is always enclosed within <table>.

✔ **Table (data) cell:** <td>

<td> is always enclosed within <tr>.

With these three elements, you can build a simple table.

The <table>, <tr>, and <td> *opening* and *closing* tags are required. If you forget to include any, your table won't display correctly in most browsers.

Layout

Tables come in many forms and at varying levels of complexity. A simple two-dimensional data table that's part of a Web page is easier to design and implement than a more complex table layout that contains an entire Web page. As you read through the following sections, you will see and appreciate this distinction clearly.

Creating a simple table

The <table> tag and its markup typically appear between the <body> tags in your document. However, you can also use them within most block elements and within the <td> and <th> tags to nest tables. (See the "Nesting tables within tables" section later in this chapter.) Use the following markup to create a simple table with two rows and two columns (four data cells) — replacing cell 1, cell 2, and so on with your text:

```
<!DOCTYPE html PUBLIC "-//W3C//DTD XHTML 1.0 Transitional//EN"
    "http://www.w3.org/TR/xhtml1/DTD/xhtml1-transitional.dtd">
<html xmlns="http://www.w3.org/1999/xhtml">
<head>
    <title>Tables</title>
</head>
<body>
 <table>
  <tr>
    <td> cell 1 </td>
    <td> cell 2 </td>
  </tr>
  <tr>
    <td> cell 3 </td>
    <td> cell 4 </td>
  </tr>
 </table>
</body>
</html>
```

The preceding example creates a table with two rows based on the sketch in Figure 11-4. The first table row encloses cells 1 and 2; the second table row encloses cells 3 and 4.

Table rows always run horizontally, and the contents of each cell — in this case, `cell 1`, `cell 2`, and so on — are contained within their own `<td>` element. Don't forget that you must close your table tags, or your table will not display correctly.

Creating a table-based Web page

To create the shell of your table-based Web page (for example, one based on the sketch from the preceding section, Figure 11-4), follow these steps:

1. **Start with the `<table>` element:**

   ```
   <table>
   ...
   </table>
   ```

   The `<table>` element can have a number of optional attributes (for example, `border="1"` or `bgcolor="black"`) — for now, however, keep it simple.

2. **Decide how many *rows* you want the table to have:**

   The following markup creates a table with two rows:

   ```
   <table>
     <tr>...</tr>
     <tr>...</tr>
   </table>
   ```

3. **Create *cells* in each row with the table data cell (`<td>`) element.**

   Each `<td>` element creates a cell, so the number of `<td>` elements in a row is the number of columns.

   The sketch in Figure 11-4 shows a two-column table with *three* cells: the first row contains one cell, and the second row contains two cells. The markup for this arrangement looks like this:

   ```
   <!DOCTYPE html PUBLIC "-//W3C//DTD XHTML 1.0 Transitional//EN"
         "http://www.w3.org/TR/xhtml1/DTD/xhtml1-transitional.dtd">
   <html xmlns="http://www.w3.org/1999/xhtml">
   <head>
       <title>Tables</title>
   </head>
   <body>
   <table>
     <tr>
       <td> contents </td>
     </tr>
     <tr>
       <td> contents </td>
       <td> contents </td>
     </tr>
   </table>
   </body>
   </html>
   ```

Other table elements

Although tables were invented to contain and display data, they're now most commonly used to control Web page layout. This chapter focuses on the elements that designers use to control layout. If you want to create a traditional table, you can use these table elements:

- <th>: The table header element displays text in boldface with a default center alignment.

  You can use the <th> element within any row of a table, but you most often find and use it in the first row at the top — or head — of a table. Except for their position and egotism, they act just like table data (<td>) tags and should be treated as such.

- <caption>: This is the table caption element. It is designed to exist anywhere inside the <table> . . . </table> tags but not inside table rows or cells (because then they wouldn't be captioning anything). This element can only occur once per table.

  Similar to table cells, captions accommodate any HTML elements that can appear in the body of a document (in other words, inline elements), but only those. By default, captions are horizontally centered with the table, and their lines wrap to fit within the table's width. The <caption> element accepts the align attribute.

- <tbody>: You can group table rows into a table body section with the table body (<tbody>) element.

  A recent addition to the HTML 4 specification, these elements allow table bodies to scroll independently of the table head (<thead>) and table foot (<tfoot>). The table body should contain rows of table

data. The <tbody> element must contain at least one table row (<tr>).

- <thead>: You can group table rows into a table head section by using the table head (<thead>) element. The table head contains information about the table's columns.

  The <thead> element must contain at least one table row.

- <tfoot>: Much like the <thead> element, you can group table rows into a table footer section by using the table footer (<tfoot>) element. The table footer contains information about the table's columns and must contain at least one table row.

  Include your footer information before the first instance of the <tbody> element so that the browser renders that information before taking a stab at all the content data cells.

- <colgroup>: This element creates an explicit column group. You specify the number of columns by using the span attribute or by using the <col> element, which we define shortly.

  You use the span attribute to specify a uniform width for a group of columns.

- <col>: The <col> element is an empty element. You use the <col> element to further define column structure. The <col> element shouldn't be used to group columns — that's the <colgroup> element's job. You use the <col> element after you define a column group and set a uniform width to specify a uniform width for a subset of columns.

Here's where tables can get a bit tricky. A simple table with an even number of rows and columns (say two rows and two columns) is a piece of cake — but you'll discover as you get more handy at designing your own pages that your needs aren't likely to produce such symmetrical tables very often. If your cell will span more than one row or column (such as the first cell in the preceding example), you have to add an attribute that tells the browser which cell does the spanning.

The number in the attribute corresponds to the number of columns or rows you want the cell to span, which means if you're creating a table like the one in our example, you have to add the colspan="2" attribute to the first <td> element. (The first cell in the table spans across two columns.)

See the section, "Adding Spans," later in this chapter for more information. But for now, assume that you're creating a table like ours. The markup looks like this:

```
<table>
  <tr>
    <td colspan="2"> contents </td>
  </tr>
  <tr>
    <td> contents </td>
    <td> contents </td>
  </tr>
</table>
```

Congratulations, you're done with your first table. Well, sort of. To effectively use tables for layout, you need to know how to control several display issues, such as borders, table widths, and the handling of white space within your table. (For example, without borders, you can't really tell the table is there — it won't show up in your browser. This isn't a bad thing or a good thing, but something that you can change if you want your borders to show up in browsers.) Keep reading for more information on completing your table and integrating it into your page.

Adding borders

A table border defines the outer edge of the table.

When the table is used to arrange elements on a page, you don't want a *visible* border. There are two ways you can turn a table border on or off:

✔ Set the border attribute within the <table> element. The value of the border attribute must be an integer that defines the border thickness in pixels.

To turn the border off, set the `border` attribute equal to `0`: `<table border="0">`

✔ Define a border using the CSS border properties.

You may define the border style, width, or color by using CSS. (See the later section, "Using CSS border properties.")

Using the (X)HTML border attribute

For an (X)HTML table, *border* refers to both

✔ Outside borders

✔ Individual cell borders

You use the `border` attribute to turn all these table borders on *or* off.

To turn the table (and cell) border on, add the `border` attribute to the `<table>` start tag, as shown in the following bold markup:

```
<!DOCTYPE html PUBLIC "-//W3C//DTD XHTML 1.0 Transitional//EN"
    "http://www.w3.org/TR/xhtml1/DTD/xhtml1-transitional.dtd">
<html xmlns="http://www.w3.org/1999/xhtml">
<head>
    <title>Tables</title>
</head>
<body>
 <table border="1">
  <tr>
    <td colspan="2"> contents </td>
  </tr>
  <tr>
    <td> contents </td>
    <td> contents </td>
  </tr>
 </table>
</body>
</html>
```

The value of the border attribute defines the thickness of the border in pixels. For example, `border="5"` produces a 5-pixel border. If you leave this attribute off, most browsers don't display a border. However, if you don't want your border visible, we suggest that you add `border="0"` to turn off the border for sure.

Where clear delineation between cell contents is desirable, such as with price charts, real data tables, and other collections of text or numerical data, borders help visitors break what they're seeing into separate bits of information. But when a table is used to organize a Web page that all hangs together nicely, turning borders off can help to reinforce this cohesiveness.

By default, most browsers use an invisible 2-pixel border on tables. When you design your table, you should do one of the following:

- ✔ Allow for those invisible 2-pixel borders in your design.

- ✔ Configure your own borders.

- ✔ Eliminate the border by setting the `border` attribute to equal 0 (`border="0"`).

Turn on the table border when you're first creating and tweaking your table. Sometimes it's difficult to see just what is going on without a border. After you've finished tweaking your table, you can turn off the border.

If you use tables to lay out content, table borders should probably be turned off when you display your Web page to the world because borders can be distracting and make text that's supposed to flow together hard to read.

Using CSS border properties

Unlike the (X)HTML border attribute, CSS allows you to define border styles for any or all of the border sides. For example, you can define a dotted gray border for the left side of the table and leave the rest of the table border invisible.

Style

As you might expect, the `border-style` property allows you to define the style (such as dotted or solid) of the border.

The style declaration used to add a border style is:

```
selector {border-style: value;}
```

The value for the `border-style` property must be one of the predefined keywords:

- ✔ dotted
- ✔ dashed
- ✔ solid
- ✔ double
- ✔ groove
- ✔ ridge
- ✔ inset
- ✔ outset

To create a solid border, use the following style declaration:

```
table {border-style: solid;}
```

Width

Similar to using the (X)HTML `border` attribute, you can define the border width in pixels. However, CSS provides you with additional width value data types to choose from. The style declaration used to add a border width is:

```
selector {border-width: value;}
```

The value for the `border-width` property can be

- ✔ **A predefined keyword:** `thin`, `medium`, or `thick`
- ✔ **An absolute or relative length**

  See the Chapter 8 sidebar, "Property measurement values," for more information. The values described in that sidebar are relevant to HTML as well as to CSS.

To set the width of a border to 1pixel, use the following style declaration:

```
table {border-width: 1px;}
```

Color

The style declaration used to define a border color is:

```
selector {border-color: value;}
```

The value for the `border-color` property must defined using a predefined color name or a hexadecimal value:

- ✔ **Color name:** `aqua`, `black`, `blue`, `fuchsia`, `gray`, `green`, `lime`, `maroon`, `navy`, `olive`, `purple`, `red`, `silver`, `teal`, `white`, or `yellow`
- ✔ **Hexadecimal value:** See Chapter 10.

To set the color of a border to black, use the following style declaration:

```
table {border-color: black;}
```

Using the catchall border property

Similar to defining font properties, you can use the shorthand `border` property to define multiple style rules at once:

```
table {border: 1px solid gray;}
```

There are five catchall `border` properties that you can use for a table or a box:

✔ `border`: Defines formatting for all four sides.

✔ `border-left`: Defines formatting for the left side.

✔ `border-right`: Defines formatting for the right side.

✔ `border-top`: Defines formatting for the top.

✔ `border-bottom`: Defines formatting for the bottom.

The border properties aren't only for use with tables, they're part of the CSS box model. They can provide borders for almost any (X)HTML element, as long as it isn't an inline element.

Adjusting height and width

Most browsers determine the width of the table cells by judging the content of the cells (images and/or text).

The browser provides as much space as possible to contain the content. However, there are limits for both images and text:

✔ Side-by-side images must fit in the width of the browser window.

For example, if you have an image that is 200 pixels wide, the cell expands to accommodate the image. However, if you have several cells in a row, each with images over 400 pixels wide, the cells only expand as far as the browser window allows.

✔ Text may expand and distort the layout.

If a cell contains a lot of text, the cell expands as far as it can until the first line break or the end of the text. That might make for a very unattractive table.

Most tables are used to help control layout, so controlling the width of cells and the table is very important. You have two ways to control width:

✔ Use the (X)HTML `width` attribute within the `<table>` or `<td>` element.

✔ Assign a width value to a `<table>` or `<td>` element using the CSS `width` property.

The (X)HTML width attribute

If you don't set table and cell width, the user's browser determines the width of every cell according to the width of its contents — no more, no less.

For example, suppose you want to put a logo in the first cell and navigational items in the cell to its left. If you don't assign the width to the first cell (containing the logo), the navigational items are placed right beside the logo, with no or almost no space between the two. To avoid that cramped look, you can use the width attribute to strategically define an exact number of pixels between the logo and navigational items.

If you're using tables for layout purposes, we recommend that you set the width for the table and cells.

Syntax

Defining width is easy when you use the width attribute. For example, you can set the width of your table at 630 pixels like this:

```
<table border="1" width="630">
...
</table>
```

The value of the width attribute can be defined in either

- ✔ Pixels (a positive integer, such as 630)

  This is an absolute value.

- ✔ Percentage of the display area width (a positive integer followed by a percent sign, such as 95%)

  This is a relative value that allows your table to be resized depending on the size of the browser window.

These values can also set the width of individual *cells*.

Markup

To add widths to the table built earlier in this chapter (and to set width for its individual cells), add the following markup shown in bold text:

```
<!DOCTYPE html PUBLIC "-//W3C//DTD XHTML 1.0 Transitional//EN"
    "http://www.w3.org/TR/xhtml1/DTD/xhtml1-transitional.dtd">
<html xmlns="http://www.w3.org/1999/xhtml">
<head>
    <title>Tables</title>
</head>
<body>
  <table border="1" width="630">
   <tr>
    <td colspan="2" width="630"> contents </td>
   </tr>
   <tr>
```

```
      <td width="400"> contents </td>
      <td width="230"> contents </td>
   </tr>
 </table>
</body>
</html>
```

Figures 11-5 and 11-6 show the difference between a site that doesn't define table and cell widths and one that uses the `width` attribute.

Figure 11-5: This image doesn't define width properties.

Figure 11-6: This image defines width properties.

If you set the pixel width smaller than the content's pixel size, the browser ignores the `width` attribute and defaults to display all the cell contents. So check all dimensions.

The CSS width property

The style declaration used to define width is:

```
selector {width: value;}
```

The value for the `width` property must be either

✔ auto

  This keyword allows the browser to determine the necessary width.

✔ An absolute or relative length:

  See the Chapter 8 sidebar "Property measurement values" for more information.

To set the width of the table displayed in Figure 11-6, use the following style declarations:

```
table {width: 630px;}
td.cellone {width: 630px;}
td.celltwo {width: 630px;}
td.cellthree {width: 630px;}
```

Padding and spacing

Determining the white space between cells is essential for proper layout. Keeping in mind the sketch from Figure 11-4, you have to determine — to the pixel — how space will be used in your table.

(X)HTML attributes

Two attributes can help you define white space by putting some space between cells: cellpadding and cellspacing. These attributes use two different techniques to put some space between cells:

- ✔ cellspacing adds space *between* cells (the border width is adjusted).
- ✔ cellpadding adds space *inside* a cell (within the cell walls).

The value for either attribute is defined in *pixels*. For example, cellpadding="5" adds 5 pixels' worth of padding to each cell.

To define either attribute, add it to the <table> start tag, as follows:

```
<table cellpadding="5" cellspacing="5">
```

When using tables for layout, without visible borders, it doesn't matter much which attribute you use. However, if you add color to your tables — or use the border for any reason — you can see a considerable difference. That's because cellpadding increases the space within the border, and cellspacing increases the width of the border itself, as shown clearly in Figures 11-7 and 11-8.

The default value for cellpadding is 1; the default for cellspacing is 2. If you don't define cellpadding and cellspacing, your users' browsers assume the defaults. Accounting for those pixels in your sketch is a good idea.

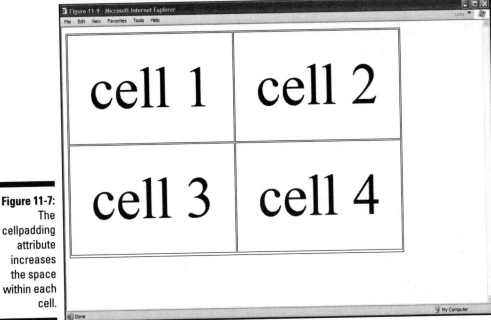

Figure 11-7:
The cellpadding attribute increases the space within each cell.

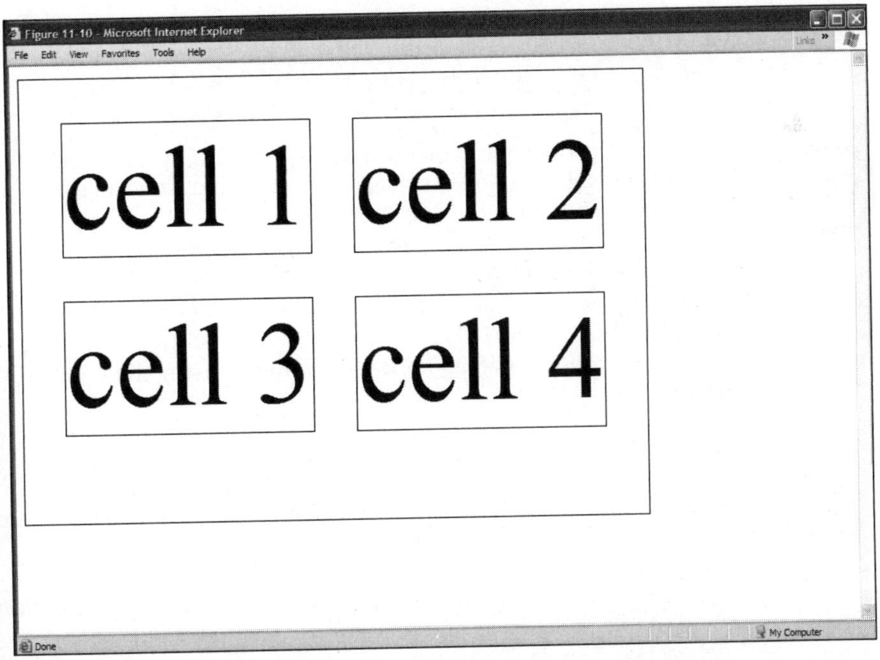

Figure 11-8:
The cellspacing attribute increases the width of the border.

Working with cellpadding and cellspacing to get your table layout just right can be a bit of a headache. Sometimes you need to create empty cells to help control layout. Although this trick is a bit of a workaround, many designers use it. You just

1. **Create a cell.**
2. **Fill the cell with either**

   - `<br />`

   - A spacer image (a transparent `.gif` that is 1 x 1 pixel) with which you can manipulate the width

CSS

You can use CSS to control cell padding and spacing between cells.

Within cells

To control the padding within cells, you use the `padding` property, like so:

```
selector {padding: value;}
```

The value for the `padding` property must be defined by an absolute or relative length, or percentage.

To set the padding of a table cell, use the following style declaration:

```
td {padding: 10px;}
```

The `padding` property can be used with most (X)HTML elements. For example, if you created a footer and assigned it a class name, you can define padding for the element using the following style rule:

```
.footer { padding: 5px;}
```

Between cells

You can control the spacing between your cells using the `border-spacing` property:

```
selector {border-spacing: value;}
```

The value for the `border-spacing` property must be defined by an absolute or relative length, or percentage:

To set the padding of a table cell, use the following style declaration:

```
td {padding: 10px;}
```

The `border-spacing` property can be used only in conjunction with the `<td>` element.

Shifting alignment

If you use tables to define your layout, you need to control their placement in the browser window. You can do this by using (X)HTML or CSS.

You use attributes that are part of the HTML standard to align your tables (horizontally) and your table contents (horizontally and vertically).

Aligning tables is similar to aligning images.

Horizontal alignment

You can horizontally align cell contents using the `align` attribute in various table elements.

✔ To align your table horizontally, use the `align` attribute with the `<table>` element.

The `align` attribute, when used with the `<table>` element, has the following possible values: `left`, `right`, or `center` of the document.

✔ You can use the `align` attribute with the `<td>` (cell) or `<tr>` (row) elements to align text within the cell or row.

The values that can be used with the `align` attribute in the `<td>` or `<tr>` elements are

✔ `align="right"`: Aligns the table or cell contents against the right side.

✔ `align="left"`: Aligns the table or cell contents against the left side. (This is the default setting.)

  • `align="center"`: Centers the table or cell contents.

  • `align="justify"`: Justifies cell contents in the middle (not widely supported).

  • `align="char"`: Aligns cell contents around a specific character (not widely supported).

The following example aligns a table in the center of the page (see Figure 11-9):

```
<!DOCTYPE html PUBLIC "-//W3C//DTD XHTML 1.0 Transitional//EN"
    "http://www.w3.org/TR/xhtml1/DTD/xhtml1-transitional.dtd">
<html xmlns="http://www.w3.org/1999/xhtml">
<head>
    <title>Tables</title>
```

```
 </head>
 <body>
  <table border="1" width="630" align="center">
   <tr>
     <td width="630" colspan="2"> contents </td>
   </tr>
   <tr>
     <td width="400"> contents </td>
     <td width="230"> contents </td>
   </tr>
  </table>
 </body>
 </html>
```

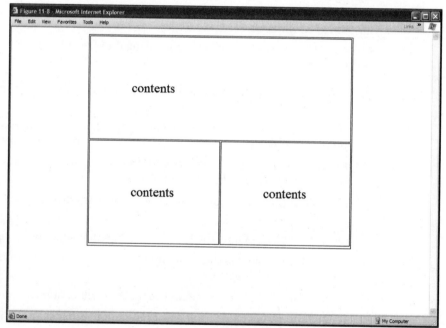

Figure 11-9:
A simple
table
centered.

Vertical alignment

You can vertically align cell contents by using the valign attribute. It can only be used with the `<tr>` (cell) and `<td>` (row) elements.

The possible values are

- valign="top": Vertically aligns cell contents to the top of the cell.

- valign="bottom": Vertically aligns cell contents to the bottom of the cell.

✔ valign="middle": Vertically centers the cell contents. (This is the default.)

✔ valign="baseline": Defines a baseline for all other cells in the same row, so alignment is the same for all cells.

You can also use the align and valign attributes with the following table elements: <col>, <colgroup>, <tbody>, <tfoot>, <th>, and <thead>.

If you set the alignment for a row (<tr>) and then set the alignment for a cell within that row (<td>), the setting you add to the cell *overrides* the setting for the row.

You are now used to learning that most X(HTML) formatting attributes are deprecated in favor of using CSS, and although the align attribute is deprecated for most (X)HTML elements, it is still allowed when used with the table elements.

You can't use the valign attribute with the <table> tag.

Using CSS to define alignment

To control table alignment by using CSS, you have access to two properties: text-align and vertical-align. They function just as the preceding align and valign attributes.

To use the text-align property, you can assign it one of the following values:

✔ right: Aligns the table or cell contents against the right side.

✔ left: Aligns the table or cell contents against the left side. (This is the default.)

✔ center: Centers the table or cell contents.

✔ justify: Justifies cell contents in the middle.

To use the vertical-align property, you can assign it one of the following values:

✔ top: Vertically aligns cell contents to the top of the cell.

✔ bottom: Vertically aligns cell contents to the bottom of the cell.

✔ middle: Vertically centers the cell contents. (This is the default.)

✔ baseline: Defines a baseline for all other cells in the same row, so alignment is the same for all cells.

You can control the alignment of an entire row by assigning alignment properties to the <tr> element.

You can't center a table by using the `text-align` property — it's only for text alignment. Currently, you have a few options for centering the entire table. None of them is ideal, but they all work:

- ✔ Use the deprecated `<center>` tags around the table.
- ✔ Use the deprecated `align` attribute within the table: `<table align="center">`.
- ✔ Enclose the table in a `<div>` element and use the `text-align` property to center its contents: `div.mytable {text-align: center;}`.

Adding Spans

Spanning is one of the main reasons tables are a flexible alternative for arranging elements in your Web page.

Spanning enables you to stretch items across multiple cells; you essentially tear down a cell wall. Whether you need to span rows or columns, you can use the concept of spanning to wrangle your table into almost any arrangement.

Column and row spanning takes careful planning. That planning should occur during the sketching phase (as we describe earlier in this chapter, in the section "Sketching Your Table").

To span cells, you add one of these attributes to the `<td>` (cell) element:

- ✔ `colspan` extends a cell *horizontally* (across multiple *columns*).
- ✔ `rowspan` extends a cell *vertically* (across multiple *rows*).

Spanning cells can be done only by using (X)HTML attributes; CSS doesn't provide equivalent functionality.

Column spans

To span columns, you use the `colspan` attribute in the `<td>` element and set the value equal to the number of cells you want to span.

Figure 11-10 illustrates a cell that spans two columns.

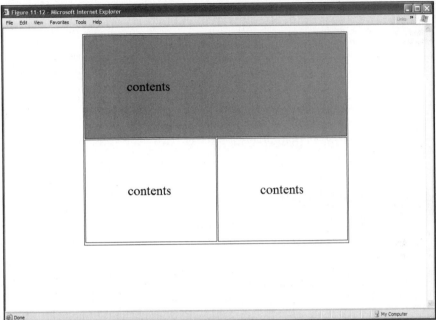

Figure 11-10:
The cell
spans two
columns.

In this example, the first cell spans the two cells in the next row. You use the
colspan attribute set to 2, as shown in the following markup, because the
cell spans two columns:

```
<!DOCTYPE html PUBLIC "-//W3C//DTD XHTML 1.0 Transitional//EN"
      "http://www.w3.org/TR/xhtml1/DTD/xhtml1-transitional.dtd">
<html xmlns="http://www.w3.org/1999/xhtml">
<head>
    <title>Tables</title>
</head>
<body>
 <table border="1" width="630">
  <tr>
    <td width="630" colspan="2"> contents </td>
  </tr>
  <tr>
    <td width="400"> contents </td>
    <td width="230"> contents </td>
  </tr>
 </table>
</body>
</html>
```

After you add a `colspan` attribute

✔ Verify that you have the appropriate number of `<td>` cells in the first row. For example, if you define a cell to span two columns, you should have one less `<td>` in that row. If you use `colspan="3"`, there should be two fewer `<td>` cells in that row.

✔ Make sure that the other rows have the appropriate number of `<td>` cells. For example, if you define a cell to span two columns, the other rows in that table should have two `<td>` cells to fill out the two columns.

Row spans

You use the `rowspan` attribute with the `<td>` tag. Figure 11-11 illustrates a cell that spans two rows.

To span rows, you use the `rowspan` attribute in the `<td>` element and set the value equal to the number of cells you want to span.

Sketch your table first so you know which cells should span which columns and rows. The example design we use throughout most of this chapter uses the `colspan` attribute with the first cell. However, the design could have been just as simple if we used a `rowspan` with the last cell that contains the navigational items. Either way, the table is efficiently laid out.

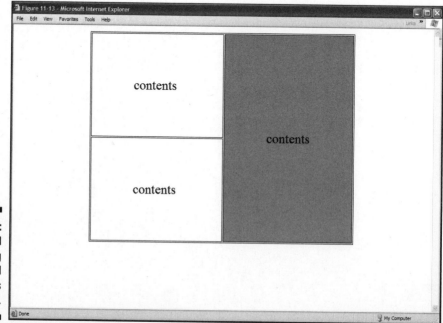

Figure 11-11:
The last cell containing navigational items spans two rows.

The modified table comes from the following markup (note the bold `rowspan`):

```
<!DOCTYPE html PUBLIC "-//W3C//DTD XHTML 1.0 Transitional//EN"
     "http://www.w3.org/TR/xhtml1/DTD/xhtml1-transitional.dtd">
<html xmlns="http://www.w3.org/1999/xhtml">
<head>
    <title>Tables</title>
</head>
<body>
 <table border="1" width="630">
  <tr>
    <td width="400"> contents </td>
    <td width="230" rowspan="2"> contents </td>
  </tr>
  <tr>
    <td width="630"> contents </td>
  </tr>
 </table>
</body>
</html>
```

Populating Table Cells

After you sketch your table and define table properties (such as width, cell padding and spacing, and cell spanning), you're ready to populate the table cells with images, hyperlinks, text, and almost any other (X)HTML element. This is a simple process: You add images, hyperlinks, and text to the `<td>` element, similar to how you add them to the `<body>` element.

The following markup shows a populated table, with data added in bold:

```
<!DOCTYPE html PUBLIC "-//W3C//DTD XHTML 1.0 Transitional//EN"
     "http://www.w3.org/TR/xhtml1/DTD/xhtml1-transitional.dtd">
<html xmlns="http://www.w3.org/1999/xhtml">
<head>
    <title>Tables</title>
</head>
<body>
 <table border="1" width="630" align="center" cellpadding="5" cellspacing="5">
  <tr>
    <td colspan="2" valign="bottom" align="left">
      <a href="http://www.ropeadope.com">
        <img src="images/ropeAdopeRecords.gif" width="249" height="94"
          alt="rope-a-dope records" border="0" />
      </a>
```

```
      </td>
    </tr>
    <tr>
      <td valign="top" align="right" width="400">
        <img src="images/gunlogo.gif" width="400" height="302" alt="rope-a-dope
        home" border="0" />
      </td>
      <td valign="top" align="left" width="230">
        <br /><br /><br />
        <img src="images/bands.gif">
        <br>
        <a href="q/">
          <img src="images/q.gif" border="0" />
        </a>
        <br />
        <a href="ilovemyself/">
          <img src="images/ilovemyself.gif" border="0" />
        </a>
        <br />
        <a href="http://www.pwolf.com">
          <img src="images/prescottCurlywolf.gif" border="0" />
        </a>
        <br /><br />
        <img src="images/organizations.gif" />
        <br />
        <a href="http://www.anthropos.org">
          <img src="images/anthropos.gif" border="0" />
        </a>
        <br /><br />
        <img src="images/distractions.gif" />
        <br />
        <a href="darth/">
          <img src="images/hubbabubba.gif" border="0" />
        </a>
        <br />
      </td>
    </tr>
  </table>
</body>
</html>
```

Testing Your Table

Testing is the final step before your table goes live. You must test your tables in all the popular browsers — including Internet Explorer, Netscape, and Opera. If you don't, your users might have to squint at your pages, or they might see your tables as one big mess.

As you're creating your table, have your browser window open at the same time. Each time you change the width of a cell or add an item to a cell, save the document and view it in the browser window. That way, when you test your table, you probably won't have too much tweaking to do.

A challenge for many designers is to create table designs that work in every browser. Thanks to many crusaders of standards, the newest versions of the most popular browsers, Netscape, Internet Explorer, and Opera, all support the HTML standard. If your audience isn't technically savvy, consider older browsers when designing your tables.

Always test your site in any browser that your users might have. For example, if your table is aligned with `align="center"` but in an old version of Internet Explorer the table remains flush with the left side, you might have to add a `<center>` tag pair to your table. However, you won't have too many problems with tables if you stick to the standard.

Table-Making Tips

We've spent years of building, maintaining, and troubleshooting tables, and in that time we've discovered some neat tricks. The following tips are a head start to creating effective tables.

Following the standards

The first — and (we think) most important — tip is to keep with the established standards. The folks involved with the Web Standards Project have campaigned for full standard support in browsers and HTML authoring applications since 1998. Their hard work should make your life easier.

Just a couple of years ago, if you built an HTML table, you would be forced to create different versions of your Web page (each version containing browser-specific elements and attributes) to define some basic table properties. As you might imagine, creating and maintaining different versions of the same Web page can drive development costs sky-high. To get around those costs, many developers would carefully craft their tables with specific markup that worked in Internet Explorer and Netscape — but what about Opera? Well, happily those are problems of the past. The newest versions of Internet Explorer, Netscape, and Opera *all* support HTML, as well as CSS and XHTML. To find out more about the fight for Web standards, visit `www.webstandards.org`.

Sanitizing markup

Efficiently written markup is easier to troubleshoot and maintain. Many designers use white space to separate elements. For example, the following markup doesn't use much white space and is hard to read:

```
<table border="1" width="630">
<tr><td width="630" colspan="2"> contents </td></tr>
<tr><td width="400"> contents </td>
<td width="230"> contents </td></tr></table>
```

Check out this clean version:

```
<table border="1" width="630">
  <tr>
    <td width="630" colspan="2"> contents </td>
  </tr>
  <tr>
    <td width="400"> contents </td>
    <td width="230"> contents </td>
  </tr>
</table>
```

The white space we include in our markup is *between* elements; not within elements. If, for example, you add white space between the <td> and </td> tags, it affects how the cell's content is displayed, which isn't generally something you want to do.

Nesting tables within tables

Many designers are forced to nest tables within tables to achieve a desired effect. This is both *legal* and *common*.

A few nested tables won't affect your users too badly. But nesting many tables within tables can lengthen download time.

To nest a table, simply add the <table> element within a <td> element as follows:

```
<!DOCTYPE html PUBLIC "-//W3C//DTD XHTML 1.0 Transitional//EN"
     "http://www.w3.org/TR/xhtml1/DTD/xhtml1-transitional.dtd">
<html xmlns="http://www.w3.org/1999/xhtml">
<head>
    <title>Nesting Tables</title>
</head>
<body>
 <table border="1">
  <tr>
```

```
    <td> contents </td>
    <td> contents </td>
  </tr>
  <tr>
    <td>
      <table border="1">
      <tr>
      <td> contents  </td>
      <td> contents  </td>
      </tr>
      <tr>
      <td> contents  </td>
      <td> contents  </td>
      </tr>
      </table>
    </td>
    <td> contents </td>
  </tr>
</table>
</body>
</html>
```

This markup produces the tables shown in Figure 11-12.

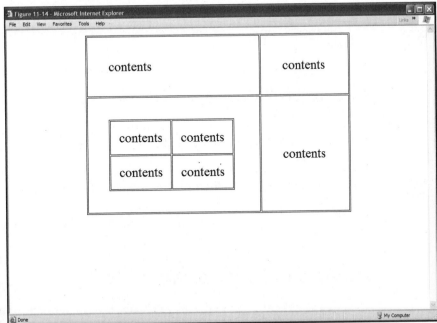

Figure 11-12:
Nested
tables.

When using nested tables

- ✔ Check cell widths — the width of the third cell should match the width of the nested table.
- ✔ Create *and test* the table you intend to nest — separately, before you add it to your primary table.

Avoiding dense tables

We recommend creativity, but be careful and don't pack a screen full of dense and impenetrable information — especially numbers. A long, unbroken list of numbers quickly drives away all but the truly masochistic — pretty much negating the purpose of the table to begin with. Put those numbers into an attractive table (better yet, *several* tables interspersed with a few well-chosen images). Watch your page's attractiveness and readability soar; hear visitors sigh with relief.

Individual table cells can be surprisingly roomy. You can position graphics in them precisely. If you're moved to put graphics in a table, be sure to

- ✔ Select images that are similar in size and looks.
- ✔ Measure those images to determine their heights and widths in pixels. (Shareware programs such as Paint Shop Pro and GraphicConverter do this automatically.)
- ✔ Use HTML markup to position these images within their table cells.

A short-and-sweet table keeps the graphics in check and guarantees that the text always sits nicely to its right.

Two more handy graphics-placement tips produce a consistent, coherent image layout:

- ✔ Size your rows and columns of cells that contain images to accommodate the *largest* graphic.
- ✔ *Center* all graphics in each cell (both vertically and horizontally).

Adding color to table cells

You can use either CSS or (X)HTML to change the background color of a cell or table. Before CSS was around, designers used the `bgcolor` attribute to change the background of table cells in much the same way it affects the background of an entire HTML document. Simply add the bgcolor attribute to any table cell to change its background color:

```
<td bgcolor="teal">...</td>
```

However, now you have a bit more flexibility to use the background property to add some color:

```
td {background: red;}
```

We cover the background property in Chapter 10.

The bgcolor attribute may be used with any of the table elements. However, the bgcolor of a cell overrides any bgcolor defined for a row or table. Note that bgcolor is also deprecated, and that most Web experts use CSS markup instead.

Marvelous Miscellany

Table 11-1 lists other table-related (X)HTML attributes that you might find in HTML files.

Table 11-1	Additional Table-related (X)HTML Attributes		
Name	*Function/ Value Equals*	*Value Types*	*Related Element(s)*
abbr	Abbreviates table header	Text	`<td><th>`
axis	Sets a comma-separated list of related table headers	CDATA	`<td><th>`
char	Defines alignment character for table elements	ISO 10646 char	`<col /><colgroup> <tbody><td><tfoot> <th><thead><tr>`
charoff	Defines offset when alignment char is used	Length (p/%)	`<col /><colgroup> <tbody><td><tfoot> <th><thead><tr>`

(continued)

Table 11-1 *(continued)*

Name	Function/ Value Equals	Value Types	Related Element(s)
`frame`	Identifies visible components in a table structure	`{"above"|"below"| "border"|"box"| "hsides"|"lhs"|"rhs"| "void"|"vsides"}`	`<table>`
`rules`	Governs the display of rule bars in a table	`{"all"| "cols"| "groups"| "none"| "rows"}`	`<table>`
`scope`	Describes scope for table header cells	`{"col"| "colgroup"| "row"| "rowgroup"}`	`<td><th>`
`summary`	Describes a table's purpose	Text	`<table>`
`span`	Sets the number of table columns to which `col` attributes apply	Number	`<col />`

Part IV
Integrating Scripts with HTML

The 5th Wave   By Rich Tennant

"See? I created a little felon figure that runs around our Web site hiding behind banner ads. On the last page, our logo puts him in a non lethal choke hold and brings him back to the home page."

In this part . . .

In this part of the book, we introduce and describe the types of scripting languages that work on Web pages, and we dig into JavaScript — by far the most popular of all Web scripting languages in use today. Scripting languages help turn static, unchanging Web pages into active, dynamic documents that can solicit and respond to user input. You start by learning basic JavaScript elements, data types, and values, and progress to topics that include rearranging Web page contents on the fly, performing calculations and displaying their results, requesting and checking user input, and a whole bunch more.

Next, you dig more deeply into JavaScript so that you can understand — and use — this scripting language in your Web pages. You also learn how to incorporate JavaScript into Web pages and how it handles and changes Web page contents on the fly. You also learn about checking your work and using cookies (those interesting but elusive data packages that adhere to Web users).

The final three chapters in this part show you ways to put JavaScript to work in your Web pages. You explore how to define and use a navigation bar, which presents users with dynamic menus of options and information to make it easier for them to move around your Web site. You learn how to use JavaScript to create and use various data-entry forms in your Web pages to solicit, check, and respond to user input. You also learn the basic concepts and techniques for creating dynamic HTML (sometimes called DHTML) and using client-side JavaScripts and pre-fabricated code to perform basic tasks, such as displaying date and time information, counting site visitors, or tabulating current statistics.

Chapter 12

Scripting Web Pages

In This Chapter

▶ Understanding what JavaScript is

▶ Exploring what JavaScript can do for your Web pages

▶ Dissecting three sample scripts

When used in conjunction with your HTML markup, *scripts* — small programs that you add to your Web page — help your Web pages respond to user actions. Scripts create the interactive and dynamic effects you see on the Web, such as images that automatically change when visitors move mouse pointers over them, additional browser windows that pop up when a page loads, and animated navigation bars.

Because scripts are mini-programs, they're often written in a programming language called JavaScript. If you are unfamiliar with the term, JavaScript may sound like a Hollywood screenplay doused with coffee. However, it is actually a scripting language built right into all the popular Web browsers.

Fortunately, because of the Nobel prize–worthy invention of "copy and paste," you don't need to be a technoguru to add scripting to your Web sites. The Web has many sites that feature canned JavaScript scripts that you can freely copy and then paste right into your Web page. (Chapter 13 lists several of the best JavaScript sites.)

In this chapter, you explore how scripting works inside your Web page by dissecting three sample scripts written in JavaScript. Chapter 13 continues this discussion by diving deeper into the JavaScript language itself.

Many good Web-page editors (such as Macromedia Dreamweaver and Adobe GoLive) have built-in tools to help you create scripts — even if you don't know anything about programming.

JavaScript is not Java

In the late 1990s, the originators of the JavaScript scripting language wanted to ride the coattails of the massive popularity of the Java programming language, so they gave it a catchy name — JavaScript. However, when they made this decision, they also introduced a lot of confusion given the similarity of the two names. To clarify, the full-featured Java programming language *isn't* a scripting language on the Web. Java is a descendent of the C and C++ programming languages. Programmers can create Java applications that can run on Windows, Macintosh, Linux, and other computer platforms:

✔ On the client side, Java is used to create *applets* (small programs that download over the Net and run inside Web browsers). Because Java is designed to be cross-platform, these applets should run identically on any Java-enabled browser.

✔ On the server side, Java is used to create many Web-based applications.

What JavaScript Can Do for Your Pages

Adding scripts to your Web site is much like those makeover reality television shows that transform a house or a person's appearance into something completely new and wonderful. So too with JavaScript. You can transform a plain and dull Web page into an interactive and dynamic Web extravaganza that will give your visitors joy and enjoyment for years to come. Okay, maybe we're exaggerating just a little bit, but you get the point.

For example, if you visit Dummies.com (`www.dummies.com`) and click the red button next to the search box without entering a term to search on, the browser displays a nice warning box that reminds you to enter a search term before you actually search, as shown in Figure 12-1.

Figure 12-1:
A script pops up a dialog box telling you what you did wrong.

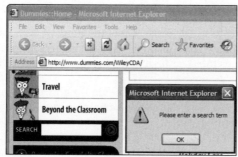

A short script verifies whether you've entered a search term before the engine runs the query:

- ✔ If you enter a search term, you don't see the warning.
- ✔ If you don't enter a search term, the script built into the page prompts the warning dialog box to appear.

This bit of scripting makes the page *dynamic,* which means that it adds programmatic functionality to your Web pages and allows them to respond to what users do on the page — for example, filling out a form or moving the mouse pointer over an image. When you add scripts to your page, the page interacts with users and changes its display or its behavior in response to what users do.

The page URL doesn't change and another browser window doesn't open when you try to search on nothing. The page responds to what you do without sending a request back to the Web server for new page. This is why the page is considered *dynamic.*

If you tried this trick without using a script (that is, without the dynamic functionality), the browser would send the empty search string back to the Web server. Then the server would return a separate warning page reminding the user to enter a search term. All the work would be done on the Web server instead of in the Web browser. This would be slower (because the request must first go to the server, and then the server must transmit the warning page back to your browser), and would feel much less fluid to the user. It's much better to just click a button on the page and instantly have an alert pop up to help the user.

In the following sections, we showcase three common ways in which JavaScript can be used in your Web pages.

Don't worry about the details of the JavaScript code in the following examples. Just focus on how JavaScript scripts can be pasted into your Web page and work alongside your HTML markup.

Arrange content dynamically

JavaScript can be used with CSS (covered in Chapters 8 and 9) to change the look of the content on a page in response to a user action. Here is an example: Two authors share a Weblog, Backup Brain (www.backupbrain.com). One of the authors prefers small, sans-serif type, and the other one finds it easier to read larger, serif type. So the Weblog has buttons that change the look of the site to match each person's preference. Of course, the site's visitors can use the buttons to switch the look of the type, too, and the site remembers the visitor's choice for future visits by setting a *cookie,* which is a small preference file written to the user's computer. Figure 12-2 shows the two looks for the page.

Figure 12-2:
Clicking the
"Change
your font"
buttons
changes
how the text
displays.

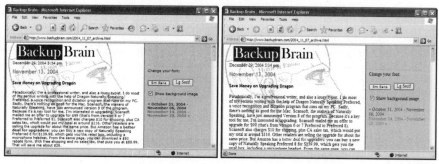

JavaScript and CSS can create this effect by switching between two style sheets:

✔ The sans-serif style sheet, `sansStyle.css`

✔ The serif style sheet, `serifStyle.css`

Listing 12-1 shows the source code of an example page that contains this switching mechanism.

✔ When a user clicks the Sm Sans button on the page, the `styleSwitcher.js` script referenced in the `<head>` element runs and switches the active style sheet to `sansStyle.css`. (Chapter 13 covers .js files.)

✔ When the user clicks the Lg Serif button, the same script switches to the `serifStyle.css` style sheet.

Listing 12-1:   Style Switching

```
<!DOCTYPE html PUBLIC "-//W3C//DTD XHTML 1.0 Transitional//EN"
      "http://www.w3.org/TR/xhtml1/DTD/xhtml1-transitional.dtd">
<html xmlns="http://www.w3.org/1999/xhtml">
<head>
    <title>Style Changer</title>
    <link href="simpleStyle.css" rel="stylesheet" rev="stylesheet" />
    <link href="sansStyle.css" rel="stylesheet" rev="stylesheet"
        title="default" />
    <link href="serifStyle.css" rel="alternate stylesheet"
        rev="alternate stylesheet" title="serif" />
    <style type="text/css" media="all">@import "complexStyle.css";</style>
    <script src="styleSwitcher.js" language="javascript1.5"
```

```
        type="text/javascript"></script>
</head>
<body>
<div class="navBar">
<br />Change your font:
<form action="none">
    <input type="button" class="typeBtn" value="Sm Sans"
        onclick="setActiveStylesheet('default')" />
    <input type="button" class="typeBtn2" value="Lg Serif"
        onclick="setActiveStylesheet('serif')" />
</form>
</div>

<div class="content" id="headContent">
<p>Replace this paragraph with your own content.</p>
</div>
</body>
</html>
```

You can see the example page for yourself at

```
www.javascriptworld.com/scripts/chap16/ex6/index.html
```

This example relies on several different files (HTML, CSS, and JavaScript). You can see the full listing for all of the files at

```
www.javascriptworld.com/scripts/script16.06.html
```

Work with browser windows

JavaScript can tell your browser to open and close windows.

You've probably seen the annoying version of this trick: advertising pop-up windows that appear when you try to leave a site.

But this technology can be used for good as well as evil. For example, you can *preview* a set of big image files with small thumbnail versions. Clicking a thumbnail image can perform such actions as

 ✔ Opening a window with a larger version of the image.

 ✔ Opening a page with a *text link* that opens a window with an illustration of that text, as shown in Figure 12-3.

The code required to do this sort of pop-up window is fairly straightforward, as Listing 12-2 shows.

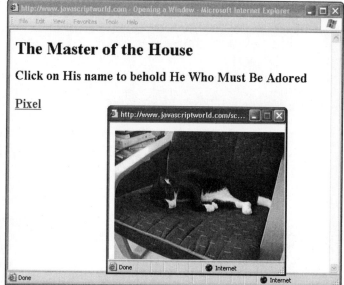

Figure 12-3:
When you click the link, a pop-up window appears with a picture in it.

Listing 12-2: Pop-up Windows

```
<!DOCTYPE html PUBLIC "-//W3C//DTD XHTML 1.0 Transitional//EN"
        "http://www.w3.org/TR/xhtml1/DTD/xhtml1-transitional.dtd">
<html xmlns="http://www.w3.org/1999/xhtml">
<head>
    <title>Opening a Window</title>
    <script language="Javascript" type="text/javascript">

    function newWindow() {
        catWindow = window.open("images/pixel2.jpg", "catWin",
          "width=330,height=250")
    }
    </script>
</head>
<body bgcolor="#FFFFFF">
    <h1>The Master of the House</h1>
    <h2>Click on His name to behold He Who Must Be Adored<br /><br />
    <a href="javascript:newWindow()">Pixel</a></h2>
</body>
</html>
```

Pop-up windows can backfire on you if you use them too much. Many Web sites use pop-up windows to deliver ads, so users are becoming desensitized (or hostile) to them and simply ignore them (or install software that prevents them). Before you add a pop-up window to your site, be sure it's absolutely necessary.

Chapter 13 has more details on creating pop-up windows with JavaScript.

Solicit and verify user input

A common use for JavaScript is to verify that users have filled out all the required fields in a form before the browser actually submits the form to the form-processing program on the Web server. Listing 12-3 places a form-checking function, checkSubmit, in the <script> element of the HTML page and references it in the onsubmit attribute of the <form> element.

Listing 12-3:   Form Validation

```
<!DOCTYPE html PUBLIC "-//W3C//DTD XHTML 1.0 Transitional//EN"
      "http://www.w3.org/TR/xhtml1/DTD/xhtml1-transitional.dtd">
<html xmlns="http://www.w3.org/1999/xhtml">
<head>
  <title>Linking scripts to HTML pages</title>
  <script type="text/javascript" language="javascript">
    function checkSubmit ( thisForm ) {
      if ( thisForm.FirstName.value == '' ) {
          alert('Please enter your First Name.');
          return false;
      }

      if ( thisForm.LastName.value == '' ) {
          alert('Please enter your Last Name.');
          return false;
      }

      return true;
    }
</script>
</head>

<body>
  <form method="POST" action="/cgi-bin/form_processor.cgi"
       onsubmit="return checkSubmit(this);">
  <p>
    First Name: <input type="text" name="FirstName" /><br />
    Last Name: <input type="text" name="LastName" /><br />
    <input type="submit" />
  </p>
  </form>
</body>
</html>
```

This script performs one of two operations if either form field isn't filled in when the user clicks the Submit button:

⮩ It instructs the browser to display a warning to let the user know he or she forgot to fill in a field.

⮩ It returns a value of false to the browser, which prevents the browser from actually submitting the form to the form-processing application.

Server-side scripting

JavaScript is a scripting language that runs inside the browser, but there are other scripting languages that run on the server side, such as Perl, ASP (Active Server Pages), PHP, Python, .NET, ColdFusion, and others. The programs written in these languages reside on the server and are called by the Web page, usually in response to a form filled out by the user. People who write these Web pages may include small snippets of code that pass bits of information from the HTML page to the program on the server. When called, the program runs and then returns a result of some sort to the user.

Amazon.com is a familiar e-commerce Web application that runs mostly on the server side using server scripts. Therefore, the Web pages that are displayed by the browser when you visit Amazon are the results of processing by server-side scripts that takes place before the page ever gets to your browser.

If the fields are filled in correctly, the browser doesn't display alerts and returns a value of `true`, which tells the browser that the form is ready to pass on to the Web server. Figure 12-4 shows how the browser displays the alert if the first name field is empty.

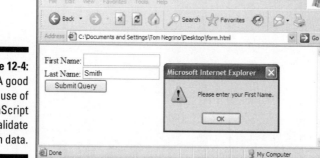

Figure 12-4:
A good use of JavaScript is to validate form data.

Although this example only verifies whether users filled out the form fields, you can create more advanced scripts that check for specific data formats (such as @ signs in e-mail addresses and only numbers in phone number fields).

When you create forms that include required fields, we recommend that you always include JavaScript field validation to catch missing data before the script can even find its way back to the server. Visitors get frustrated when they take the time to fill out a form only to be told to click the Back button in their browsers to provide missing information. When you use JavaScript, the script catches any missing information before the form page disappears so users can quickly make changes and try to submit again.

But wait . . . there's more!

You can do much more with JavaScript. The following list highlights several common uses of the scripting language:

- ✔ Detect whether a user has a browser plug-in installed that handles multi-media content
- ✔ Build slide shows of images
- ✔ Automatically redirect the user to a different Web page
- ✔ Add conditional logic to your page, so that if the user performs a certain action, other actions are triggered
- ✔ Create, position, and scroll new browser windows
- ✔ Create navigation bars and change the menus on those bars dynamically
- ✔ Automatically put the current date and time on your page
- ✔ Combine JavaScript and CSS to animate page elements

One of the more innovative uses of JavaScript is in Gmail, the free Web-based e-mail service from Google, which you can find at `www.gmail.com`. Gmail uses JavaScript to load an entire e-mail user interface into the user's browser, which makes Gmail much more responsive to user actions than most other Web-based mail programs. Gmail uses JavaScript to keep the number of times the page needs to fetch additional information from the Gmail servers to an absolute minimum. By doing much of the processing in the user's browser, the Gmail Web application feels much more like an e-mail program that you run on your computer. Figure 12-5 shows the JavaScript-powered Gmail interface. It's a great example of the power of JavaScript.

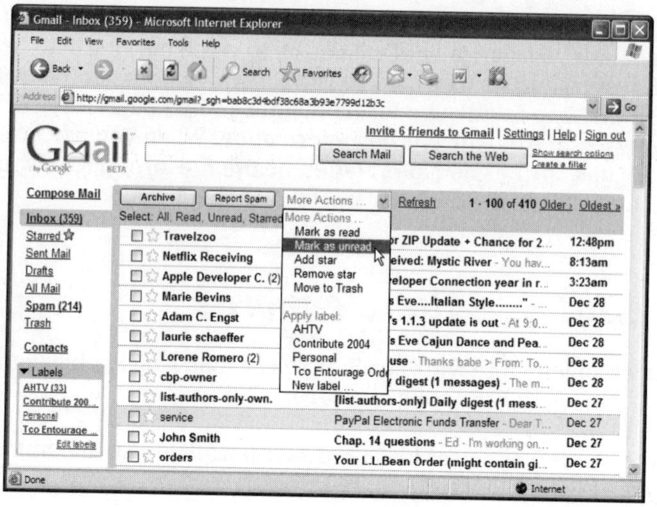

Figure 12-5: The Gmail interface is powered by JavaScript.

Chapter 13

The Nuts and Bolts of JavaScript

- -

In This Chapter

▶ Putting scripts in your pages

▶ Using external script pages

▶ Delving into the JavaScript language

▶ Where to learn more

- -

A lot of good "canned JavaScript" is available for free on the Web; you know what we mean — scripts written by someone else that you simply copy and paste into your HTML page. But, as good as canned scripts can be, copy-and-paste goes only so far. Sooner or later, you are going to encounter unique needs that can't be fulfilled with a free script.

Canned JavaScript is much like canned SPAM: Great for convenience, but you probably don't want to live on an exclusive diet of it. Instead, knowing how to script — or at least how to tweak a prewritten script — is as important as knowing how to fix some good ol' fashioned home cooking.

In this chapter, you "open the can" of the JavaScript language and have a look at what's inside. (Don't worry; you won't encounter any pink meaty substances along the way.) You discover how to plug scripts into your pages, how to bundle your scripts into external JavaScript files to save time and effort, and how the nuts and bolts of the JavaScript language work. Finally, at the end of this chapter, we point you to good sources of additional information about JavaScript. These will come in handy as your scripting needs grow more advanced.

Including Scripts in Web Pages

Because a JavaScript script is a totally separate animal from HTML markup, you have to contain this JavaScript beast inside an HTML container tag,

`<script>` and `</script>`. You can put a script in one of two places on an HTML page:

- ✔ Within the `<head>` and `</head>` tags (this is called a *header script*)
- ✔ Within the `<body>` and `</body>` tags (this is called a *body script*)

Header scripts contain code that you either want to be processed before the page loads or else want to have available to be called by other scripts in your Web page. Body scripts are executed when the `<body>` tag is processed. Typically, body scripts are used to generate HTML content for the page.

Listing 13-1 shows an example of a header script. This simple script pops up a welcoming message box when the user loads the page.

Listing 13-1: Header Script

```
<!DOCTYPE html PUBLIC "-//W3C//DTD XHTML 1.0 Transitional//EN"
     "http://www.w3.org/TR/xhtml1/DTD/xhtml1-transitional.dtd">
<html xmlns="http://www.w3.org/1999/xhtml">
<head>
   <title>My JavaScript page</title>
     <script language="Javascript" type="text/javascript">
      alert("Welcome to my JavaScript page!")
     </script>
</head>
<body bgcolor="#FFFFFF">
   <h2>This script pops up a message box for the user.</h2>
</body>
</html>
```

The preceding `<script>` tag has two attributes:

- ✔ `language="Javascript"` tells the browser which scripting language the document uses.
- ✔ `type="text/javascript"` tells the browser that the script is plain text in JavaScript.

The script itself, `alert("Welcome to my JavaScript page!")`, is straight-forward. The `alert()` method displays a message box that pops up on top of the browser window and shows a customized message to the Web page visitor. You specify the message you want displayed by enclosing the text within quotation marks and putting the text string inside the `alert()` method's parentheses, as shown in Listing 13-1. (***Note:*** Curly quotes and single quotes won't work.) Make sure you close the script with the `</script>` tag, and your script is ready to go.

Using the Same Script on Multiple Pages

If you have a single Web page that uses a JavaScript script, it's handy to be able to contain all of the scripting code inside a single `<script>` tag. However, suppose you have a boatload of pages, each of which needs to call the same script. You can always copy and paste the script into each page, but there are two downsides to that approach. First, you have to add the script to each page and make sure it is set up correctly and working. Second, anytime you make any tweaks to the script, you are forced to update each and every HTML page that uses it. If you have two pages, that's no big deal. But if you have more than three, it can lead to a maintenance migraine.

However, this headache can be avoided — even without ibuprofen! Instead, you can use an external JavaScript file, also called a `.js` file (pronounced "dot jay ess"). A `.js` file is an ordinary text file that stores your JavaScript scripts. You can store one or more of your JavaScript scripts in a single `.js` file and access them from multiple HTML pages.

To use the same script on multiple pages, you should

1. **Put the script in an external JavaScript file.**

   If you have the script already inside your HTML page, remove all the JavaScript code inside the `<script>` tag and paste it into a separate file.

2. **Reference the file in any HTML page when you need the script.**

   Define a `<script>` tag in the head section of your Web page, but don't add any code inside it. Instead, use the `src` (for *source*) attribute in the `<script>` tag to call the external `.js` file.

Listing 13-2 shows the reference to the external file.

Listing 13-2:   External Script Reference

```
<!DOCTYPE html PUBLIC "-//W3C//DTD XHTML 1.0 Transitional//EN"
        "http://www.w3.org/TR/xhtml1/DTD/xhtml1-transitional.dtd">
<html xmlns="http://www.w3.org/1999/xhtml">
<head>
     <title>My JavaScript page</title>
<script src="external.js" language="JavaScript" type="text/javascript">
</script>
</head>
(the rest of your HTML page goes here)
```

You don't need to include anything between the opening and closing script tags. In Listing 13-2, the name of the source file, `external.js`, is placed between double quotes. You can reference this file, `external.js`, with either a relative or absolute link, so you can refer to external JavaScript files in other directories on your server, or even on other servers (if you have access to those servers).

Adding the `src` attribute to the `<script>` tag tells the browser to look for that external file in the specified path. The resulting Web pages look and act like the scripts are in the header or body of the page's script tags, though the script is in the external `.js` file.

With this technique, you need to change a JavaScript only once on your site in the external file, not in each individual page on the site. All of the pages that reference the external file automatically receive the updated code. It's a big timesaver when updating your site.

If you use a script on only one page, it's often easier simply to put the script on the page in a body or header script.

If you have multiple external `.js` files, you can use any or all of them on any HTML page. Just include multiple `<script>` references on the page. It's perfectly okay for a page to include multiple scripts and to both refer to external `.js` files and include its own scripts inside `<script>` tags.

When you have multiple `<script>` tags defined in your Web page, the browser processes them in the order in which they are declared. If, for some reason, you have an external `.js` file that conflicts with a script inside a `<script>` tag, the last one defined wins.

There is nothing magical about the inside of the `.js` file itself — it is pure JavaScript code. No HTML tags are allowed. Listing 13-3 shows an example of a script in an external `.js` file. This script implements button rollovers for a Web page. When the user moves the mouse pointer over a button image, the image changes to highlight the choice.

Listing 13-3:   An External JavaScript File

```
homeOff = new Image
productsOff = new Image
contactOff = new Image
pressOff = new Image

homeOver = new Image
productsOver = new Image
contactOver = new Image
pressOver = new Image

homeOff.src = "images/home_off.jpg"
productsOff.src = "images/products_off.jpg"
```

```
  contactOff.src = "images/contact_off.jpg"
pressOff.src = "images/press_off.jpg"

homeOver.src = "images/home_over.jpg"
productsOver.src = "images/products_over.jpg"
contactOver.src = "images/contact_over.jpg"
pressOver.src = "images/press_over.jpg"

function imgOver(thisImg) {
    document[thisImg].src = "images/" + thisImg + "_over.jpg"
}

function imgOut(thisImg) {
    document[thisImg].src = "images/" + thisImg + "_off.jpg"
}
```

Note that the contents of the .js file shown in Listing 13-3 could be copied directly into a `<script>` tag and function identically.

Exploring the JavaScript Language

If you travel to a country whose people don't speak your native tongue, you usually buy a pocket language guide to help you make your way through the country. You don't necessarily need to know all the particulars and idiosyncrasies of the language, but you do need to know the essentials — phrases like "Where's the bathroom?" or "Where can I get an espresso?" — in order to survive.

In the same way, if you want to work with JavaScript, you don't need to become a hotshot scripting guru. You do, however, need to know enough about the scripting language to do the programming equivalent of ordering a meal or asking where the bathroom is.

Like any other programming language, JavaScript is made up of several components, including

- ✔ Basic syntax rules
- ✔ Commands, values, and variables
- ✔ Operators and expressions
- ✔ Statements
- ✔ Loops
- ✔ Functions

✔ Arrays

✔ Object orientation

Each of these is explored in the following sections.

Basic syntax rules

Every language has its own set of rules to make it possible to communicate. English, for example, uses periods to end sentences, quotation marks to denote quotes, and exclamation points to indicate something exciting is happening! JavaScript is no exception.

Below are some of the basic syntax rules that you should understand as you begin to discover what the scripting language is all about.

Statements

Just as an English or French document is composed of sentences, JavaScript scripts are composed of one or more *statements*. For example, the script in Listing 13-1 has a single statement, whereas the script in Listing 13-3 has over 20. Statements can end simply by putting the next statement on the following line. You can also optionally end a statement with a semicolon.

Capitalization

JavaScript is a case-sensitive language. The text you type in a script must not only be spelled correctly but must also be in the correct case. For example, the `alert()` method we use earlier in this chapter is in the correct syntax for that method. If we use `Alert()` or `ALERT()`, the script won't work.

White space

JavaScript ignores spaces and tabs (usually called *white space*) between statements, but it's a good idea to use space to make your code more readable. For example, the following two code examples function in the same way, but the first is much easier to read than the second.

✔ The following code separates and organizes statements with spaces and line breaks, so it is easy to read and understand:

```
if (document.images) {
    arrowRed = new Image
    arrowBlue = new Image

    arrowRed.src = "images/redArrow.gif"
    arrowBlue.src = "images/blueArrow.gif"
}
```

✔ The following code separates statements with semicolons and doesn't use spaces and line breaks for organization, so it's harder to read:

```
if (document.images) {arrowRed = new Image; arrowBlue = new Image;
arrowRed.src ="images/redArrow.gif"; arrowBlue.src = "images/
blueArrow.gif"}
```

Comments

Comments are text within your script that's ignored by the browser when the script runs. Comments are invaluable help to

✔ **Other people who are trying to figure out your code.**

✔ **You.** Months after you write the script, comments can make the code much easier for you to change.

Single-line comments

You can add comments to your JavaScript by adding two slashes to a comment that fits all on one line, like this:

```
//The code that runs below displays a snazzy pop-up window
```

Multiple-line comments

If your comment is lengthy and you need to span more than one line, you can either start each line with two slashes or else enclose your comments with /* and */ marks.

```
/* The code that runs below displays a really nifty, snazzy,
   jazzy, wicked-cool pop-up window.
   Last modified: June 10, 2005    */
```

Variables and data types

In JavaScript, you can execute various commands that are built into the language itself, such as alert(), shown in Listing 13-1. However, you often use commands to act on pieces of information, known as *values*. For example, alert() displays a string value that is contained within its parentheses. A value can be either a literal value (such as a number or a string of alphanumeric characters) or a variable. Each value is categorized by its type.

Variables

A *variable* is a placeholder for a value. For example, the variable favPerson contains the string value *Gilligan*. In JavaScript, you can write this as favPerson = "Gilligan".

The equals sign is read as "is set to." In other words, the variable favPerson now contains the value "Gilligan." (The equals sign is an *assignment operator,* which is explained later in this chapter.) When assigning a value to a variable, keep in mind the following rules:

- ✔ The variable name is always on the left side of the equals sign.
- ✔ The variable value is always on the right side.

Here are examples of variables and the value that each contains:

```
x = 5
first_Time = false
formZipcode = "92683"
```

In the preceding example, x contains the numeric value of 5. However, the formZipcode variable contains a text string, not a number, because the string value is enclosed in double quotes.

If you need to perform mathematical operations on a variable, assign a number value to it, not a quoted string.

The actual act of creating a variable and assigning it a value is called *declaring* the variable. So, to declare the variable pi to be equal to 3.14, you write this:

```
pi = 3.14
```

When you declare a variable, remember that

- ✔ **JavaScript is case-sensitive.**

  myname, MyName, and myName are treated as three separate variables because they each have different capitalization.

- ✔ **Variable names can use only letters, numbers, and underscores.**

  They can't contain spaces or other punctuation.

- ✔ **Variable names can't start with a number.**

- ✔ **Variable names can't be the same as a reserved word.**

  Reserved words are special keywords, such as if or with, that are used by JavaScript for its core functionality. Make sure you avoid naming a variable the same as one of these words. A complete list of reserved words is available at www.javascripter.net/faq/reserved.htm.

Data types

When you work with a literal value or variable, JavaScript categorizes it as a particular data type. Table 13-1 shows the common types of values.

Table 13-1	Data Types	
Type	*Description*	*Example*
Number	Any numeric value	`42`
String	Text characters inside quote marks	`"My name is Inigo Montoya"`
Object	A JavaScript object, which can be defined by the language or else created on your own	`window`
Function	Value returned by a function	`myFunction()`
Boolean	A true or false value	`true`
Null	Empty; has no value	`null`

Operating on expressions

As the preceding sections discuss, a literal value (such as 5 and `"Lightbulb"`) or a variable can represent a value of a particular type. However, in JavaScript, a complete statement, called an *expression,* can also return a value. For example, consider the following two expressions:

```
2+1+2                           // Evaluates to a value of 5
"A" + "three" + "hour" + "tour" // Evaluates to "Athreehourtour"
```

As you can see from these two examples, JavaScript often uses symbols as you evaluate, manipulate, and work with expressions. These symbols are called *operators*. In the examples shown above, the + symbol is used to either add numeric values or to concatenate two or more strings together into a single one.

JavaScript has several different types of operators, including assignment, arithmetic, counting, and comparison types.

Assignment operators

Assignment operators put values into variables. For example, x = 8 assigns the value of 8 to the variable x. Table 13-2 shows the assignment operators, although as you can see, they really combine assignment and arithmetic functionality.

Table 13-2	Assignment Operators	
Operator	*Assignment*	*Description*
=	x = y	Sets x to the value of y
+=	x += y	Same as x=x + y
-=	x -= y	Same as x = x - y
*=	x *= y	Same as x = x * y
/=	x /= y	Same as x = x / y

Arithmetic operators

When you feel like crunching numbers, use arithmetic operators. You'll quickly recognize these symbols from your high-school math class. Expressions with the most common operators are listed in Table 13-3.

Table 13-3	Arithmetic Operators	
Operator	*Example*	*Description*
+	x + y (numeric)	Adds x and y together
-	x - y	Subtracts y from x
*	x * y	Multiplies x and y together
/	x / y	Divides x by y
-	-x	Reverses the sign of x

Counting operators

JavaScript provides operators that are especially designed for counting either up or down while a process runs. The same operator can

- ✔ Retrieve a variable
- ✔ Count up or count down

Table 13-4 shows the counting operators.

Table 13-4	Counting Operators
Operator	*Description*
++x	Increases x by 1 (same as x=x+1) before an assignment

Operator	Description
x++	Increases x by 1 after an assignment
--x	Decreases x by 1 (same as x = x - 1) before an assignment
x--	Decreases x by 1 after an assignment

Changing before an assignment

When you place the ++ or -- operators *before* the variable, the value of the variable changes *before* you use the variable. For example, if x is 8, y= ++x changes the variables in this order:

1. Set x to 9.
2. Set y to 9.

Changing after an assignment

When you place the ++ or -- operators *after* the variable, the value of the variable changes *after* you use the variable. For example, if x is 8, y=x++ changes the variables in this order:

1. Set y to 8.
2. Set x to 9.

Comparison operators

Comparison operators tell you whether expressions on both sides of the operator are the same or different. The result of a comparison operation is either true or false. Table 13-5 shows the comparison operators.

Table 13-5		Comparison Operators
Operator	**Example**	**Description**
==	x == y	Returns true if x and y are equal
!=	x != y	Returns true if x and y are not equal
>	x > y	Returns true if x is greater than y
>=	x >= y	Returns true if x is greater than or equal to y
<	x < y	Returns true if x is less than y
<=	x <= y	Returns true if x is less than or equal to y

(continued)

Table 13-5 *(continued)*		
Operator	**Example**	**Description**
	x || y	Returns true if either x or y is true
&&	x && y	Returns true if both x and y are true
!	!x	Returns true if x is false

Working with statements

As discussed in the "Basic syntax rules" section, JavaScript statements are the basic units of a script. Two common types are expression statements and conditional statements.

Expression statement

An expression statement returns a value. For example, consider the following statement:

```
fullName = firstName + " " + lastName
```

The result of this expression is that the variable `fullName` is assigned the concatenated value of

- ✔ The value of the variable `firstName`
- ✔ A space
- ✔ The value of the variable `lastName`

The plus signs indicate that the result is concatenated together to form a string.

Conditional statement

A conditional statement can check your data and decide what to do. It has three steps:

1. *Test* a value.

   The result of the test is always either true or false.

2. *Select* an action according to the result of the test.

3. *Perform* the selected action.

The most common conditional statements are the `if` and `if/else` statements. Consider the following `if` statement:

```
if ( x = "Boxen" ) {
    y = 1
    alert( "You are a smarty! The correct answer is Boxen. Well done!")
}
```

The `if` statement tests the expression inside the parentheses and determines whether or not `x = "Boxen"`. If the test evaluates to `true`, then the statements inside the curly braces are executed. If the test evaluates to `false`, then these lines are bypassed.

The `if/else` statement can also be used to specify code to be processed when the `if` test evaluates to false:

```
if ( x = "Boxen" ) {
    y = 1
    alert( "You are a smarty! The correct answer is Boxen. Well done!")
}
else {
    y = 0
    alert( "You are totally wrong! The correct answer is Boxen. Bad!")
}
```

A second example helps illustrate the steps involved in an `if/else` conditional statement:

```
if (confirm("Are you sure you want to do that?")) {
alert("You said yes")
}
else {
alert("You said no")
}
```

Here's how the statement works:

1. The `if` portion of the statement displays a dialog box that asks the user to confirm a choice (using the `confirm()` method).

2. The `confirm()` method returns either `true` or `false`, depending on the user's response.

   - If the user clicks the OK button in the dialog box, the `confirm()` method returns `true`.

   - If the user clicks the Cancel button, the `confirm()` method returns `false`.

3. The code then performs an action based on the value that the `confirm()` method returns.

   - If the method returns `true`, an alert appears with the message, "You said yes," as shown in Figure 13-1.

   - If the method returns `false`, an alert appears with the message, "You said no."

Figure 13-1:
Confirming a
user action.

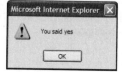

Loops

When you need to repeat an action in a JavaScript script, you use a *loop*. For example, a script that uses a loop can

✔ Make sure every character in a zip code field is a number.

✔ Check every item in a list for a specific value

for loop

The `for` loop repeats steps a specific number of times.

If you don't know how many times you need to repeat some steps, use a `while` loop instead of a `for` loop.

The `for` loop in Listing 13-4 calculates a multiplication table. Figure 13-2 shows the result in the browser.

Listing 13-4: A for Loop

```
<!DOCTYPE html PUBLIC "-//W3C//DTD XHTML 1.0 Transitional//EN"
        "http://www.w3.org/TR/xhtml1/DTD/xhtml1-transitional.dtd">
<html xmlns="http://www.w3.org/1999/xhtml">
<head>
<title>A For Loop</title>
</head>
<body>
<script type="text/javascript" language="javascript">

document.write("<h3>Multiplication table for 7</h3>")

for (loopCount = 0; loopCount <= 10; loopCount++)
{
```

```
document.write("7 X ",loopCount," = ", 7 * loopCount,"<br />");
}
</script>
</body>
</html>
```

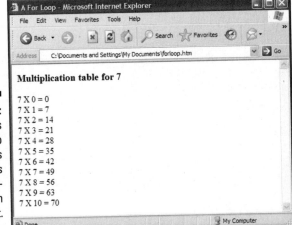

Figure 13-2:
This script's
for loop
calculates
and displays
the multi-
plication
result.

A `for` loop has three steps:

1. The *initialization step* sets the beginning value of the loop variable.

   In Listing 13-4, `loopCount = 0` is the initialization step.

2. The *limiting step* tells the loop when to stop looping.

   In Listing 13-4, `loopCount <= 10` is the limiting step. The loop repeats as long as the value of `loopCount` is less than or equal to 10.

3. The *increment step* tells the loop to increase the variable `loopCount` by a specific amount after the `for` block (the set of statements contained inside the curly braces) is executed.

   In Listing 13-4, `loopCount++` is the increment step. It increases the value of `loopCount` by 1 each time through the loop.

while loop

A `while` loop repeats steps until you get a certain kind of result (such as finding a name in a list).

If you know exactly how many times you need to repeat steps, use a `for` loop instead of a `while` loop.

Listing 13-5 shows the construction of the `while` loop.

Listing 13-5:   A while Loop

```
<!DOCTYPE html PUBLIC "-//W3C//DTD XHTML 1.0 Transitional//EN"
        "http://www.w3.org/TR/xhtml1/DTD/xhtml1-transitional.dtd">
<html xmlns="http://www.w3.org/1999/xhtml">
<head>
<title>A While Loop</title>
</head>
<body>
<script type="text/javascript" language="javascript">
con = confirm("Do you want to continue?")
while(con == false)
{
document.write("Continuing to wait<br />");
    con = confirm("Do you want to continue?")
}
</script>
</body>
</html>
```

A `while` loop works as follows:

1. The `while` statement evaluates the expression inside its parentheses.

   In Listing 13-5, `con == false` is evaluated. The value of `con` is dependent on whether the user clicks the yes or no button in a confirmation message box.

2. As long as the expression evaluates to `true`, the code contained inside the curly braces (the `while` block) is repeated.

   In Listing 13-5, notice that the `confirm` statement is triggered again at the end of the `while` block to determine whether the loop should continue.

Functions

A *function* is a grouped set of JavaScript statements that

- ✔ Is identified by a name
- ✔ Is sectioned off from the rest of the script
- ✔ Performs a specific task
- ✔ Must be called by other parts of the script to execute

Functions are useful when you want organize your code into separate units or when you use a bit of code more than once in a script. For example, a user may enter information into a form. You can use a function to save that information, perform a calculation on it, and allow other parts of the script to call the function to retrieve the result of the calculation.

A function consists of

✔ The *function declaration,* which contains the keyword function, a unique function name, and parentheses. Optionally, you can pass values into the function by adding arguments inside the parentheses.

✔ The *function block,* which is a set of one or more statements surrounded by curly braces.

The basic structure of a function looks like this:

```
function name_of_function(argument) {
    // One or more statements
}
```

Here is an example of a function:

```
function alertMessage() {
alert("Please enter a value in this field.")
}
```

When your page loads into the browser and your script is processed by the browser, the function code doesn't run automatically. Instead, it has to be explicitly called in your script. Therefore, to trigger the alertMessage() function, you need to call it by name:

```
alertMessage()
```

Listing 13-6 shows a script with a function that is used to display a variety of alerts, depending on which button the user presses.

Listing 13-6:   Calling a Function

```
<!DOCTYPE html PUBLIC "-//W3C//DTD XHTML 1.0 Transitional//EN"
        "http://www.w3.org/TR/xhtml1/DTD/xhtml1-transitional.dtd">
<html xmlns="http://www.w3.org/1999/xhtml">
<head>
<title>Function calling</title>
<script language="javascript" type="text/javascript">
function saySomething(message) {
alert(message)
}
</script>
</head>
```

(continued)

Listing 13-6 *(continued)*

```
<body>
<h2>Famous Quotes</h2>
<hr />
<form action="#">
<input type="button" value="George Orwell" onclick=
  "saySomething('To write or even speak English is not a science but
   an art.')" />
<input type="button" value="Arthur Conan Doyle" onclick=
  "saySomething('We cannot command our love, but we can our actions.')" />
<input type="button" value="H.G. Wells" onclick=
  "saySomething('If we do not end war, war will end us.')" />
</form>
</body>
</html>
```

The result of this script is shown in Figure 13-3.

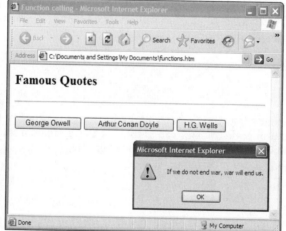

Figure 13-3:
An alert
pops up as
a result of
clicking the
H.G. Wells
button.

In the script, when the user clicks one of the buttons on the page, the say
Something function is called and is passed the information in quotes, which
the function stores in the variable message. The function then displays the
alert, with the value of message, which is the quotation it was passed.

Arrays

An *array* is a collection of values. Arrays are useful because you can use them
to manipulate and sort groups of things.

The location of information in an array is based on a numbered position called the *index*. The numbering of the index always starts at 0 and goes up. JavaScript has a special object — the Array object — just to handle arrays.

Creating arrays

To create an instance of an array, you must use the new operator along with the Array object, like this:

```
x = new Array()
```

You can fill in the array when you create the Array object, separating the array elements with commas, like so:

```
theDays = new Array("Monday", "Tuesday", "Wednesday", "Thursday", "Friday",
                    "Saturday", "Sunday")
```

Accessing arrays

Once the array has been created, you can write to it and read from it by using the [] operator. By placing a position number in this operator, you can access the data stored at that index number.

For example, the value of theDays[2] in the preceding example is Wednesday (array positions always begin with 0, so Monday is 0).

Reading elements

To read an element from an array, create a variable and assign it a value from the array, like this:

```
thisDay = theDays[6]
```

The value of thisDay is now Sunday.

Writing elements

To write a value to the array, follow these steps:

1. Identify the index of the value you want to change.

2. Assign a new value to the array element, like this:

   ```
   theDays[0] = "Mon"
   ```

Looping

All arrays have a length property, which is very useful for discovering how many elements the array contains, and is often used to loop through the array elements, like this example:

```
planets = new Array ("Mercury", "Venus", "Earth", "Mars")
for (i = 0; i < planets.length; i++)
alert (planets[i]);
```

This causes the browser to display a series of four alert boxes, each containing one of the names of the `planets` array. The value of `planets.length` is 3 (since numbering starts at 0), and the script steps through each element of the array until the value of the counting variable `i` is greater than 3, at which time the script ends.

Objects

Most JavaScript scripts are designed to "give life" to objects that exist inside your browser. A rollover brings an image link to life. A validated e-mail address field is smart about what kind of e-mail address it will accept. A document displays new text on the fly based on a response from the Web page visitor.

Within JavaScript, you work with a variety of objects, such as the browser window, a button, a form field, an image, or even the document itself. Because JavaScript's primary calling is to work with objects, the scripting language is called an *object-based language.*

Think, for a moment, of an object that exists in the real world, such as a car or an MP3 player. Each of these objects has characteristics that describe the object, such as its color, weight, and height. Many objects also have a behavior that can be triggered. A car can be started; an MP3 player can be played.

These real-world analogies can be applied to JavaScript. Objects you work with have descriptive qualities (called *properties*) and behaviors (called *methods*). For example, a `document` object represents the HTML page in your browser. It has properties, such as `linkColor`, `title`, and `location`, as well as methods, such as `open()`, `clear()`, and `write()`. (Methods always have parentheses following their names.)

JavaScript uses periods (or dots) to access an object's properties or methods:

```
object.property
object.method()
```

For example, to get the `title` of the `document` and assign it to a variable, you write this:

```
mytitle = document.title
```

To call the `clear` method of the document, you write this:

```
document.clear()
```

Events and Event Handling

Events are actions that either the browser executes or the user performs while visiting your page. Loading a Web page, moving the mouse over an image, closing a window, and submitting a form are all examples of events.

JavaScript deals with events by using commands called *event handlers*. Any action by the user on the page triggers an event handler in your script. Table 13-6 is a list of JavaScript's event handlers.

Table 13-6	Event Handlers
Event Handler	*Description*
onabort	User cancels a page load.
onblur	An element loses focus because the user focuses on a different element.
onchange	User changes the contents of a form element or selects a different check box, radio button, or menu item.
onclick	User clicks an element with the mouse.
ondblclick	User double-clicks an element with the mouse.
onerror	Browser encounters an error in the scripts or other instructions on the page.
onfocus	An element becomes the focus of the user's attention, like a form field when you start typing in it.
onkeydown	User presses and holds a key on the keyboard.
onkeypress	User presses and immediately releases a key on the keyboard.
onkeyup	User releases a depressed key.
onload	Browser loads an HTML page.
onmousedown	User moves the mouse pointer over an element, presses the mouse button down, and holds it down.
onmousemove	User moves the mouse pointer anywhere on the page.
onmouseout	User moves the mouse pointer off an element.
onmouseover	User moves the mouse pointer over an element.

(continued)

Table 13-6 *(continued)*

Event Handler	Description
onmouseup	User releases a held mouse button.
onreset	User clicks a form's Reset button.
onresize	User resizes the browser window.
onselect	User selects a check box, radio button, or menu item from a form.
onsubmit	User clicks a form's Submit button.
onunload	Browser stops displaying one Web page because it's about to load another.

Not all objects support every event handler. For example, the onload handler is supported by only the window and image objects. The onsubmit event handler is supported by only the form object.

A common way to deal with event handlers is to use them as an attribute of an HTML element. This is called an *inline* event handler. Here is an example of the onsubmit inline event handler being used as an attribute of a <form> tag:

```
<form onsubmit="submitIt(this)" action="submitForm.cgi">
```

This example calls the submitIt function when the user clicks the form's Submit button. You can also embed JavaScript commands in the HTML, like this:

```
<input type="button" value="Click Me!"
    name="button1" onclick="alert("That tickles!");" />
```

A third way to use event handlers is to express them in JavaScript code, like this:

```
document.button1.onclick = function () { alert("That tickles!")}
```

Chapter 15 offers examples of event handlers.

Document Object Model (DOM)

JavaScript gives you the tools to manipulate the objects in a Web page. The Document Object Model (DOM) is the specification for how all those objects are represented. The DOM is a Web standard, defined by the World Wide Web Consortium (W3C; more information than you can imagine about the DOM specification is available at www.w3.org/DOM).

The DOM allows JavaScript to programmatically access and manipulate the contents of a document. The DOM defines

- Each object on a Web page
- Attributes associated with those objects
- Methods that you can use to manipulate those objects

By using the DOM, JavaScript can *dynamically* update the content, structure, and style of Web pages. This means that you can use JavaScript to produce effects in your Web pages, such as

- Rewriting your document on the fly
- Changing styles and style sheets
- Page layout

Marvelous Miscellany

Table 13-7 lists other script- and forms-related (X)HTML markup attributes that you might find in HTML files.

Table 13-7	Other Script- and Forms-related (X)HTML Attributes		
Name	*Function/Value Equals*	*Value Types*	*Related Element(s)*
declare	Declares document object without invoking it	"declare"	<script>
defer	Allows user agent to defer script execution	"defer"	<script>

References and Resources

This part of the book presents the basics of the JavaScript language and how to add and adapt scripts that you find on the Web to your own HTML pages. But the JavaScript language is more powerful than that.

If you want to start writing your own code, you need more information. The best place to get your questions answered is online. Many resources on the Web can help you use JavaScript. Visit www.dummies.com/extras, click "HTML 4 For Dummies, 5th Edition" in the list, and go to the Chapter 13 link for a detailed list of Web sites and books that can help you create and use JavaScript.

Chapter 14

Working with Forms

Most of the HTML you write helps you display content and information for your users. Sometimes, however, you want a Web page to *gather* information from users instead of giving static information to them. HTML *form markup tags* give you a healthy collection of elements and attributes for creating forms to collect information from visitors to your site.

This chapter covers the many different uses for forms. It also shows you how to use form markup tags to create just the right form for soliciting information from your users, reviews your options for working with the data you receive, and gives you some tips for creating easy-to-use forms that really help your users provide the information you're looking for.

Uses for Forms

The Web contains millions of forms, but every form is driven by the same set of markup tags. Web forms can be short or long, simple or complex, and they have myriad uses. But they all fall into one of two broad categories:

✔ **Search forms** that let users search a site or the entire Web

✔ **Data collection forms** that provide information for such uses as online shopping, technical support, site preferences, and personalization

Before you create any form markup, you need to determine what kind of data your visitors will search for on your site and/or what kind of data you need to collect from visitors. Your data drives the form elements you use — and how you put them together on a page.

Searches

Search forms help you give visitors information.

The following search forms are from the friendly folks at the Internal Revenue Service (IRS). The difference between these search forms is the data the IRS site needs from you for its search:

✔ The IRS home page (shown in Figure 14-1) is a simple search form that uses two different single-field forms to help visitors search for general information and tax forms. This type of form can produce dozens of relevant responses. Visitors can both

- Choose the best option.
- Look at more than one option.

✔ A more complicated search form, such as the Get Refund Status page (as shown in Figure 14-2), produces only *one* specific response. It searches IRS records for the status of *your* refund. This page demands detailed information because the IRS doesn't want you to see anyone else's refund; therefore, it both

- Finds the data visitors need.
- Hides data that visitors shouldn't see.

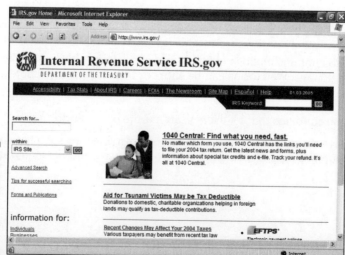

Figure 14-1:
The IRS home page uses two short search forms.

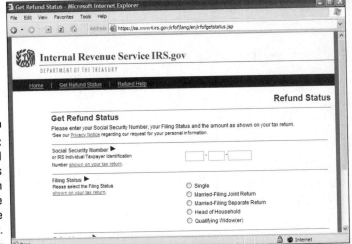

Figure 14-2:
The refund status search form is a little more complex.

Searches come in all shapes and sizes, so the search forms that drive those searches come in all shapes and sizes, too. A short keyword search might do the trick, or you might need a more sophisticated search method.

Data collection

Data collection forms receive information you want to process or save. When you create a form that collects information, the information you need drives the structure and complexity of the form:

✔ If you need just a little information, the form may be short and (relatively) sweet.

The Library of Congress (LC) uses a form to collect information from teachers to subscribe to a free electronic newsletter, as shown in Figure 14-3. The LC doesn't need much information to set up the subscription, so the form is short and simple.

✔ If you need a lot of information, your form may be several pages long.

RateGenius uses long and detailed forms to gather the information it needs to help customers get the best possible loan rate. The page in Figure 14-4 is just the first of several that a visitor must fill out to provide all the necessary information.

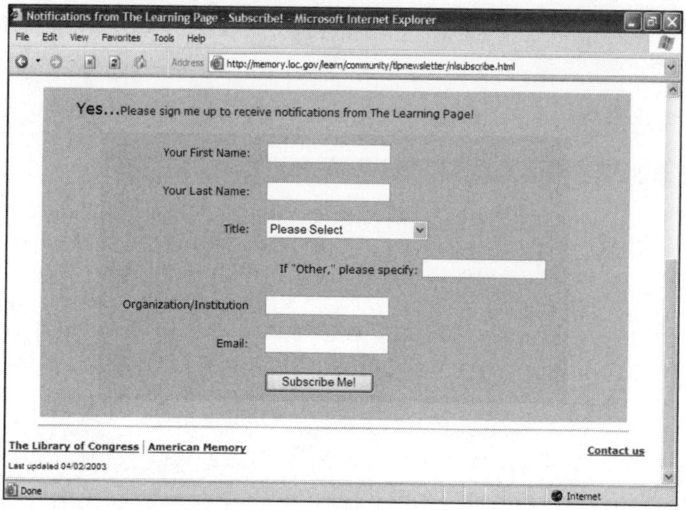

Figure 14-3:
A free
subscription
form
collects
basic
information.

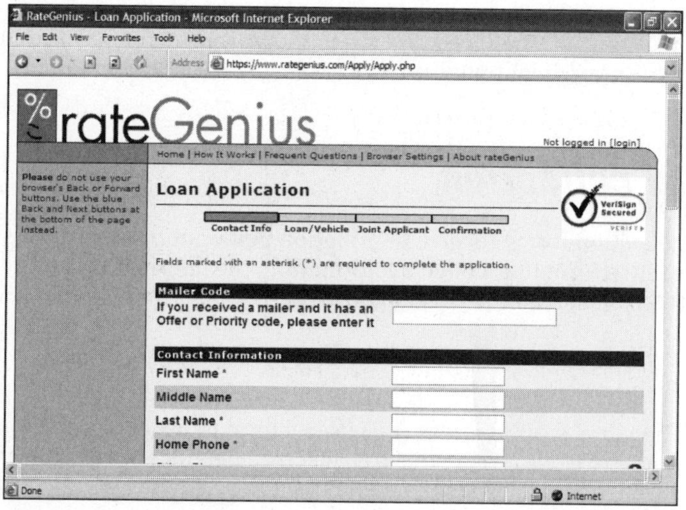

Figure 14-4:
An online
car loan site
uses many
detailed
forms to
collect
necessary
data.

Creating Forms

HTML form markup tags and attributes can

✓ **Define the overall form structure.**

Every form has the same basic structure.

✓ **Tell the Web browser how to handle the form data.**

✔ **Create input objects (such as text fields and drop-down lists).**

Which input elements you use depends on the data you're collecting.

Structure

All of the input elements associated with a single form are

✔ Contained within a `<form>` tag

✔ Processed by the same *form handler*

A *form handler* is a program on the Web server (or a simple `mailto` URL) that manages the data a user sends to you through the form. A Web browser can only *gather* information through forms; it doesn't know what to do with the information once it has it. You must provide some other mechanism to actually *do* something useful with the data you collect. This chapter covers form handlers in detail later.

Attributes

You always use these two key attributes with the `<form>` tag:

✔ `action`: The URL of the form handler.

✔ `method`: How you want the form data to be sent to the form handler.

Your form handler dictates which of these values to use for `method`:

- `get` sends the form data to the form handler on the URL.

- `post` sends the form data in the Hypertext Transfer Protocol (HTTP) header.

Webmonkey offers a good overview of the difference between `get` and `post` in its "Good Forms" article:

```
http://hotwired.lycos.com/webmonkey/99/30/index4a_page3.html
```

Markup

The markup in Listing 14-1 creates a form that uses the `post` method to send user-entered information to a form handler (`guestbook.cgi`) to be processed on the Web server.

Listing 14-1:   A Simple Form Processed by a Form Handler

```
<!DOCTYPE html PUBLIC "-//W3C//DTD XHTML 1.0 Transitional//EN"
        "http://www.w3.org/TR/xhtml1/DTD/xhtml1-transitional.dtd">
<html xmlns="http://www.w3.org/1999/xhtml">
<head>
    <title>Forms</title>
```

(continued)

```
        <meta http-equiv="Content-Type" content="text/html; charset=ISO-8859-1" />
    </head>
    <body>
        <form action="cgi-bin/guestbook.cgi" method="post">

        <!-- form input elements go here -->

        </form>
    </body>
</html>
```

The value of the action attribute is a URL, so you can use absolute or relative URLs to point to a form handler on your server.

Input tags

The tags you use to solicit input from your site visitors make up the bulk of any form. HTML supports a variety of different input options — from text fields to radio buttons and from files to images.

Every input control associates some value with a name:

- ✔ When you create the control, you give it a name.
- ✔ The control sends back a value based on what the user does in the form.

For example, if you create a text field that collects a user's first name, you might name the field firstname. When the user types his or her first name in the field and submits the form, the value associated with firstname is whatever name the user typed in the field.

The whole point of a form is to gather values associated with input controls, so the way you set the name and value for each control is important. The following sections explain how you should work with names and values for each of the input controls.

Input fields

You can use a variety of input fields in your forms.

For input elements that require a user to *select* an option (such as a check box or radio button), rather than typing something into a field, you define both the name and the value. When the user selects a box or a button and clicks the Submit button, the form returns the name and value assigned to the element.

Text

Text fields are single-line fields that users can type information into.

- ✔ You use the `<input />` element to define a text field and the `type` attribute with a value of `text`.

  ```
  <input type="text" />
  ```

- ✔ You use the `name` attribute to give the input field a name.

  ```
  <input type="text" name "firstname" />
  ```

- ✔ The user supplies the value when he or she types in the field.

This markup creates two text input fields — one for a first name and one for a last name:

```
<form action="cgi-bin/guestbook.cgi" action="post">
  <p>First Name: <input type="text" name="firstname" /></p>
  <p>Last Name: <input type="text" name="lastname" /></p>
</form>
```

In addition to the `<input />` elements, the preceding markup includes paragraph (`<p>`) elements and some text to label each of the fields. By themselves, most form elements won't give the user many clues about the type of information you want. You also must use HTML block and inline elements to format the appearance of your form. Figure 14-5 shows how a browser displays this HTML.

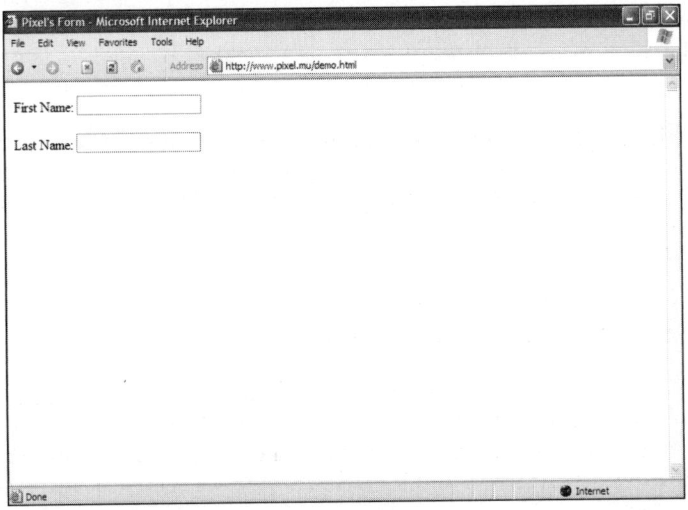

Figure 14-5:
Text entry fields in a form.

You can control the size of a text field with these attributes:

- ✔ size: The length (in characters) of the text field
- ✔ maxlength: The number of characters the user can type into the field

The following markup creates a form that sets both fields to a size of 30 and a maxlength of 25. Each field will be about 30 characters long; even so, a user can type only 25 characters into each field, as shown in Figure 14-6.

```
<form action="cgi-bin/guestbook.cgi" action="post">
<p>First Name: <input type="text" name="firstname" size="30"
             maxlength="25" /></p>
<p>Last Name: <input type="text" name="lastname" size="30"
             maxlength="25" /></p>
</form>
```

Passwords

A password field is a text field that doesn't display what the user types. Someone looking over the user's shoulder sees each keystroke represented on the screen by a *placeholder character,* such as an asterisk or bullet.

You create a password field by using the <input /> element with a type attribute set to password, as follows:

```
<form action="cgi-bin/guestbook.cgi" action="post">
<p>First Name: <input type="text" name="firstname" size="30"
             maxlength="25" /></p>
<p>Last Name: <input type="text" name="lastname" size="30" maxlength="25" /></p>
<p>Password: <input type="password" name="psswd" size="30" maxlength="25" /></p>
</form>
```

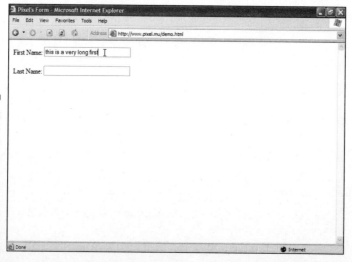

Figure 14-6:
You can specify the length and maximum number of characters for a text field.

Password fields are programmed like text fields.

Figure 14-7 shows how a browser replaces what you type with bullets. Some browsers may replace the text with asterisks or some other character. It depends on the browser's default.

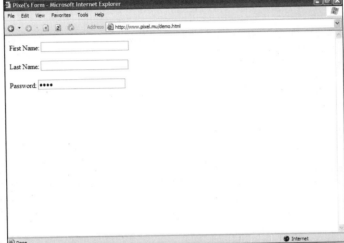

Figure 14-7:
Password fields mask the text a user enters.

Check boxes and radio buttons

If only a few possible values are available to the user, you can give him or her a collection of options to choose from:

- ✔ **Check boxes:** Choose *more* than one option.
- ✔ **Radio buttons:** Choose only *one* option.

If many choices are available, use a *drop-down list* instead of radio buttons or check boxes.

To create radio buttons and check boxes, you

- ✔ Use the `<input />` element with the `type` attribute set to `radio` or `checkbox`.
  - If the attribute value is `radio`, a round radio button appears.
  - If it's `checkbox`, a check box appears.

  Radio buttons differ from check boxes in that users can select a single radio button from a set of options but can select any number of check boxes (including none).

✔ Create each option with these attributes:

- The `name` attribute to give the option a name.

- The `value` attribute to specify what value is returned if the user selects the option.

You can use the `checked` attribute (with a value of `checked`) to specify that an option should be already selected when the browser displays the form. This is a good way to specify a default selection in a list.

This markup shows how to format check box and radio button options:

```
<form action="cgi-bin/guestbook.cgi" action="post">
<p>What are some of your favorite foods?</p>
<p><input type="checkbox" name="food" value="pizza" checked="checked" />
    Pizza<br />
   <input type="checkbox" name="food" value="icecream" />Ice Cream<br />
   <input type="checkbox" name="food" value="eggsham" />Green Eggs and Ham<br />
</p>

<p>What is your gender?</p>
<p><input type="radio" name="gender" value="male" />Male<br />
   <input type="radio" name="gender" value="female" checked="checked" />
    Female</p>
</form>
```

In the preceding code, each set of options uses the same name for each input control but gives a different value to each option. You give each item in a set of options the same name to let the browser know they are part of a set. Figure 14-8 shows how a browser displays this markup.

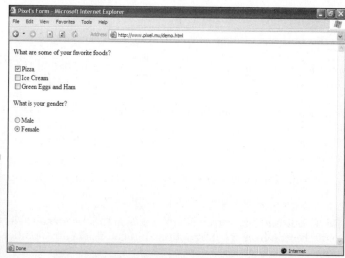

Figure 14-8:
Check boxes and radio buttons.

Hidden fields

A *hidden field* gives you a way to collect name and value information that the user can't see along with the rest of the form data. Hidden fields are useful if you want to keep track of information associated with the form (such as its version or name).

If your Internet service provider (ISP) provides a generic application for a guest book or feedback form, you might have to put your name and e-mail address in the form's hidden fields so the data goes specifically to you.

To create a hidden field, you

- ✔ Use the `<input />` element with its `type` attribute set to `hidden`.
- ✔ Supply the name and value pair you want to send to the form handler.

Here's an example of markup for a hidden field:

```
<form action="cgi-bin/guestbook.cgi" action="post">
<input type="hidden" name="e-mail" value="me@mysite.com" />
<p>First Name: <input type="text" name="firstname" size="30"
         maxlength="25" /></p>
<p>Last Name: <input type="text" name="lastname" size="30" maxlength="25" /></p>
<p>Password: <input type="password" name="psswd" size="30" maxlength="25" /></p>
</form>
```

As a general rule, using your e-mail address in a hidden field is just asking for your address to be picked up by spammers. If your ISP says that this is how you should do your feedback form, ask them if they have any suggestions for how you can minimize the damage. Surfers to your page can't see your e-mail address, but spammers' spiders can read the underlying tags.

File uploads

A form can receive documents and other files, such as images, from users. When the user submits the form, the browser grabs a copy of the file and sends it with the other form data. To create this *file upload field,*

- ✔ Use the `<input />` element with the `type` attribute set to `file`.

  The file itself is the form field value.
- ✔ Use the `name` attribute to give the control a name.

Here's an example of markup for a file upload field:

```
<form action="cgi-bin/guestbook.cgi" action="post">
<p>Please submit your resume in Microsoft Word or plain text format:<br />
   <input type="file" name="resume" />
</p>
</form>
```

Browsers render a file upload field with a browse button that allows users to surf their local hard drive and select a file to send to you, as in Figure 14-9.

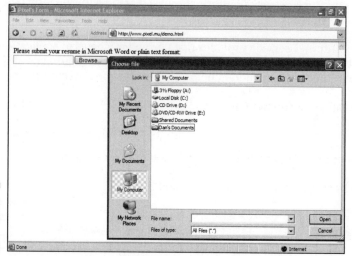

Figure 14-9:
A file upload
field.

When you accept users' files through a form, you can receive files that are either huge or are infected by viruses. Consult with whoever is programming your form handler to discuss options for protecting the system where files are saved. Several barriers can help minimize your risks, including

✔ Virus-scanning software

✔ Restrictions on file size

✔ Restrictions on file type

Drop-down lists

Drop-down lists are a great way to give users lots of options in a little screen space. You use two different tags to create a drop-down list:

✔ `<select>` holds the list.

Use a `name` attribute with the `<select>` element to name the entire list.

✔ A collection of `<option>` elements identifies the list options.

The `value` attribute assigns a unique value for each `<option>` element.

Here's an example of markup for a drop-down list:

```
<form action="cgi-bin/guestbook.cgi" action="post">
<p>What is your favorite food?</p>
<select name="food">
   <option value="pizza">Pizza</option>
   <option value="icecream">Ice Cream</option>
   <option value="eggsham">Green Eggs and Ham</option>
</select>
</form>
```

The browser turns this markup into a drop-down list with three items, as shown in Figure 14-10.

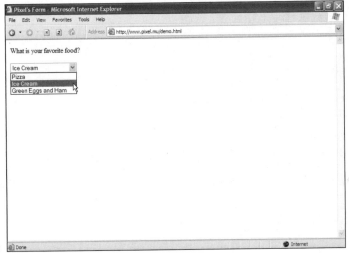

Figure 14-10:
A drop-down list.

You can enable users to select more than one item from a drop-down list by changing the *default settings* of your list:

✔ If you want your user to be able to choose more than one option (by holding down the Alt [Windows] or ⌘ [Mac] key while clicking options in the list), add the `multiple` attribute to the `<select>` tag. The value of `multiple` is `multiple`.

   Because of XHTML rules, standalone attributes cannot stand alone; therefore, the value is the same as the name of the attribute.

✔ By default, the browser displays only one option until the user clicks the drop-down menu's arrow to display the rest of the list. Use the `size` attribute with the `<select>` tag to specify how many options to show.

   If you specify fewer than the total number of options, the browser includes a scroll bar with the drop-down list.

You can specify that one of the options in the drop-down list be already selected when the browser loads the page, just as you can specify a check box or radio button to be checked. Simply add the `selected` attribute to have a value of `selected` for the `<option>` tag you want as the default.

The following markup

- ✔ Allows the user to choose more than one option from the list
- ✔ Displays two options
- ✔ Selects the third option in the list by default

```
<form action="cgi-bin/guestbook.cgi" action="post">
<p>What are some of your favorite foods?</p>
<select name="food" size="2" multiple="multiple">
 <option value="pizza">Pizza</option>
 <option value="icecream">Ice Cream</option>
 <option value="eggsham" selected="selected">Green Eggs and Ham</option>
</select>
</form>
```

Figure 14-11 shows how adding these attributes modifies the appearance of the list in a browser.

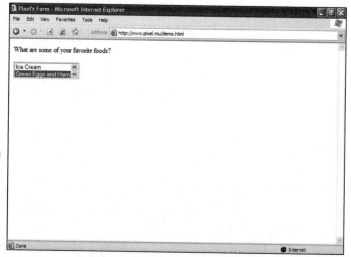

Figure 14-11:
A drop-down list with modifications.

Multi-line text boxes

If a single-line text field isn't enough room for responses, create a *text box* instead of a text field:

✔ The <textarea> element defines the box and its parameters.

✔ The rows attribute specifies the height of the box in rows based on the font in the text box.

✔ The cols attribute specifies the width of the box in columns based on the font in the text box.

The text the user types into the box provides the value, so you need only give the box a name with the name attribute:

```
<form action="cgi-bin/guestbook.cgi" action="post">
  <textarea rows="10" cols="30" name="comments">
    Please include any comments here.
  </textarea>
</form>
```

Any text you include between the <textarea> and </textarea> tags appears in the text box in the browser, as shown in Figure 14-12. The user then enters information in the text box and overrides your text.

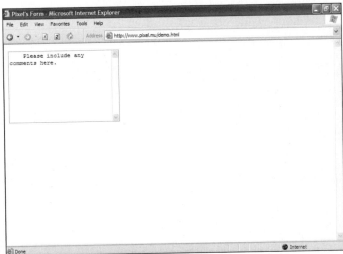

Figure 14-12:
A text box.

Submit and reset

Submit and reset buttons help the user tell the browser what to do with the form. You can create buttons to either submit or reset your form using the <input /> element with the type and value attributes:

✔ **Submit**

Visitors need to tell a browser that they are done with a form and want to send the contents. You create a button to *submit* the form to you by using this markup:

```
<input type="submit" value="Submit" />
```

You don't use the name attribute for the submit and reset buttons. You use the value attribute instead to specify how the browser labels the buttons for display.

✔ **Reset**

Visitors need to clear the form if they want to start all over again or decide not to fill it out. You create a button to reset, or *clear,* the form by using the following markup:

```
<input type="reset" value="Clear" />
```

You can set the value to anything you want to appear on the button. In our example, we set ours to Clear. You can use something that's more appropriate to you if you'd like.

Here's an example of markup to create Submit and Reset buttons named Send and Clear, respectively:

```
<form action="cgi-bin/guestbook.cgi" action="post">
<p>First Name: <input type="text" name="firstname" size="30"
            maxlength="25" /></p>
<p>Last Name: <input type="text" name="lastname" size="30" maxlength="25" /></p>
<p>Password: <input type="password" name="psswd" size="30" maxlength="25" /></p>

<p>What are some of your favorite foods?</p>
<p><input type="checkbox" name="food" value="pizza" checked="checked" />
    Pizza<br />
    <input type="checkbox" name="food" value="icecream" />Ice Cream<br />
    <input type="checkbox" name="food" value="eggsham" />Green Eggs and Ham<br />
</p>

<p>What is your gender?</p>
<p><input type="radio" name="gender" value="male" />Male<br />
    <input type="radio" name="gender" value="female" checked="checked" />
    Female</p>

<p>
    <input type="submit" value="Send" />
    <input type="reset" value="Clear" />
</p>
</form>
```

Figure 14-13 shows how a browser renders these buttons in a form.

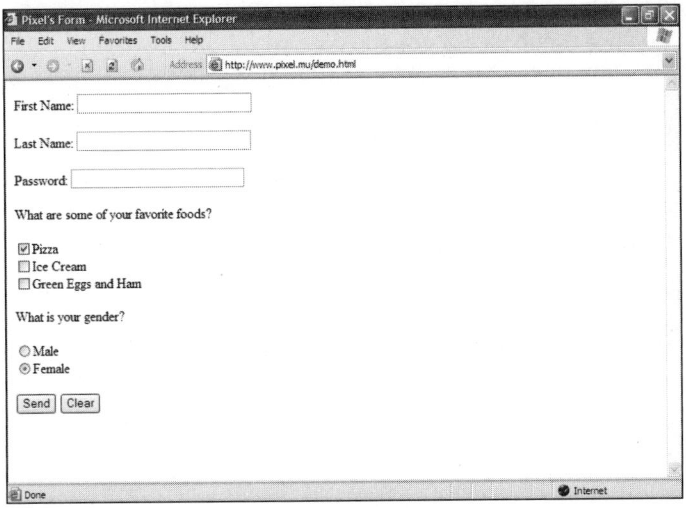

Figure 14-13: Submit and reset buttons labeled as Send and Clear.

Customizing

If you don't like the Submit and Reset buttons that a browser creates, you can substitute your own graphical buttons by using

✔ The `<input />` element with a `type` of `image`.

✔ An `src` attribute that specifies the image's location.

✔ A `value` that defines the result of the field:

• For an image that submits the form, set `value` to `submit`.

• For an image that clears the form, set `value` to `reset`.

TIP

Use the `alt` attribute to provide alternative text for browsers that don't show images (or for users who can't see them).

The following markup creates customized submit and reset buttons:

```
<p><input type="image" value="submit" src="submit_button.gif" alt="Submit" />
    <input type="image" value="reset" src="reset_button.gif" alt="Clear" />
</p>
```

Validation

No matter how brilliant your site's visitors, there's always a chance that they'll enter data you aren't expecting. JavaScript to the rescue!

Form validation is the term for checking the data the user enters before it's put into your database. Check the data with both *JavaScript* and Common Gateway Interface *(CGI)* scripts on your server.

JavaScript

You can validate entries in JavaScript before data goes to the server. This means that visitors don't wait for your server to check the data — they're told quickly (before they click Submit, if you want) if there's a problem.

You can learn more about JavaScript and your forms so you can use them on your Web site at

- ✔ www.w3schools.com/js/default.asp
- ✔ www.quirksmode.org/js/forms.html
- ✔ http://webmonkey.wired.com/webmonkey/programming/javascript

CGI

You need to validate your form data on the server side because users can surf with JavaScript turned off. (They'll have a slower validation process.) Find out more about CGI in the next section and at

- ✔ www.4guysfromrolla.com/webtech/LearnMore/Validation.asp
- ✔ www.cgi101.com/book

Processing Data

Getting form data is really only half of the form battle. You create form elements to get data from users, but then you need to do something with that data. Of course, your form and your data are unique every time, so no single, generic form handler can manage the data for every form. Before you can find (or write) a program that handles your form data, you must know what you want to do with it. For example,

- ✔ If you just want to receive comments from a Web form by e-mail, you might need only a simple `mailto:` URL.
- ✔ If a form gathers information from users to display in a guest book, you
    - • Add the data to a text file or a small database that holds the entries.
    - • Create a Web page that displays the guest-book entries.

✔ If you need a shopping cart, you need programs and a database that can handle inventory, customer-order information, shipping data, and cost calculations.

Your Web hosting provider — whether it's an internal IT group or an ISP to which you pay a monthly fee — has the final say in what kind of applications you can use on your Web site to handle form data. If you want to use forms on your site, be sure that your hosting provider supports the applications you need to run on the server to process form input data (which will normally use `post` or `get` methods that we discuss earlier in this chapter). Chapter 3 includes more information on finding the right ISP to host your pages.

Using CGI scripts and other programs

Typically, form data is processed in some way or another by a Common Gateway Interface (CGI) script written in some programming language, such as Perl, Java, AppleScript, or one of many other languages that run on Web servers. These scripts make the data from your form useful by

✔ Putting it into a database

✔ Creating customized HTML based on it

✔ Writing it to a flat file

If you aren't familiar with CGI scripts and how they work, the "CGI Scripts for Fun and Profit" article on Webmonkey provides an excellent overview:

```
http://hotwired.lycos.com/webmonkey/99/26/index4a.html
```

You don't have to be a programmer to make the most of forms. Many ISPs support (and provide) scripts for processing common forms such as guest books, comment forms, and even shopping carts. Your ISP may give you

✔ All the information you need to get the program up and running

✔ HTML to include in your pages

You can tweak the markup that manages how the form appears in the canned HTML you get from an ISP, but don't change the form itself — especially the *form tag names and values.* The Web server program uses these to make the entire process work.

Several online script repositories provide free scripts that you can download and use along with your forms. Many of these also come with some generic

HTML you can dress up and tweak to fit your Web site. You simply drop the program that processes the form into the folder on your site that holds programs (usually called cgi-bin), add the HTML to your page, and you're good to go. Some choice places on the Web to find scripts you can download and put to work immediately are

- ✔ **Matt's Script archive:** `www.scriptarchive.com/nms.html`
- ✔ **The CGI Resource Index:** `http://cgi.resourceindex.com`
- ✔ **ScriptSearch:** `www.scriptsearch.com`

If you want to use programs that aren't provided by your ISP on your Web site, you need complete access to your site's cgi-bin folder. Every ISP's setup is different, so read your documentation to find

- ✔ Whether your ISP allows you to use CGI scripts in your Web pages
- ✔ Languages the ISP supports (Perl is a safe bet, but it's safer to be sure.)

Sending data by e-mail

You can opt to receive your form data from e-mail instead of using a script or other utility to process a form's data. You get just a collection of name and value pairs in a text file sent to your e-mail address, but that isn't necessarily a bad thing. You can include a short contact form on your Web site that asks people to send you feedback (a feature that always looks professional); then you can simply include, in the action URL, the e-mail address you want the data sent to:

```
<form action="mailto:me@mysite.com" action="post">
```

Many spam companies get e-mail addresses by trolling Web sites looking for `mailto` URLs. Consider setting up a special e-mail account just to receive comments so the e-mail address you use every day won't have yet another way to get pulled onto spam mailing lists.

Designing User-Friendly Forms

Designing *useful* forms is a different undertaking from designing *easy-to-use* forms. Your form may gather the data that you need, but if it's hard for visitors to use, they may abandon it before they're done.

As you use the markup elements from this chapter, along with the other elements that drive page layout, keep the following guidelines in mind:

✔ **Provide textual cues for all your forms.** Be clear about

- Information you want

- Format you need

For example, tell users such inputting details as whether

- Dates must be entered as mm/dd/yy (or as mm/dd/yyyy).

- The number of characters a field can take is limited.

Characters can be limited with the maxlength attribute.

✔ **Use field width and character limits to provide visual clues.** For example, if users should enter a phone number as *xxx-xxx-xxxx*, consider creating three text fields — one for each part of the phone number.

✔ **Group similar fields together.** A logical grouping of fields makes filling out a form easier. It's confusing if you ask for the visitor's first name, then birthday, then last name.

✔ **Break long forms into easy-to-manage sections.** Forms in short chunks are less intimidating and more likely to be completed.

Major online retailers (such as Amazon.com) use this method to get the detail they need for orders without making the process too painful.

✔ **Mark required fields clearly.** If some parts of your form *can't* be left blank when users submit the form, mark those fields clearly.

You can identify required fields by

- Making them bold

- Using a different color

- Placing an asterisk beside them

✔ **Tell users what kind of information they need for the form.** If users need any information in their hands before they fill out your form, a *form gateway* page can detail everything users should have before they start filling out the form.

The RateGenius Apply For a Loan page, shown in Figure 14-14, lays out clearly for visitors about to fill out a long form exactly what information to prepare before starting.

The series of forms RateGenius uses to gather information for car loans and loan refinancing are excellent examples of long forms that collect a variety of different kinds of data by using all the available form markup elements. Visit www.rategenius.com to review its form techniques.

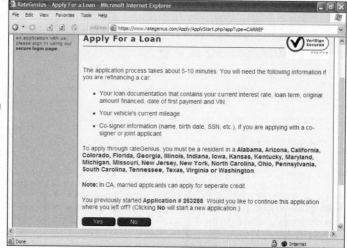

Figure 14-14:
A form
gateway
page helps
users
prepare to
fill out a
long form.

Marvelous Miscellany

Table 14-1 lists other forms-related (X)HTML markup attributes that you
might find in HTML files.

Table 14-1	Other Forms-related (X)HTML Attributes		
Name	*Function/Value Equals*	*Value Types*	*Related Element(s)*
Accept	Lists acceptable MIME types for file upload	CS Media types	`<form>` `<input />`
accept-charset	Lists character encodings	SS Encodings	`<form>`
Checked	Preselects option for select lists	"checked"	`<input />`
Disabled	Disables form elements	"disabled"	`<button>` `<input>` `<optgroup>` `<option>` `<select>` `<textarea>`

Name	Function/Value Equals	Value Types	Related Element(s)
enctype	Specifies encoding method for form input data	Media type	`<form>`
for	Points to ID reference from other attributes	Idref	`<label>`
label	Identifies a group of options in a form	Text	`<optgroup>`
label	Specifies an option name in a form	Text	`<option>`
method	HTTP method to use when submitting a form	{"get"| "put"}	`<form>`
multiple	Permits multiple option selection in a form	"multiple"	`<select>`
name	Names a specific form control	CDATA	`<button>` `<textarea>`
name	Names a specific form input field	CDATA	`<select>`
name	Names a form for script access	CDATA	`<form>`
readonly	Blocks editing of text fields within a form	"readonly"	`<input />` `<textarea`
size	Specifies number of lines of text to display for a drop-down menu	Number	`<select>`
tabindex	Defines tabbing order for form fields	Number	`<a><area />` `<button>` `<input />` `<object>` `<select>` `<textarea>`
type	Defines button function in a form	{"button"| "reset"| "submit"}	`<button>`

(continued)

Table 14-1 *(continued)*

Name	*Function/Value Equals*	*Value Types*	*Related Element(s)*
type	Specifies type of input required for form input field	{"button"| "checkbox"| "file"| "hidden"| "image"| "password"| "radio"| "reset"| "submit"| "text"}	\<input />
value	Supplies a value to send to the server when clicked	CDATA	\<button>
value	Associates values with radio buttons and check boxes	CDATA	\<input />

Chapter 15

Fun with Client-Side Scripts

***

In This Chapter

▶ What is DHTML?

▶ Image and text rollovers

▶ Adding dynamic content

▶ Showing pop-up windows

▶ Using Web cookies

***

*I*f you are the outdoor type, you can get an adrenaline rush by climbing a mountain, mountain biking, or perhaps inventing a new sport, such as parafishing or sewer snorkeling. But if you are reading this book, chances are you are sitting in front of your computer trying to create a Web site. If so, then we have an idea for the ultimate Web adrenaline rush: Dynamic HTML!

Dynamic HTML, also known as *DHTML,* is techie talk for a useful and powerful set of technologies. It's the combination of HTML, Cascading Style Sheets (CSS), the Document Object Model (the DOM), and JavaScript. If you're using those four technologies together, you're writing DHTML.

DHTML is like a printed document in which the DOM acts as the nouns, Java-Script as the verbs, CSS as the adjectives, and HTML as the paper itself. The individual parts are useful, but it's in combination that they become truly powerful. If you can put them all together, you can speak DHTML.

In this chapter, we explore how to use DHTML and its component technologies to bring active content to your Web pages. Specifically, we explore how to create rollovers, add dynamic content to your page, display pop-up windows, and tap into the power of cookies.

Adding Rollovers to Your Pages

If you are new to HTML, a rollover probably sounds like a pet trick. But, in actuality, a rollover is perhaps the most common use of DHTML on the Web. A rollover brings your Web page to life when a mouse hovers over an image or text.

Image rollovers with JavaScript

If all JavaScript scripts went to school, the image rollover would certainly be the BMOC, the Big Man on Campus. It's definitely the most popular use for JavaScript. Without image rollovers, your image buttons look dull and drab; visitors to your site might even assume that your buttons aren't actually live links if those buttons don't change in some fashion when a cursor moves over them. But, with image rollovers, your pages let loose a dash of adrenaline with each mouse hover.

Consider the two-states of the image rollover shown in Figures 15-1 and 15-2:

- Figure 15-1 shows a button in its inactive *(off)* state.
- Figure 15-2 shows the same button when the cursor is moved over it. That's the active *(on)* state.

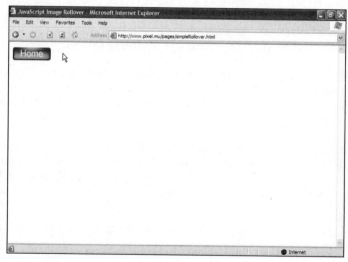

Figure 15-1:
A very simple button.

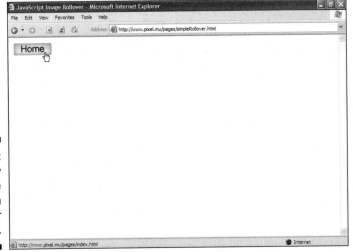

Figure 15-2:
A very
simple
button with
the cursor
over it.

Listing 15-1 shows the code for a JavaScript image rollover.

Listing 15-1:   JavaScript Image Rollover

```
<!DOCTYPE html PUBLIC "-//W3C//DTD XHTML 1.0 Transitional//EN"
    "http://www.w3.org/TR/xhtml1/DTD/xhtml1-transitional.dtd">
<html xmlns="http://www.w3.org/1999/xhtml">
<head>
    <title>JavaScript Image Rollover</title>
    <meta http-equiv="Content-Type" content="text/html; charset=ISO-8859-1" />
    <script type="text/javascript" language="javascript">
        function chgImg(imgField,imgState) {
            document[imgField].src = "images/" + imgField + imgState + ".gif"
        }
    </script>
</head>
<body>
    <a href="index.html" onmouseover="chgImg('homeButton','On')"
        onmouseout="chgImg('homeButton','Off')">
        <img src="images/homeButtonOff.gif" width="65" height="15"
            border="0" alt="Go Home" name="homeButton" /></a>
</body>
</html>
```

The `images` subdirectory holds two separate image files with identical dimensions:

- ✔ `homeButtonOff.gif` appears when the button is in the *off* state (when the page loads).
- ✔ `homeButtonOn.gif` appears when the button is in the *on* state (when the cursor is over the button).

If you want to add JavaScript rollovers to your existing Web page, follow these steps:

1. **Decide on an attribute name for the rollover button.**

   You want to give each button a unique name. For example, if you have a button for an About page, you might call it `aboutMeButton`. Call a button linked to your Home page `homeButton`.

2. **Create your button images in your favorite image-editing application.**

   You need two identically sized images for each button.

3. **Name the `On` and `Off` button image files with the attribute.**

   For example, the `aboutMeButton` button needs two image files:

   ```
   aboutMeButtonOn.gif
   aboutMeButtonOff.gif
   ```

4. **Put the button image files into an images subdirectory under the directory of the page that will contain the rollovers.**

5. **Add the JavaScript code in Listing 15-1 to your page.**

   That's everything between (and including) the `<script>` and `</script>` tags. It goes inside the `<head>` tags at the top.

6. **Add the *off* versions of each image to your page.**

7. **Add the `name` attribute to each `<img>` tag on your page.**

8. **Surround each `<img>` tag with an `<a href>` `</a>` tag.**

9. **Add these event handlers to each `<a href>` tag:**

   Add the following attributes to use `homeButton`:

   ```
   onmouseover="chgImg('homeButton','On')"
   onmouseout="chgImg('homeButton','Off')"
   ```

   Next, add these attributes to use `aboutMeButton`:

   ```
   onmouseover="chgImg('aboutMeButton','On')"
   onmouseout="chgImg('aboutMeButton','Off')"
   ```

With this image rollover script, note the following behavior:

✔ For dialup visitors to your Web site, this rollover script takes a moment to download the active image file the first time the visitor hovers the mouse over the image.

However, you can *preload* the active states of your images; that is, tell JavaScript to load all the *on* versions of your buttons when the page initially loads. This technique enables your page to instantaneously swap between images when rolled over. Listing 15-2 shows the added code to preload the images.

Recent versions of Microsoft Internet Explorer (5.*x* and 6.*x*) contain a bug that can make preloading ineffective. Under certain circumstances, the browser will ignore images already downloaded into your local cache and instead request the image all over again each time a visitor moves the mouse over the rollover image. If you encounter this problem, consider a text rollover instead, which is discussed in the "Text rollovers with CSS" section later in this chapter.

✔ This script depends on the buttons having particular names; if you want more flexibility, the code has to be written to handle it.

✔ This script causes trouble with certain ancient browsers, particularly Netscape versions 1 and 2 and Internet Explorer versions 1, 2, and 3.

Listing 15-2: Enhanced JavaScript Image Rollover with Preloader

```
<!DOCTYPE html PUBLIC "-//W3C//DTD XHTML 1.0 Transitional//EN"
    "http://www.w3.org/TR/xhtml1/DTD/xhtml1-transitional.dtd">
<html xmlns="http://www.w3.org/1999/xhtml">
<head>
    <title>JavaScript Image Rollover</title>
    <meta http-equiv="Content-Type" content="text/html; charset=ISO-8859-1" />
    <script type="text/javascript" language="javascript">

        //Preloads images
        if (document.images) {
          homeButtonOn = new Image
          homeButtonOff = new Image
          homeButtonOn.src = "images/homeButtonOn.gif"
          homeButtonOff.src = "images/homeButtonOff.gif"
        }

        function chgImg(imgField,imgState) {
            document[imgField].src = "images/" + imgField + imgState + ".gif"
        }
    </script>
</head>
<body>
    <a href="index.html" onmouseover="chgImg('homeButton','On')"
        onmouseout="chgImg('homeButton','Off')">
        <img src="images/homeButtonOff.gif" width="65" height="15"
            border="0" alt="Go Home" name="homeButton" /></a>
</body>
</html>
```

Text rollovers with CSS

For years, the only option available for creating a rollover effect was to create button images and then "activate" them using JavaScript (as discussed in the

"Image rollovers with JavaScript" section previously). However, as CSS has finally gained acceptance with the newer versions of browsers, you have an alternative way to create rollovers without using any images at all.

Text rollovers have advantages and disadvantages when compared to JavaScript image rollovers:

- ✔ **Good news:** Text is faster and more meaningful to search engines, and it's always easier to just add text to a page than it is to create two images and then add them to a page, as with an image rollover. Plus, you don't need to worry about preloading your images.

- ✔ **Bad news:** Although you can control the text font, style, and border, you can't do all the nifty visual tricks that you can with images, such as anti-aliasing. In addition, this method works only in reasonably current browsers. (However, if your target viewing audience uses a browser that was released in this century, you should be fine.)

Figure 15-3 shows a plain-Jane Web page with two rollover text links: *Home* and *About Me*. Moving the cursor over one of the images, as shown in Figure 15-4, causes the rolled-over version of the text to display. Listing 15-3 displays the HTML and CSS required for this rollover effect.

The page can still display whether you've visited the linked page or not. Figure 15-5 shows how the page appears after you've been to this site's home page. And although that image is grayed out, it's still a link, so rolling over it still gives the same effect as in Figure 15-4.

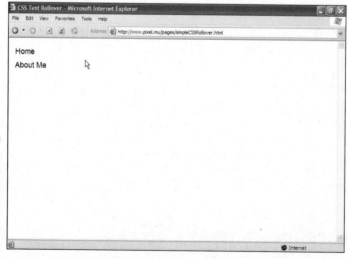

Figure 15-3:
A page with text rollovers handled with CSS.

Figure 15-4:
Moving the
cursor over
the link text
changes the
text and
background
colors.

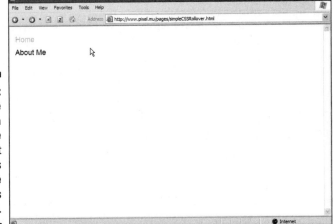

Figure 15-5:
After you've
been to a
page, the
link text
color shows
that the
page was
visited.

Listing 15-3:   A Text Rollover with CSS

```
<!DOCTYPE html PUBLIC "-//W3C//DTD XHTML 1.0 Transitional//EN"
    "http://www.w3.org/TR/xhtml1/DTD/xhtml1-transitional.dtd">
<html xmlns="http://www.w3.org/1999/xhtml">
<head>
    <title>CSS Text Rollover</title>
    <meta http-equiv="Content-Type" content="text/html; charset=ISO-8859-1" />
    <style type="text/css">
        h4 {font: 18px geneva, sans-serif; margin: 0; color: #000;
            background: #FFF;}
```

(continued)

Listing 15-3 *(continued)*

```
        a {text-decoration: none;}

        div#navbar {width: 100px;}
        div#navbar a {display:block; margin: 0; padding: 0.3em;}
        div#navbar a:hover {background: #FFF; color: #000;}
        div#navbar a:link {color: #000; background-color: transparent;}
      div#navbar a:link:hover {color: #FFF; background: #000;}
        div#navbar a:visited {color: #CCC; background-color: transparent;}
        div#navbar a:visited:hover {color: #CCC; background: #000;}
    </style>
</head>
<body>
<div id="navbar">
    <h4><a href="index.html">Home</a></h4>
    <h4><a href="aboutMe.html">About Me</a></h4>
</div>
</body>
</html>
```

In this example, we've made the text change from black on white to white on black when the cursor hovers over the link so that it's easy for you to see what's going on in the black-and-white figures. You likely want your site to use a more colorful approach.

Adding this type of navigation to your site couldn't be simpler:

1. **Within the** `<head>` **tags, add the preceding code (from Listing 15-3) inside and including the** `<style>` **and** `</style>` **tags.**

2. **Add links inside individual** `<h4>` **tags.**

3. **Make sure that the entire menu is inside a** `<div>` **tag with an** `id` **attribute of** `navbar`.

If you add the CSS to your site via a link to a site-wide external style sheet (see Chapters 8 and 9 for more information on style sheets), you can add, change, or delete menu bar links on your site at any time without having to touch a single line of CSS or JavaScript. You simply add or modify your `<a href>` tags. Slick, huh?

Displaying Dynamic Content on Your Page

Web pages can take advantage of JavaScript to change by themselves without requiring any user input or updating from the Web server. To demonstrate how JavaScript can do this, we create a simple clock that can automatically update itself every second. We first show you how to do this using JavaScript and HTML and then how to do this an even better way using JavaScript and the DOM.

HTML and JavaScript

You can create a JavaScript-enabled clock by using JavaScript and an ordinary HTML <input> tag. Listing 15-4 displays the code that you need to make this happen, and Figure 15-6 displays the results on-screen.

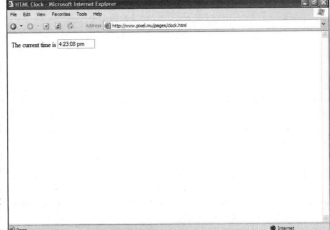

Figure 15-6: This page displays the current time, updated every second, inside a text field.

Listing 15-4:   A Simple HTML and JavaScript Clock

```
<!DOCTYPE html PUBLIC "-//W3C//DTD XHTML 1.0 Transitional//EN"
    "http://www.w3.org/TR/xhtml1/DTD/xhtml1-transitional.dtd">
<html xmlns="http://www.w3.org/1999/xhtml">
<head>
    <title>HTML Clock</title>
    <meta http-equiv="Content-Type" content="text/html; charset=ISO-8859-1" />
    <script type="text/javascript" language="javascript">
        window.onload = theClock

        function theClock() {
            now = new Date;

            theTime = ((now.getHours() > 0 && now.getHours()
                    < 13)) ? now.getHours() : (now.getHours() == 0)
                    ? 12 : now.getHours()-12;
            theTime += (now.getMinutes() > 9) ? ":" + now.getMinutes() : ":0"
```

(continued)

Listing 15-4 *(continued)*

```
                              + now.getMinutes();
            theTime += (now.getSeconds() > 9) ? ":" + now.getSeconds() : ":0"
                              + now.getSeconds();
            theTime += (now.getHours() < 12) ? " am" : " pm";

            document.myForm.myClock.value = theTime;
            setTimeout("theClock()",1000);
        }
    </script>
</head>
<body>
<form action="#" name="myForm">
The current time is
<input type="text" name="myClock" readonly="readonly" size="11" />
</form>
</body>
</html>
```

In Listing 15-4, the clock is updated inside a form text field so that JavaScript can write out to the page without having to reload the entire page every second. Wherever the text field is on your page, that's where the time appears. The clock shows the time set on the user's computer, not the time on the Web server that's serving the pages.

To add this clock to your page, just

1. **Copy everything from the beginning `<script>` tag to the ending `</script>` tag in Listing 15-4.**

   The complete code listings for this book are available at `www.dummies.com/extras`.

2. **Paste the code into the `<head>` section of your page.**

3. **Add the `<form>` and `<input>` tags (including the `name` attribute on each) on your page where you want your clock to appear.**

The very first thing that JavaScript does when the Web page loads is set the window's `onload` event handler to trigger the `theClock` function. This is no big deal — unless you want to run another script when the page loads. However, this script is written in such a way that it never comes back to run anything else, since the clock is constantly updating itself.

JavaScript and DOM

When you add both JavaScript and some DOM manipulation to your page, you can update the text of the page itself, as shown in Listing 15-5. Figure 15-7 shows a clock that updates every second, but it looks visually just like the rest of the text on the line.

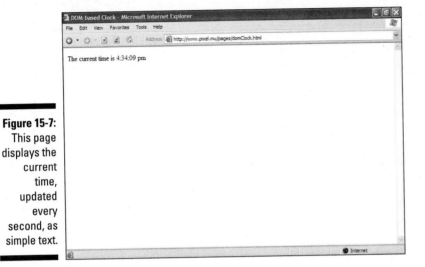

Figure 15-7:
This page
displays the
current
time,
updated
every
second, as
simple text.

Listing 15-5: A Slightly More Complex JavaScript and DOM Clock

```
<!DOCTYPE html PUBLIC "-//W3C//DTD XHTML 1.0 Transitional//EN"
        "http://www.w3.org/TR/xhtml1/DTD/xhtml1-transitional.dtd">
<html xmlns="http://www.w3.org/1999/xhtml">
<head>
    <title>DOM-based Clock</title>
    <meta http-equiv="Content-Type" content="text/html; charset=ISO-8859-1" />
    <script type="text/javascript" language="javascript1.5">
      window.onload = theClock

    function theClock() {
        now = new Date;

        theTime = ((now.getHours() > 0 && now.getHours() < 13)) ?
          now.getHours() : (now.getHours() == 0) ? 12 : now.getHours()-12;
        theTime += (now.getMinutes() > 9) ? ":" + now.getMinutes() : ":0"
          + now.getMinutes();
        theTime += (now.getSeconds() > 9) ? ":" + now.getSeconds() : ":0"
          + now.getSeconds();
        theTime += (now.getHours() < 12) ? " am" : " pm";

        clockSpan = document.getElementById("myClock");
        clockSpan.replaceChild(document.createTextNode(theTime),
          clockSpan.firstChild);

        setTimeout("theClock()",1000);
```

(continued)

Listing 15-5 *(continued)*

```
        }
    </script>
</head>
<body>
The current time is <span id="myClock">?</span>
</body>
</html>
```

The script in Listing 15-5 is virtually identical to Listing 15-4, except for a couple of different lines of JavaScript. Using the DOM, the script can grab that text and replace it with new text every second.

> ✔ **The good news:** You can style that text with CSS and have it appear just like everything else on the page. The visual look is far superior to putting the dynamic text inside an `<input>` tag.

> ✔ **The bad news:** Older browsers don't support the `<span>` tag, so if your visitors use legacy versions of Netscape or Microsoft browsers, consider using the HTML and JavaScript version instead.

Other examples in this book show the initial `<script>` tag with the `language` attribute set to `javascript`. This particular script specifies `javascript1.5`, which tells the browser to ignore everything that's going on if you aren't using a modern browser. If you come into this page with an older browser, you won't get an error, but you won't get the dynamic effects, either.

To add the DOM-enabled scripted clock to your page, follow these steps:

1. **Add everything between the beginning and ending `<script>` tags to the `<head>` section of your page.**

2. **Add a `<span>` tag with an `id` attribute of `myClock` anywhere on your page.**

    The clock appears!

Are you getting errors when you try to add the DOM-powered clock to your page? Some browsers have a problem with either *nothing* or a *space* in the `<span>` tag. Solution: As with the example shown in Listing 15-5, put something (anything) inside the `<span>` tag for when it's initially loaded. In this case, there's a question mark, but it won't ever be visible to the Web page visitor.

Displaying Pop-up Windows

Pop-up windows are both one of the most useful and one of the most abused tools on the Web. Having a way to provide some extra information to site visitors without making them leave a page is very useful. Unfortunately, so many unethical people have given pop-ups (particular advertising pop-ups) a bad name that many Web surfers install pop-up blockers. Consequently, if you add pop-up windows to your site, make sure that they aren't the only way that your visitors have of getting information.

Figure 15-8 shows a simple pop-up window containing the clock from Listing 15-5. This little window is a nice, floating, constantly updated clock that can stay up even after you've left the calling page. Listing 15-6 shows how to create this pop-up window, which is a new browser window that doesn't have an address bar, menu bar, scroll bars, status bar, or toolbars, as shown in Figure 15-8.

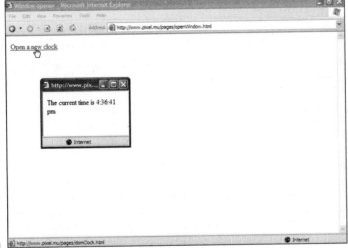

Figure 15-8: Clicking the link opens a new browser window.

Listing 15-6:   Opening a New Browser Window

```
<!DOCTYPE html PUBLIC "-//W3C//DTD XHTML 1.0 Transitional//EN"
        "http://www.w3.org/TR/xhtml1/DTD/xhtml1-transitional.dtd">
<html xmlns="http://www.w3.org/1999/xhtml">
<head>
    <title>Window opener</title>
    <meta http-equiv="Content-Type" content="text/html; charset=ISO-8859-1" />
    <script type="text/javascript" language="javascript">
        function OpenWindow (newPage) {
            window.open(newPage,"newWin","width=200,height=50,resizable=yes");
        }
```

(continued)

Listing 15-6 *(continued)*

```
    </script>
</head>
<body>
<a href="domClock.html"
    onclick="OpenWindow(this.href);return false">Open a new clock</a>
</body>
</html>
```

The "Open a new clock" link, when clicked, calls a tiny JavaScript function that opens a new window that's 200 pixels wide, 50 pixels high, and resizable.

Follow these steps to add this new window to your own site:

1. **Add everything from the beginning to the ending `<script>` tags to the `<head>` of your page.**

2. **In the body, figure out where you want the link to be.**

3. **Add the `onclick` event handler attribute to the `<a href>` tag around the text or image.**

You can have multiple links on the same page that each open a new window, and they can all have identical `onclick` handlers and call the same JavaScript function.

The script is coded so that all the different bars are turned off. You can change the code so that the sizes are different or various fields either are or aren't displayed by varying the contents of the last field in the `window.open` function. Table 15-1 shows the valid entries for this parameter; just put them all, separated by commas (but not spaces), into a single string, and you get exactly the results you want.

The default for every parameter is `no`, so there's no difference between setting an entry to `no` and just leaving it off entirely.

Table 15-1	JavaScript's Window Parameters	
Name	*Values (Default in Italics)*	*Description and Value*
`location`	yes, *no*	Should the new window display the location bar (also known as the address bar)?
`menubar`	yes, *no*	Should the new window display the menu bars? (Applies only to Windows and Unix.)

Name	Values (Default in Italics)	Description and Value
resizable	yes, *no*	Should the user be allowed to resize the new window?
scrollbars	yes, *no*	Should the user be allowed to scroll the new window?
status	yes, *no*	Should the new window display the status bar?
toolbar	yes, *no*	Should the new window display the toolbar?
height	Numeric	The height of the new window in pixels
width	Numeric	The width of the new window in pixels

Working with Cookies

Every time we start talking about cookies, we are tempted to rush off to the fridge for a glass of milk and get ready for dipping. But then we remind ourselves that Web cookies, as useful as they can be, actually taste pretty bland. In fact, they taste far more like chicken than that famous Toll House recipe. Although they might not be tasty, you can still find cookies to be helpful as you create your Web site.

A cookie lets you store information on visitors' computers that you can recall at a later time. Cookies can be one of the most powerful ways to maintain "state" within your Web pages.

The code in Listing 15-7 reads and writes two cookies when a visitor loads the page:

- pageHit contains a count of the number of times the visitor has loaded the page.
- pageVisit contains the last date and time the visitor visited.

Figure 15-9 shows how the page appears on the initial visit, and Figure 15-10 shows how the page looks on subsequent visits.

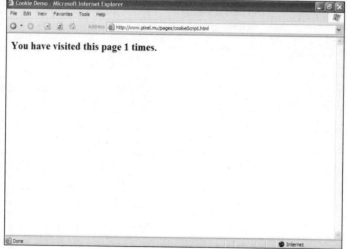

Figure 15-9:
The cookie knows you've never been to this page before.

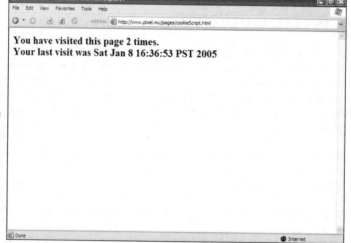

Figure 15-10:
The cookies know not only that you've been here before but when.

Listing 15-7:   Cookie-Handling Script

```
<!DOCTYPE html PUBLIC "-//W3C//DTD XHTML 1.0 Transitional//EN"
        "http://www.w3.org/TR/xhtml1/DTD/xhtml1-transitional.dtd">
<html xmlns="http://www.w3.org/1999/xhtml">
<head>
    <title>Cookie Demo</title>
```

```
<meta http-equiv="Content-Type" content="text/html; charset=ISO-8859-1" />
<script type="text/javascript" language="javascript">
now = new Date
expireDate = new Date
expireDate.setMonth(expireDate.getMonth()+6)

hitCt = parseInt(cookieVal("pageHit"))
hitCt++
lastVisit = cookieVal("pageVisit")
if (lastVisit == 0) {
   lastVisit = ""
}

document.cookie = "pageHit="+hitCt+";expires=" + expireDate.toGMTString()
document.cookie = "pageVisit="+now+";expires=" + expireDate.toGMTString()

function cookieVal(cookieName) {
    thisCookie = document.cookie.split("; ")
    for (i=0; i<thisCookie.length; i++) {
        if (cookieName == thisCookie[i].split("=")[0]) {
            return thisCookie[i].split("=")[1]
        }
    }
    return 0
}
</script>
</head>
<body>
<h2>
    <script type="text/javascript" language="javascript">
    document.write("You have visited this page " + hitCt + " times.")
    if (lastVisit != "") {
        document.write("<br />Your last visit was " + lastVisit)
    }
    </script>
</h2>
</body>
</html>
```

Unlike preceding examples, Listing 15-7 has a `<script>` section in both the head and the body:

 ✔ Cookies are read and written in the header script when the page loads.

 ✔ The body script dynamically writes out the contents of the page itself.

Follow these steps to add the cookie-handling script to your page:

1. **Copy both** `<script>` **sections and put them into the appropriate parts of your page.**

2. **Change the** `<body>` **section to contain the text that you want the page to display.**

   The lines inside the `document.write()` statements write the text out to the document on the fly.

A cookie has an expiration date, after which it's no longer available. This example creates cookies that expire in six months. If you want your cookie to last more or less time, adjust the line in the JavaScript code near the top that sets the value of `expireDate`.

Marvelous Miscellany

You can use the (X)HTML `<object>` element to embed content inside a Web page. It provides a general mechanism to embed content of all kinds, from another text file to numerous types of active content, such as programs written in languages other than JavaScript (that works with the `<script>` element, as you already know) and multimedia (such as Flash animations). This is advanced stuff for Web-page builders, so we list only object-related (X)HTML attributes in Table 15-2 and then conclude with pointers to details on using this element.

If you want to use programming languages, such as Perl, Python, Java, and so forth, or various types of multimedia in your Web pages, you should cozy up to the `<object>` element.

Table 15-2	Object-related (X)HTML Attributes		
Name	*Function/ Value Equals*	*Value Types*	*Related Element(s)*
`archive`	Identifies location (URI) for archive file	URI	`<object>`
`classid`	Identifies object implementation URI	URI	`<object>`

Name	Function/ Value Equals	Value Types	Related Element(s)
codebase	Identifies base URI for classid, data, and archive	URI	<object>
codetype	Identifies content type for code	Media type	<object>
data	Identifies object data by location	URI	<object>
standby	Specifies message that displays while object is loading	Text	<object>
type	Identifies content type for object data	Media type	<object>

The following resources address the (X)HTML <object> tag nicely:

- W3Schools offers (X)HTML tag information online; <object> coverage includes links to a complete tag list at www.w3schools.com/tags/tag_object.asp.

- Juicy Studio offers a detailed discussion of the <object> element at www.juicystudio.com/tutorial/html/object.asp.

- In the HTML 4 Recommendation, the W3C includes "Objects, Images, and Applets" at www.w3.org/TR/REC-html40/struct/objects.html.

Part V
HTML Projects

The 5th Wave   By Rich Tennant

"Evidently he died of natural causes following a marathon session animating everything on his personal Web site. And no, Morganstern—the irony isn't lost on me."

In this part . . .

In this part of the book, you can explore, understand, and see some typical Web page projects, including all the markup and underlying scripts, graphics, and other materials that go into their makeup. They're ready-to-use examples that you can edit or customize for your own needs and circumstances, so these projects are designed to function as templates of a sort that you can adapt and use as your own Web pages.

Here, you find typical implementations of a personal Web page ("About me") and a company profile page ("About my company"). You also find an eBay auction page, a product marketing page, and a product catalog page that incorporates an honest-to-gosh shopping cart application. This is where everything in Parts II, III, and IV is put to work in useful, attractive Web pages that you can tailor for your own needs.

Chapter 16

The About Me Page

*I*t's time to build your very own page, one that tells the world who you are and what you're like.

You only get one chance to make a good first impression, and your site is how people all over the world can get to know who you are. So put your best foot forward and make your home page reflect exactly the image you want to project.

Overview and Design Considerations

Every Web site should start with a plan of its goals and intended audience, and a simple home page is no exception. Think about

✔ Who will visit the site

✔ What you want them to get out of it

✔ How often you want to update the site

✔ Content to include

Audience analysis

Your site will be your public face to the world, so analyze who you think will be visiting and what you want them to get out of a visit. For instance, a site that amuses and entertains your friends might be exactly what you don't want a prospective employer to see!

Even if you don't give people the URL of your site, they're still likely to find it through search engines. *Googling* (searching the Web, particularly via Google.com) prospective employees and dates is more common than not. Do you really want your parents and siblings, or your co-workers, to read all the details about what you did last weekend?

Component elements

At its simplest, a home page consists of nothing but a single HTML text file. If you're a great designer, that's sufficient. Chances are, though, that you'll want to add an image or two to give the site some visual interest. The two examples of home pages in this chapter each use three files: the home page and two small graphics.

Page Markup

After you have a template for a Web page (see the "Using *HTML 4 For Dummies* page templates" sidebar), just fill in the blanks. Include your content in new *headings* (<h2> tags in the following examples) and new *paragraphs* (with their corresponding <p> tags).

Your home page

Listing 16-1 is the HTML code for a typical home page. Figure 16-1 shows how it looks when displayed in a browser.

Listing 16-1:   A Home Page

```
<!DOCTYPE html PUBLIC "-//W3C//DTD XHTML 1.0 Transitional//EN"
        "http://www.w3.org/TR/xhtml1/DTD/xhtml1-transitional.dtd">
<html xmlns="http://www.w3.org/1999/xhtml">
<head>
    <title>My Home Page</title>
    <meta http-equiv="Content-Type" content="text/html; charset=ISO-8859-1" />
</head>
<body>
    <h1><img src="crosskick.gif" alt="crosskick.gif" width="125"
        height="125" align="middle" hspace="20" />Welcome to my home page!</h1>
    <h2>About me:</h2>
    <p>My name is Sean. I'm a high school student, and I'm interested in
```

```
      math, science, and sports.</p>
   <h2>Sites I like:</h2>
   <p>My parents have a weblog: <a href="http://www.backupbrain.com">
      Backup Brain</a></p>
   <p>My cat has a Web site: <a href="http://www.pixel.mu">Pixel.mu</a></p>
   <h2>Send me email: <a href="mailto:sean@example.com">
         img src="email.gif" alt="email.gif" width="60" height="60"
         align="middle" border="0" /></a></h2>
</body>
</html>
```

This page is about as simple as it gets: There's no style information, no JavaScript, only two images, and not a lot of text. But it's enough to give you an idea of what kind of person put up the site and what he's like.

Figure 16-1:
A simple
home page.

This page contains two small graphics:

- ✔ `crosskick.gif` is a simple image that adds a splash of color while hinting about the page owner's favorite sport.

- ✔ `email.gif` is a button that visitors can click. When a visitor clicks it, her e-mail client will pop up in a window with a preaddressed e-mail.

It isn't hard to go from a super-simple site to a site that's considerably more attractive without getting horribly complex. Listing 16-2 and Figure 16-2 show a site with a lot more style and only a little more complexity.

Listing 16-2:   Another Home Page

```
<!DOCTYPE html PUBLIC "-//W3C//DTD XHTML 1.0 Transitional//EN"
      "http://www.w3.org/TR/xhtml1/DTD/xhtml1-transitional.dtd">
<html xmlns="http://www.w3.org/1999/xhtml">
<head>
    <title>My Home Page</title>
    <meta http-equiv="Content-Type" content="text/html; charset=ISO-8859-1" />
    <style type="text/css">
        body {color: #000; background-color: #9C6;}
        h1 {font: 48px "monotype corsiva", fantasy;}
        h2 {margin-top: 20px; font: 20px "trebuchet ms", verdana,
            arial, helvetica, geneva, sans-serif;}
        p {margin-left: 20px; font: 14px/16px verdana, geneva, arial,
            helvetica, sans-serif}
    </style>
</head>
<body>
    <h1><img src="dancer.gif" alt="dancer.gif" width="125" height="122"
        align="middle" hspace="20" />Welcome to my home page!</h1>
    <h2>About me:</h2>
    <p>My name is Susan. I'm a high school student, and I'm interested in math,
        science, and sports.</p>
    <h2>Sites I like:</h2>
    <p>There's a good site about Web design at
        <a href="http://www.wise-women.org">Wise-Women.org</a></p>
    <p>My cat has a Web site: <a href="http://www.pixel.mu">Pixel.mu</a></p>
    <h2>Send me email: <a href="mailto:susan@example.com">
        <img src="email2.gif" alt="email2.gif" width="60"
        height="60" align="middle" border="0" /></a></h2>
</body>
</html>
```

Text and tags within the <body> element are about the same as inside the
first example, but the result is different because of the style rules in the
<head>.

The style rules set a background color for the page and specify the fonts to
be used. Although the two pages have almost identical content, the latter
page gives a much stronger impression of the person's individuality.

Looking good

Adding cool fonts and bright colors to your page is a good way to add visual
interest — but it makes your site look tacky if it's overdone.

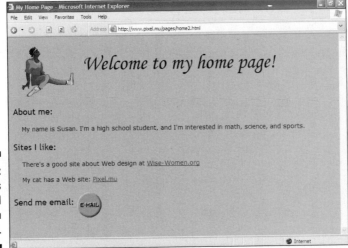

Figure 16-2:
Our less
simple and
more stylish
home page.

Follow these tips for a colorful, professional-looking page:

✔ **Pick a graphic and use its colors elsewhere on the page.**

The colors in the image of the woman in Figure 16-2 are used elsewhere on the page:

- The background color of the image is the background color for the entire page (so the image's background blends into the page).
- The color of her blouse is used as the color of the e-mail icon.

✔ **Check your page on other computers to make sure your colors really look the way you want them to look.**

Colors often appear differently on different monitors, and not everyone's monitor is set up correctly.

✔ **Be selective when choosing fonts and font colors.**

- A font on your computer might not be on other computers.

  Give alternate fonts as a backup in your style rules.

- Don't use too many different fonts on one page or it'll end up looking like a ransom note.

- Use font colors that contrast with your background so people can read what you've written.

Listing 16-3 is a bare-bones template with comments that tell you where to add your own content. Start with this, and where you end up is limited only by your imagination and creativity.

Listing 16-3:   A Home Page Template

```
<!DOCTYPE html PUBLIC "-//W3C//DTD XHTML 1.0 Transitional//EN"
        "http://www.w3.org/TR/xhtml1/DTD/xhtml1-transitional.dtd">
<html xmlns="http://www.w3.org/1999/xhtml">
<head>
    <title>My Home Page</title>
    <meta http-equiv="Content-Type" content="text/html; charset=ISO-8859-1" />
    <style type="text/css">
        body {color: #000; background-color: #FFF;}

        /* Add additional style rules here */

    </style>
</head>
<body>
    <h1>Welcome to my home page!</h1>

    <h2>About me:</h2>
    <!-- Add something here about you and your interests -->

    <h2>Sites I like:</h2>
    <!-- Add links here to sites that you like to visit -->

    <h2><a href="mailto:yourName@example.com">Send me email!</a></h2>
</body>
</html>
```

Using *HTML 4 For Dummies* page templates

Part V of this book (Chapters 16–19) contains page templates designed specifically so that you can easily copy and modify them to suit your tastes. You can either

✔ Type them in yourself

✔ Download them from www.dummies. com/extras

If you're looking for more templates, you can find great ones for copying, pasting, and adding your content in most WYSIWYG HTML editors. Chapter 20 covers these.

Chapter 17

The eBay Auction Page

Whether you are trying to buy or sell a car, a rare CD, or a bologna sandwich that bears an uncanny likeness to Calvin Coolidge, eBay has become the 21st century's answer to the street marketplace. In fact, with more than 50 million active participants, eBay is sometimes referred to as "the world's garage sale." However, if these staggering numbers are leaving you starry-eyed over your expected profits, be careful: With millions of items for sale, it's easy for your "Coolidge-looking bologna sandwich" to get lost in the crowd.

Given this reality, the more attractively your auction item is presented and the better the description is written, the greater the chances your item will sell and at a higher price.

In this chapter, we show you how to effectively use HTML to make your eBay auction look wicked cool. You'll discover how to

✔ Highlight parts of your description.

✔ Add pictures.

Although eBay is the most popular online auction site, you can use HTML in your item descriptions on most other online auction sites as well, such as Half.com, Yahoo! Auctions, and ubid.

Designing Your Auction Page

Online auction sites let you include a few specific elements in your auction item page, such as

- ✔ **Title** (and sometimes a subtitle)
- ✔ **Description**

    This chapter focuses on the item description because that's where your HTML markup can enhance the look of the description and add pictures.

- ✔ **Pictures**

Figure 17-1 shows an example of an auction description from eBay that uses HTML to add style and an embedded picture.

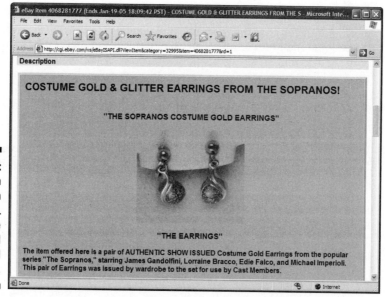

Figure 17-1: This auction description uses HTML to style the text and add a centered picture.

Auction sites typically allow you to use a series of online forms to list items for sale. If you want to use HTML in your item description, you include the HTML markup in the text field the auction site gives you for the description, as shown in Figure 17-2.

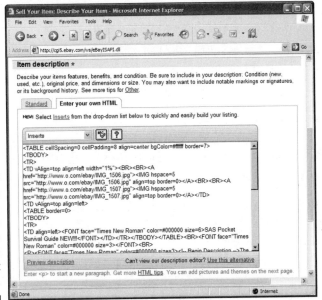

Figure 17-2:
Entering
HTML in the
online
description
form field at
eBay.

eBay allows you to use HTML for style only in the item description; you can't use it in the title or subtitle lines.

Because the auction site itself creates much of an online auction page, you don't have to create the entire page of HTML markup. You just need to create markup for the item description part of the page. That means that you

✔ Don't need to include the `<html>`, `<title>`, or `<body>` tags

✔ Can't include any scripts in the description

When you create your auction item page, be aware that all browsers are not created equally.

✔ If you use Microsoft Internet Explorer 6 as your browser, eBay gives you an HTML editor that allows you to style text directly and then turns it into HTML markup, as shown in Figure 17-3.

✔ Other browsers, including Mozilla Firefox and Safari on the Macintosh, display a simple text form in which to enter or paste your HTML markup.

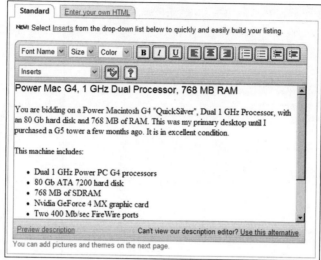

Figure 17-3:
Using
eBay's
HTML editor
to style your
text in
Internet
Explorer 6.

When designing your item's title and description, don't immediately rush to add fancy HTML formatting. Instead, your first task is to create a description that effectively presents your product. Before you worry about the HTML markup, write a compelling title and description. Consider the following tips when you write your text:

- ✔ **Write a great, descriptive title.** A good title includes words that clearly and specifically identify what you are selling. eBay's search engine uses these titles to help people find your item, and you won't sell what buyers can't find.

- ✔ **Look at completed listings to see successful descriptions.** Use those ideas to stimulate your own.

  However, don't plagiarize other people's descriptions (or rip off their pictures).

- ✔ **Spell words in the title and description correctly.** Misspelled words will not be found by visitors searching for your item.

  In fact, we've bought equipment worth thousands of dollars for a fraction of its worth that got no other bids because the sellers misspelled the items' names in the auction title.

- ✔ **Be sure that you're listing the item in the proper auction category.** If you list it in the wrong category, your item will get lost, buried, obscured, masked . . . well, you get the idea.

- ✔ **Resist the temptation to use large fonts and lots of styles.** Buyers want to see your item description and photographs as quickly as possible. Keep your text and images direct, visually uncluttered, and to the point.

✔ **Use good photographs.** Items with pictures sell much better:

- The photo of your item (more than one is usually better) should be sharp, with the item's important features clearly visible.

- Make sure that your image files are a reasonable size; buyers hate large photos that take a long time to load or that require scrolling.

Use a photo-editing program to reduce the pictures that your digital camera or scanner produces to a smaller size and lower-resolution jpeg file. You want a size that loads quickly and can be viewed without scrolling, as discussed in Chapter 7.

✔ **Avoid animation and music like the plague.** Serious bidders click off of your item in a flash if you have either of these annoyances in your item description.

Presentation Issues to Consider

When you create your listings, remember that a variety of users will view your page using different browsers and operating systems. With that in mind, the following are some helpful tips for creating your listing:

✔ **Design your page so it works with as many browsers as possible.** Any Web browser may view your listing. (For example, you can't assume that your buyers have a browser capable of properly rendering CSS.)

✔ **Use an appropriate font size.** The font size that you use should be large enough to be legible at a variety of screen resolutions. Standard font sizes such as a 10- to 12-point font are good examples. Some buyers won't bother to read your item description if it is in a tiny font size. At the same time, don't make the font size too large. Large fonts can make your auction item page look amateurish.

✔ **Don't use huge type that requires users to scroll the page a lot.** For example, four headings that are all in a 48-point font would be way too much.

✔ **Use backgrounds that don't distract your users from the text and images on the Web site.**

Avoid colored or patterned backgrounds because

- People who are colorblind might have problems reading them.

- Colored backgrounds can make your page hard to read when printed on a monochrome printer. (Many users print auctions for inventory records.)

- They can make your page look amateurish.

Using a Template for Presenting Your Auction Item

In this section, we provide a handy HTML template that enables you to display pictures of your item alongside its description:

- **A left column contains two pictures of the auction item.**

  The example assumes that you're hosting the image files on a Web server that you control. You should prepare the image files and upload them to your server before you begin using the template.

- **A right column contains text describing the item.**

Listing 17-1 shows the HTML markup for the auction item description. You can type it in any text editor, replacing the parts set off by the HTML comment tags with the appropriate information as indicated in the comment tag text.

Listing 17-1: Auction Item HTML Template

```
<!-- Begin Description Table -->
<!-- Picture column -->

<table align="center" cellpadding="8" border="7"
      cellspacing="0" bgcolor="#FFFFFF">
<tr>
<td valign="top" align="Left" width="1%"><br /><br />

<!-- First picture goes below; replace URL with the location of your picture -->

<img border="0" align="top" hspace="5"
     src="http://www.example.com/images/image1.jpg"
     alt="Alternative image text" />

<br /><br />

<!-- Next picture goes below; replace URL with the location of your picture -->

<img border="0" align="top" hspace="5"
     src="http://www.example.com/images/image1.jpg"
     alt="Alternative image text" /></td>

<!-- Text column -->

<td valign="top" align="Left">

<!-- This table-within-a-table for the headline makes your description
```

```
    look better -->

<table border="0" >
  <tr><td align="Left" ><font face="Times New Roman" color="#000000" size="6">
    Your Exciting Item Title Goes Here!</font>
  </td></tr>
</table><br />

<p><font face="Times New Roman" color="#000000" size="3">

<!-- Begin Description -->

Replace this text with the description of your auction item.

<!-- End Description -->

</font></p>

<p><font face="Times New Roman" color="#000000" size="2">

<!-- Enter your payment terms and details here. -->

</font></p>

<p><font face="Times New Roman" color="#000000" size="2">

<!-- Enter your shipping terms and details here. -->

</font></p>

</td>
</tr>
</table>

<!-- End Description Table -->
```

In Figure 17-4, you can see the results of the preceding auction item description template. We sold many copies of this item successfully on eBay.

Many auction sites, including eBay, host pictures for your item — often for free. For example, eBay hosts one picture for free, but you pay for extra pictures. You might also consider looking into sites such as Andale (www.andale.com) that offer image-hosting services for online auction sellers.

Figure 17-4:
The
template as
it appeared
on eBay.

Chapter 18

A Company Site

Companies large and small differ on their office dress policy — from being required to wear three-piece suits in the office to being allowed to work in a SpongeBob T-shirt and torn cutoffs. However, all companies, despite the differences in formality, want to present themselves effectively to the outside world. As such, they want their Web sites to reek of confidence, capability, and professionalism. No one feels good about handing over their hard-earned money to a company whose Web site looks cheesy and tacky (unless the company sells cheese and tacks).

In this chapter, you explore the basics of creating a company Web site and look at the typical elements you want to utilize as you design your own company's site.

Issues to Consider When Designing Your Site

When you start to plan your company's Web site, the most important task is to consider the kind of people who are going to visit your Web site — potential or existing customers, clients, or partners. After you determine a list of the types of visitors, brainstorm about what they will want from your Web site.

Working with the concept of *personas,* in which you envision a few of the site's visitors and what they each want to get from the site, can be valuable. As you lay out the site, think about how each of these imaginary people interacts with your design. Will they find what they're looking for?

If you are designing a site for a company that has many departments, you will discover that they have different goals. For instance, marketing wants the front page of the site to be a gigantic Flash animation showing all the company's products, whereas management wants every page on the site to look exactly like a corporate brochure and to be identical in every browser known to man.

Your job, as a Web designer and developer, is not only to design the site but also to educate people around you as to what is actually possible and feasible — while staying within a certain budget.

Basic Elements of a Company's Web Site

As you consider creating a company's Web site, keep in mind the following basic elements that you typically want to include in your site. Our site consists of six files:

- **The initial Web page,** index.html, is the site's home page. It contains the basic marketing message about the company and its products.

  A site's home page can have any of a variety of file names, such as index.html, default.html, and home.html. You want to check with your Webmaster or your Web-hosting provider to determine the exact filename you should use. However, in general, the filename index.html will almost always work.

- **The products page,** products.html, contains summary information about each of the company's products.

- **The contact us page,** contact.html, contains a form that the visitor can fill out in order to give his or her opinion to the company.

- **The press page,** press.html, contains

  - Links to the press releases generated by the company

  - Information that marketing thinks members of the press might want

  This page isn't discussed in the rest of the chapter, but you can easily modify the basic HTML template discussed for the other site pages to create this unique page.

✔ **An image,** `building.gif`, is displayed on the site's home page to give visitors the initial impression of the company and its site. This could be any image, from a company logo to pictures of employees in action.

✔ **A style sheet,** `stylesheet.css`, contains the formatting instructions for each page of the site.

Every page links to this style sheet by using the `<link>` tag. A change in this file changes the appearance of every page on the site.

The home page

Listing 18-1 shows the home-page markup for MegaCorp, our fictitious company. Figure 18-1 shows how it looks when displayed in a browser.

Listing 18-1: Our Company's Home Page (index.html)

```
<!DOCTYPE html PUBLIC "-//W3C//DTD XHTML 1.0 Transitional//EN"
    "http://www.w3.org/TR/xhtml1/DTD/xhtml1-transitional.dtd">
<html xmlns="http://www.w3.org/1999/xhtml">
<head>
    <title>MegaCorp Home Page</title>
    <meta http-equiv="Content-Type" content="text/html; charset=ISO-8859-1" />
    <link rel="stylesheet" href="stylesheet.css" />
</head>
<body>
<div id="navbar">
    <h4>Home &larr;</h4>
    <h4><a href="products.html">Products</a></h4>
    <h4><a href="press.html">Press</a></h4>
    <h4><a href="contact.html">Contact Us</a></h4>
</div>
<div id="main">
<h1>
<img src="building.gif" height="145" width="145" alt="Our building"
  hspace="10" align="middle" />Welcome to MegaCorp Online</h1>
<!-- Insert text for your company here -->
</div>
<div id="footer">
    All contents of this site &copy; 1999-2005 MegaCorp International,
    All Rights Reserved
</div>
</body>
</html>
```

As you look at the markup in Listing 18-1, you can see that it doesn't contain any information about colors, fonts, or how the page itself should be displayed. All that information is in the style sheet, which allows the most flexible approach to updating the site in the future.

Figure 18-1:
Our
company's
home page.

The navigation used in the home page and for the other site pages is based on the text rollover example discussed in Chapter 15. These rollovers are simple, are fast-loading, and can be *spidered* (automatically searched for keywords) by search engines such as Google. They also *degrade* (they work even if they don't do the fancy stuff) nicely in older browsers.

If you want to use this template for your home page, just

- Change the contents of the `<title>` and `<h1>` tags.
- Add the company's description where the template shows the HTML comment "Insert text for your company here."

A few slightly tricky things are going on in the navigation section (the part inside the `<div>` with the `id` of `navbar`):

- Each option is placed inside an `<h4>` tag, but only the last three are also within an `<a>` tag. That's because we don't want visitors to try to rollover and then click a Home link because they're already at the home page. Similarly, on each of the other pages, the link corresponding to the current page is disabled.

- The word *Home* on this page is followed by a leftward-pointing arrow (`&larr;`). That's another way of showing visitors which page they're currently on.

- The arrow and the word *Home* are separated by a nonbreaking space ` `. This special space keeps these two pieces in the same line, even if a browser is set oddly.

✔ The navigation menu shown in Listing 18-1 and the text rollover menu shown in Chapter 15 are slightly different — this one's modified to display each link the same whether the visitor has been to that page or not. You can compare the two styles and use the one you prefer.

Why use this type of navigation? Because it's simple to add, remove, or modify elements:

✔ Delete a line of markup, and the other menu items move up to fill the gap.

✔ Add a line with matching markup, and it automatically appears just as it should.

The products page

Listing 18-2 and Figure 18-2 show the company's products page and demonstrate how the overall look is the same, yet slightly different, for an interior site page.

Listing 18-2: Our Company's Products Page (products.html)

```
<!DOCTYPE html PUBLIC "-//W3C//DTD XHTML 1.0 Transitional//EN"
    "http://www.w3.org/TR/xhtml1/DTD/xhtml1-transitional.dtd">
<html xmlns="http://www.w3.org/1999/xhtml">
<head>
    <title>MegaCorp's Products</title>
    <meta http-equiv="Content-Type" content="text/html; charset=ISO-8859-1" />
    <link rel="stylesheet" href="stylesheet.css" />
</head>
<body>
<div id="navbar">
    <h4><a href="index.html">Home</a></h4>
    <h4>Products &larr;</h4>
    <h4><a href="press.html">Press</a></h4>
    <h4><a href="contact.html">Contact Us</a></h4>
</div>
<div id="main">
<h1 align="center">MegaCorp's Products</h1>
<p>Say something here about your products</p>
<ul>
    <li>Product 1 goes here</li>
    <li>Product 2 goes here</li>
</ul>
</div>
<div id="footer">
    All contents of this site &copy; 1999-2005 MegaCorp International,
    All Rights Reserved
</div>
</body>
</html>
```

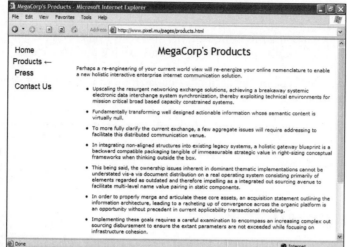

Figure 18-2:
Our
company's
products
page.

To use the template shown in Listing 18-2, perform the following steps:

1. **Customize the title, heading, and navigation bar for your page.**

2. **Add descriptive text within the <p> that describes your products.**

3. **Describe each product specifically within the individual <li> tags.**

You can add links to subpages from within the individual product descriptions. If you do this, use this page as a template for the individual product pages, but make sure the Products link is enabled in the navigation bar. That way, site visitors can retrace their steps back to where they came from without clicking the Back button.

It's all greeked to me

If you would like to mock up a page for which you don't yet have actual content, we recommend using greeked text. *Greeked text* is placeholder text that typically starts with the Latin phrase "Lorem Ipsum."

If you want to add greeked text to your page, check out www.lipsum.com, which will let you choose such options as the number of words, paragraphs, and bytes of greeked text you need. Then you can copy and paste the placeholder text into your page.

The contact page

This simple page allows visitors to the site to send their feedback directly to the company. All it asks for is a name, an e-mail address, and the message to be sent, as shown in Listing 18-3 and Figure 18-3.

Listing 18-3:   Contact Our Company (contact.html)

```
<!DOCTYPE html PUBLIC "-//W3C//DTD XHTML 1.0 Transitional//EN"
    "http://www.w3.org/TR/xhtml1/DTD/xhtml1-transitional.dtd">
<html xmlns="http://www.w3.org/1999/xhtml">
<head>
    <title>Contact MegaCorp</title>
    <meta http-equiv="Content-Type" content="text/html; charset=ISO-8859-1" />
    <link rel="stylesheet" href="stylesheet.css" />
</head>
<body>
<div id="navbar">
    <h4><a href="index.html">Home</a></h4>
    <h4><a href="products.html">Products</a></h4>
    <h4><a href="press.html">Press</a></h4>
    <h4>Contact Us &larr;</h4>
</div>
<div id="main">
<h1 align="center">Contact MegaCorp</h1>
<h2>MegaCorp values your opinions!</h2>
<form action="mailto:contact@example.com" method="post" enctype="text/plain">
    <p>Name: <input type="text" size="20" /></p>
    <p>Email: <input type="text" size="20" /></p>
    <p>Your message:<br />
    <textarea name="Message" rows="10" cols="30"></textarea></p>
    <input type="submit" value="Submit" /> 
    <input type="reset" value="Reset" />
</form>
</div>
<div id="footer">
    All contents of this site &copy; 1999-2005 MegaCorp International,
    All Rights Reserved
</div>
</body>
</html>
```

You could make the contact page considerably smarter by adding a little JavaScript that verifies whether valid information is entered into each of the fields. You want to make sure that

✔ A name was entered.

✔ Some text was entered in the message `<textarea>` field.

✔ Something resembling an e-mail address was given in the e-mail address field. (But there's no way to verify that the e-mail address belongs to the person filling out the form.)

Embedding an e-mail address into the HTML markup like this is generally a bad idea. It works, but spammers usually find the e-mail address in the HTML file and abuse it. In the long run, it's smarter to use a Common Gateway Interface (CGI) that handles the address on the server side. See Chapter 14 for more information on forms handling or contact your Webmaster or Web host for assistance.

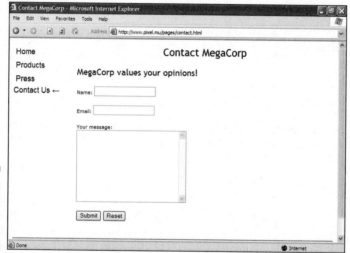

Figure 18-3:
Contacting
our
company.

The style sheet

Listing 18-4 is a very basic version of a style sheet. All the HTML pages in this Web site reference this style sheet. The great advantage of using a style sheet to define your formatting instructions is that you can update this one file to give the whole site an entirely new look.

Listing 18-4:   The Site-wide Style Sheet (stylesheet.css)

```
body {color: #000; background-color: #FFF}
body, p {font: 11px/14px verdana, geneva, arial, helvetica, sans-serif}

h1 {font: 24px "trebuchet ms", verdana, arial, helvetica, geneva, sans-serif}
h2 {font: 20px "trebuchet ms", verdana, arial, helvetica, geneva, sans-serif}
```

```
h4 {font: 18px geneva, sans-serif; margin: 0; color: #000;
   background-color: #FFF}
   a {text-decoration: none}

div#navbar {width: 120px; float: left}
div#navbar a {display:block; margin: 0}
div#navbar a:link, a:visited  {color: #000}
div#navbar a:hover {color: #FFF; background-color: #000}

div#main {width: 80%; float:right}

div#footer {border-color: gray; border-width: 2px 0px 0px 0px;
            border-style: solid; color: gray; padding: 6px 0px 10px 0px;
            display: block; float: none; clear: both;
            margin: 20px 0px 0px 0px}

li {margin-bottom: 10px}
```

As shown in Figure 18-1 earlier in the chapter, the site's style sheet changes the menu items from white-on-black to black-on-white when the cursor moves over them. That works well for this book because it's in black and white. For a live Web site, change this to something a little less stark by changing the colors in the line that starts with `div#navbar a:hover`. You can also modify the style sheet to change such attributes as

- The whole page background
- The navigation background color
- Fonts

Chapter 19

A Product Catalog

*I*n days gone by, a product catalog was a big production and investment. Not only was the cost of producing a printed color catalog high, but sending it out to every George, Jerry, and Kramer out there in the world meant only the big companies could afford it. Unless your name was J. Peterman, J.C. Penney, or Eddie Bauer, you had no way to reach a broad audience with your catalog.

The Internet, of course, changed all this. Now, whether you are part of a big or a small company, you can economically produce and maintain a professional-looking catalog on your Web site. And, without a significant investment, you can even sell directly to your customers from an online store.

This chapter covers the basics of creating a product catalog and selling your goods on the Web.

Dissecting a Product Catalog

A product catalog usually includes these components:

▸ **A navigation interface** to help the user move easily through the catalog.

The navigation interface is normally a menu system. Navigation interfaces are discussed briefly in Chapter 3.

✔ **At least one category page,** with several items listed in each category.

Choosing a category from the menu system brings the user to a category page, which identifies individual items with

- Thumbnail images
- A brief description

The image and title of an item are linked to that item's detail page. The user clicks the link for detailed information about an item.

The site may allow the user to purchase items from the category page. (Some sites require purchases from the item's detail page.)

✔ **A detail page for each item in the catalog,** which usually displays

- At least one large image of the item.
- A detailed description of the item.
- A button that adds the item to the site's *shopping cart,* if the site allows purchases. (This chapter covers shopping carts later.)

Design basics

Whether you *sell* directly to online buyers or just *show* your retail store's inventory, keep these design principles in mind:

✔ **Keep your catalog clean.** Your online store should encourage users to *browse*. Users should see many items quickly and easily get more detail on items that interest them.

✔ **Make your site design colorful, interesting, and fun.** (But keep the size of the graphics as small as possible — less than 30k per photo — so pages download quickly.)

✔ **Make it easy to get around.** Your site navigation should be easy, logical, and obvious. If site visitors find interesting items quickly, they buy. Otherwise, they lose interest and find what they want elsewhere.

✔ **Provide detail.** Visitors can't see or touch the item, so printed detail is a must. There aren't any space limitations on the Web (unlike a printed catalog), so you can include all the detail users might want on an item. (Information about shipping charges, returns, and contact should be easy to find, too.)

✔ **Make buying easy if you're selling.** Streamline the buying process as much as possible. An online purchase shouldn't take more than three screens. You'll make more sales and gain repeat customers.

An amazing number of online stores use shopping cart software that seems positively *user-hostile*. Buyers must fill out page after page of selection and confirmation screens before completing the sale.

This chapter's example of a product catalog uses the following resources:

✔ Two templates for the product catalog:

- A category page with small images of items within that category

- A detail page for one example item

✔ The navigational menu system

Figure 19-1 shows an example category page for a fictional outdoor equipment store, Adventure Tools. Site visitors can click either the thumbnail picture of the item or the item's name to go to the item's detail page.

After a visitor clicks an item in the category page, the item detail page appears, as shown in Figure 19-2. This page contains the all-important Add to Cart button, which allows the visitor to purchase the item.

Figure 19-1: A category page from the online catalog.

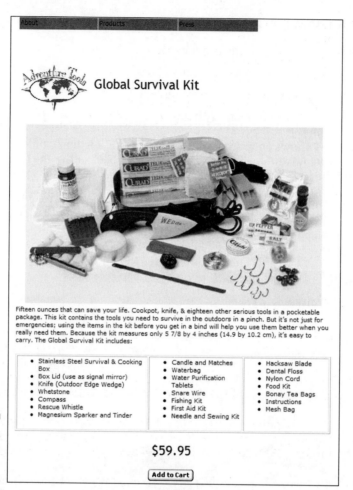

Figure 19-2:
An item
detail page.

Choosing a Shopping Cart

If you want people to purchase from your site, you need a *shopping cart*. The cart allows buyers to purchase items and pay for them (usually with a credit card or a bank account transaction).

The shopping cart software (which runs on a Web server) leads the buyer through the steps of buying a product online:

1. The buyer selects an item and adds it to the shopping cart.

2. If the buyer wants to shop for other items, he or she can continue shopping and place other items in the shopping cart.

3. When ready to purchase, the buyer chooses to move to the *checkout* process.

   At checkout, the shopping cart software

   - Totals the purchases

   - Adds shipping costs (if necessary)

   - Leads the buyer through the payment process of entering such details as a credit card number and shipping address

In concept, a shopping cart for an online store is fairly simple. But in execution, it can get complex. This chapter surveys only the basics of e-commerce. If you are going to dive into it fully, we recommend these books:

   ✔ *Starting an Online Business For Dummies* (Wiley)

   ✔ *MySQL/PHP Database Applications* (Wiley)

PayPal

In this chapter, we focus on using the shopping cart from a well-known e-commerce site, PayPal. Owned by eBay, PayPal's shopping cart is free for you to use on your Web site. Your customers can purchase multiple items with a single payment, and you can accept credit card and bank account payments. (PayPal charges you a transaction fee when you receive a payment.)

PayPal offers a button generator that takes information about the name and price of an item you have for sale and creates HTML markup for an Add to Cart button that you then insert directly into your product catalog page.

This button generator and the PayPal shopping cart require a PayPal Premier or Merchant account. (PayPal Personal accounts can't accept debit or credit card payments; they just send and receive transfers from bank accounts.)

Other e-commerce solutions

PayPal is one of the easiest shopping carts to implement on your site, but many others are available.

The following technologies require a more serious business and financial commitment to setting up your online presence.

Hosting e-commerce services

Hosted e-commerce services let you build an online storefront on your site but let the service provider deal with the technical aspects of your store and transaction processing.

A good example of the online storefront service is Yahoo! Merchant Solutions (`http://smallbusiness.yahoo.com/merchant`). You can create a storefront hosted on a Yahoo! server with such features as your own domain name, a product catalog, site-building tools (that let you avoid using raw HTML if you want), a secure shopping cart, e-mail order confirmations, integration with UPS for shipping, and order statistics tools. An online store on Yahoo! is fairly easy to set up and operate, especially if you're more merchant than Web developer. Prices start at about $40 a month.

Do-it-yourself software

If you are really a technical guru and aren't faint of heart, you can install full-featured shopping cart software on your own Web server and configure it manually.

If you choose this option, you need the technical know-how, a Web server, and constant Internet connection for hosting your e-commerce Web site.

One do-it-yourself shopping cart software package is Zen Cart (`www.zen-cart.com`). It's a free, open-source shopping cart written in PHP. Stores created with Zen Cart are almost infinitely customizable and have many useful features, such as allowing customer reviews of your products and the ability to customize tax and shipping rates for everywhere you sell your items.

If you use Zen Cart, you should expect to spend at least a few days setting up your store before you're ready for business. You need to know how to upload and install the Zen Cart software on your server, how to rename files and set Unix permissions on your server, and how to create a MySQL database. Then you need to create or modify the page templates for your store and set up many other server-side parameters.

In general, we recommend you stick with PayPal or a hosted e-commerce solution to avoid the complexity of trying to do it all yourself.

Incorporating a PayPal shopping cart

Creating the HTML markup for the shopping cart is easy; use the PayPal site's button generator, and then copy and paste the markup into your Web page.

To use the PayPal shopping cart, you must be a PayPal Premier or Merchant account holder. After you have an account established, you can create your own Add to Cart button and View Cart button by performing the instructions shown in the following sections.

Add to Cart button

Follow these steps to insert an Add to Cart button on your page:

1. **In your Web browser, go to the PayPal site:** `https://www.paypal.com`.

   This site is secure, so all transactions are encrypted between the site and your browser.

2. **Log in to your Premier or Merchant account.**

   Your account overview appears, as shown in Figure 19-3. We blur out the name and e-mail for security reasons.

Figure 19-3:
Logging in
to your
PayPal
account.

PayPal   Log Out | Help

| My Account | Send Money | Request Money | Merchant Tools | Auction Tools |

Overview | Add Funds | Withdraw | History | Resolution Center | Profile

Activate Account   **U.S. Premier Account Overview**

Add auction account

Name: ▒▒▒▒▒▒▒▒▒
Email: ▒▒▒▒▒▒▒▒▒ (Add email)
Status: Verified (35)

3. **Click the Merchant Tools tab.**

4. **On the Merchant Tools page, click the PayPal Shopping Cart link.**

5. **On the PayPal Shopping Cart page, fill out the information about the item you want to sell, as shown in Figure 19-4.**

   You must enter the item name, the price, and the currency you accept. An item number (used in reports that PayPal provides for you after the sale) and the default country for the buyer's payment form are optional.

Figure 19-4:
Enter your
item's
information.

Enter the details of the item you wish to sell (optional)

Item Name/Service: Global Survival Kit

Item ID/Number: KT001
(optional)

Price of Item/Service
you want to sell: 59.95   ($2,000.00 USD limit for new buyers) [?]

Currency: U.S. Dollars   [?]

If you want your buyer's payment form to default to a specific country, select a country below.
Otherwise, do nothing and your buyers can choose for themselves.

Buyer's Country: United States   [?]
(Optional)

6. **In the Select an Add to Cart Button section, click to select the button style shown, as in Figure 19-5.**

Select an Add to Cart button

Your customers will use the image you select below to add items to their shopping cart before they checkout.

⦿ [Add to Cart]   Choose a different button

Or customize your button! Just enter the exact URL of any image on your website.

◯ Yes, I would like to use my own image

Button Image URL: http://

If you don't like the style shown, click the Choose a Different Button link to pick a different button style.

You can *create* a button image and use it with the PayPal shopping cart:

    a. Create the button graphic in an image-editing program.

    b. Upload the graphic to a Web server.

    c. Select the Yes, I Would Like to Use My Own Image radio button on the PayPal Shopping Cart page.

    d. Fill in the URL for the graphic on your Web server.

7. **Click the Create Button Now button at the bottom of the page.**

8. **On the Add a Button to Your Website page, select *all* the text in the Add to Cart Button Code field (as shown in Figure 19-6), and then choose Edit⇨Copy in your browser.**

Add a button to your website

Copy your custom HTML code
The HTML code below contains your "Add to Cart" button. Copy the code and paste it into onto your webpage. When your customers press the buttons they will be taken to a webpage listing the items they have added to their cart.

Add to Cart Button code

```
<form target="paypal"
action="https://www.paypal.com/cgi-
bin/webscr" method="post">
<input type="image"
src="https://www.paypal.com//en_US/i/bt
n/x-click-but22.gif" border="0"
```

9. **Switch to your HTML page editor and paste the cart code where you want the button to appear, as in Figure 19-7.**

Figure 19-7:
Pasting the
code into
your HTML
page.

10. **Save and preview the HTML page you just modified in your Web browser to see the button on the page, as shown in Figure 19-8.**

Figure 19-8:
The
completed
Add to Cart
button on
the page.

View Cart button

If you add a View Cart button on your page, as shown in Figure 19-8, follow these steps:

1. **Go to the PayPal Add a Button to Your Website page.**

   This HTML markup was generated at the same time as the Add a Button HTML markup.

2. **Select *all* the text in the View Cart Button Code field.**

3. **Copy and paste the code into your HTML page.**

Page Markup

Listing 19-1 includes the markup for the category page.

Listing 19-1: Category Page Template

```
<!DOCTYPE html PUBLIC "-//W3C//DTD XHTML 1.0 Transitional//EN"
        "http://www.w3.org/TR/xhtml1/DTD/xhtml1-transitional.dtd">
<html xmlns="http://www.w3.org/1999/xhtml">
<head>
<title>Your Title Here</title>
<meta http-equiv="Content-Type" content="text/html; charset=ISO-8859-1" />
<!-- External stylesheet for the menu system -->
<link rel="stylesheet" href="menu.css" />
<!-- Stylesheet for this page -->
   <style type="text/css">
      body {color: #000; background-color: #FFF;}
      body, p {font-family: tahoma, verdana, arial; font-size: 12px;}
      hr {color: #369; height: 1px}
      h1 {font: 24px "trebuchet ms", verdana, arial, helvetica, geneva,
         sans-serif;}
      h2 {margin-bottom: 0px; margin-top: 0px; font-size: 18px; color:
         #DBEAF5;}
      .darkline {background: #4682B4;}
      .cright {font-family: Tahoma, Verdana, sans-serif; font-size: 12px;
            color: #FFF; background: #4682B4; text-align: right;}
      body,p {font: 11px/14px verdana, geneva, arial, helvetica,
            sans-serif;}
      .style1 {font-size: 14px;}
   </style>
</head>
<body bgcolor="#ffffff">
<!-- External script references for the menu system -->
<script language="JavaScript" src="menu.js" type="text/javascript"></script>
<script language="JavaScript" src="menu_items.js"
   type="text/javascript"></script>
<script language="JavaScript" src="menu_tpl.js" type="text/javascript"></script>
<script language="JavaScript" type="text/javascript">
<!--//
   new menu (MENU_ITEMS, MENU_POS, MENU_STYLES);
//-->
</script>
<div style="height: 50px;"> </div>
<!-- Enter your logo image and category headline below. -->
<h1 align="left"><img src="yourlogo.gif" alt="Alternative text" hspace="10"
   align="middle" />Your Headline </h1>
<p align="left" class="style1">
<!-- Replace this comment with a description of the category. -->
</p>
<p align="left" class="yourstyle"> </p>
<table width="642" height="352" border="0" align="left">
   <tr>
      <!-- First item picture -->
   <td width="300" height="204"><img src="item1small.jpg"
```

```
       alt="Alternative text" align="bottom" /></td>
  <td width="28"> </td>
    <!-- Second item picture -->
  <td width="300"><img src="item2small.jpg" alt="Alternative text"
     align="bottom" /></td>
  </tr>
  <tr>
  <td height="35"><h1 align="center">Item 1 Name</h1>
  <h1 align="center">Item 1 price</h1>
  <p align="left">Item 1 short description.</p></td>
  <td> </td>
  <td height="35">
  <h1 align="center"><br />Item 2 Name</h1>
  <h1 align="center">Item 2 price</h1>
  <p align="left">Item 2 short description.</p></td>
  </tr>
</table>
<p> </p>
</body>
</html>
```

Listing 19-2 includes the markup for the detail page template.

Listing 19-2:   Detail Page Template

```
<!DOCTYPE html PUBLIC "-//W3C//DTD XHTML 1.0 Transitional//EN"
      "http://www.w3.org/TR/xhtml1/DTD/xhtml1-transitional.dtd">
<html xmlns="http://www.w3.org/1999/xhtml">
<head>
   <title>Your Page Title Here</title>
   <meta http-equiv="Content-Type" content="text/html; charset=ISO-8859-1" />
   <!-- External stylesheet for the menu system -->
   <link rel="stylesheet" href="menu.css" />
   <!-- Stylesheet for this page -->
      <style type="text/css">
        body {color: #000; background-color: #FFF;}
        body, p {font-family: tahoma, verdana, arial; font-size: 12px;}
        hr {color: #369; height: 1px;}
        h1 {font: 24px "trebuchet ms", verdana, arial, helvetica, geneva,
           sans-serif;}
        h2 { margin-bottom: 0px; margin-top: 0px; font-size: 18px; color:
           #DBEAF5;}
        .darkline { background: #4682B4;}
        .cright {font-family: Tahoma, Verdana, sans-serif; font-size: 12px;
           color: #FFF; background: #4682B4; text-align: right;}
        body,p {font: 11px/14px verdana, geneva, arial, helvetica, sans-serif;}
        .style1 {font-size: 14px;}
      </style>
```

(continued)

Listing 19-2 *(continued)*

```
</head>
<body bgcolor="#ffffff">
   <!-- External script references for the menu system -->
<script language="JavaScript" src="menu.js" type="text/javascript"></script>
<script language="JavaScript" src="menu_items.js"
   type="text/javascript"></script>
<script language="JavaScript" src="menu_tpl.js"
   type="text/javascript"></script>
<script language="JavaScript" type="text/javascript">
   <!--//
   new menu (MENU_ITEMS, MENU_POS, MENU_STYLES);
   //-->
</script>
<div style="height: 50px;"> </div>
<h1 align="left">
   <!-- Add your logo and headline below. -->
<img src="yourlogo.gif" alt="Alternative text" hspace="10"
   align="middle" />Your Headline Here</h1>
<!-- Begin detail table -->
<table width="604" height="352" border="0" align="left">
   <tr>
<!-- Add your item's detail picture here. -->
<td width="598" height="204"><div align="center"><img src="item-pic.jpg"
      alt="Alternative text" align="top" /></div></td>
</tr>
<tr>
<td height="35"><p align="left">
   <!-- Replace this comment with your item description. -->
</p>
<h1 align="center">Replace with your item's price.</h1>
<h1 align="center">
   <!-- Begin PayPal Add to Cart button code -->
   <!-- Replace this comment with the pasted Add to Cart button code. -->
   <!-- End PayPal Add to Cart button code -->
   <!-- Begin PayPal View Cart button code -->
   <!-- Replace this comment with the pasted View Cart button code. -->
   <!-- End PayPal View Cart button code -->
</h1></td>
</tr>
</table>
<p> </p>
</body>
</html>
```

Part VI
The Part of Tens

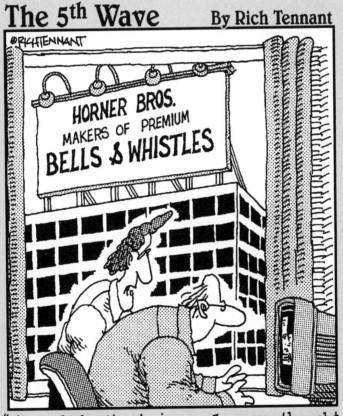

The 5th Wave   By Rich Tennant

HORNER BROS.
MAKERS OF PREMIUM
BELLS & WHISTLES

"As a Web site designer I never thought
I'd say this, but I don't think your
site has enough bells and whistles."

In this part . . .

Here we point you at some undeniably cool HTML tools, cover top do's and don'ts for HTML markup, and help you catch potential bugs and errors in your Web pages. With our tongues planted firmly in our cheeks (that makes it kind of hard to talk, you know), we try to recap some of the most important advice and information in this book. Enjoy!

Chapter 20

Ten Cool HTML Tools

*H*TML documents are made of plain old text. You can make one with a basic text editor like Notepad. Once upon a time, that was all Web authors used.

As the Web has evolved, so have the tools used to create Web pages. Nowadays, Web authoring is so complex that a simple text editor is a big headache unless

✔ You don't care about graphics and HTML validation.

✔ You're on a quick in-and-out mission to make small changes to an existing HTML document.

As you get more experience with HTML, you'll build your HTML toolbox. This chapter helps you stock that toolbox. Some of these tools may already be on your system, quietly waiting to help you create amazing Web pages.

When you go shopping for items for your HTML toolbox, look for good buys. Students and educators often qualify for big discounts on major-brand software, but careful shopping can save on just about any software purchase. Try comparison-shopping at sites like CNET Shopper (www.shopper.com) or PC Magazine (http://pcmag.shopping.com).

HTML Editors

This book explains how to create and maintain (X)HTML pages with nothing more complicated than a pocketknife and a ball of string. But HTML editors can turn the chore of creating complicated (X)HTML pages into an easy task.

HTML editors come in two flavors. The flavor you need depends on the complexity of the Web page you are creating or editing.

- ✔ **Helper editors** have fewer capabilities.
- ✔ **WYSIWYG** (what you see is what you get) **editors** do everything but your laundry.

Helper editors

An HTML helper works like it sounds. It helps you create HTML, but it doesn't do all the markup work for you.

In a helper, HTML is displayed "raw" — tags and all. You can reach right into the code and tweak it (if you have *HTML 4 For Dummies*).

But good helpers save time and lighten your load. Functions like these make HTML development easier and more fun:

- ✔ Tags are a different color than content.
- ✔ The spell checker knows tags aren't misspelled words.

Use a helper editor when you're building complex tables or multilevel lists. The more complex your markup, the more help a helper editor can provide!

HomeSite+: The champ

HomeSite+ is an HTML editor suitable for both beginners and professionals. It requires HTML knowledge to use, but it assists you at every step.

If you have Macromedia Dreamweaver MX, you have HomeSite+ (`www.macromedia.com/software`).

We like the HomeSite+ interface. You can

- ✔ Browse images directly in the editor.
- ✔ Customize the toolbars and menus for your personal needs.

✔ Create a browser view instantly by clicking a tab.

✔ Move and use context menus with a right-click of your mouse.

Text is easy to enhance and modify with

✔ Color-coded HTML

✔ Integrated spell checker

✔ Search-and-replace tools to update whole projects, folders, and files

✔ Internal HTML validation

✔ Extensive online help with accessing documentation on HTML and other popular scripting languages

HomeSite+ helps you perform

✔ Project management

✔ Link verification

✔ File uploads to a remote Web server

If you don't have HomeSite+, try one of the following challengers as your helper editor instead.

Contenders

There are many more good HTML helper editors than there are good WYSI-WYG editors. Here's our slate of alternatives.

BBEdit

BBEdit rules the Macintosh world. It comes in two versions:

✔ The free product formerly known as BBEdit Lite is still free, but has been superseded by a newer, free text editor called TextWrangler.

✔ BBEdit ($200 retail)

If you don't need the powerful and specialized set of HTML editing, preview, and cleanup tools of BBEdit, use TextWrangler and save! (A detailed features comparison that also includes BBEdit Lite is available online at `www.barebones.com/products/bbedit/threeway.shtml`.)

If you use a Macintosh, check BBEdit out at `www.barebones.com`.

HTML-Kit

HTML-Kit is a compact Windows tool with

- ✔ Menu-driven support for both HTML and Cascading Style Sheets (CSS) markup
- ✔ A nice preview window for a browser's-eye view of your markup

If you want to download HTML-Kit, go to `www.chami.com/html-kit`.

WYSIWYG editors

A WYSIWYG editor creates HTML for you as you create and lay out Web page content on your computer display (often by dragging and dropping visual elements, or working through GUI menus and options), shielding your delicate eyes from naked markup along the way. These tools look much like word processors or page-layout programs; they do a lot of the work for you.

WYSIWYG editors make your work easier and save hours of endless coding — you have a life, right? — but you should only use WYSIWYG editors in the initial design stage. For example, you can use a WYSIWYG editor to create a complex table in under a minute and then use a helper to refine and tweak your HTML markup directly.

Dreamweaver: the champ

Dreamweaver is the best WYSIWYG Web development tool for Macintosh and PC systems. Many (if not most) Web developers use Dreamweaver. Dreamweaver is an all-in-one product that supports

- ✔ Web site creation
- ✔ Maintenance
- ✔ Content management

The current version is Dreamweaver MX 2004. It also belongs to a suite of products, Studio MX 2004, that work together to provide a full spectrum of Internet solutions. Studio MX also includes Fireworks MX 2004, Flash MX 2004, ColdFusion MX, and Freehand MX.

Dreamweaver has an easy-to-follow-and-learn dialog box so you can style Web pages with CSS without even knowing what a style rule is! Many of the benefits of Dreamweaver stem from its sleek user interface and its respect for clean HTML. You can learn more about Dreamweaver by visiting the Macromedia Web site at `www.macromedia.com`.

If you're too low on funds for a top-of-the-line WYSIWYG HTML editor like Dreamweaver MX (suggested retail price is about $500, but discounts of up to $200 are available), there are other possibilities. You can ponder the suggestions in the next section or go a-searching on the Web (the search string "WYSIWYG HTML editor" should do nicely) to find lots more still!

Contenders

WYSIWYG editors generate allegiances that can seem as pointless as the enmity between owners of Ford and Chevy trucks. Both of the following editors have fans, and they can both produce great Web pages.

- ✔ **FrontPage 2003** is Microsoft's latest version of its award-winning Web site builder. It's in all MS Office 2003 versions.

  `www.microsoft.com/frontpage/`

- ✔ **GoLive** cs is Adobe's latest version of its Web publishing toolset. It's included in Adobe Creative Suite Premium.

  `www.adobe.com/products/golive`

Graphics Tools

Graphics applications are beasts. They can do marvelous things, but learning how to use them can be overwhelming at first.

If you aren't artistically inclined, consider paying someone else to do your graphics work. Graphics applications can be pricey and complicated. But you should have some kind of high-function (if not high-end) graphics program to tweak images should you need to. Our highest rating goes to Adobe Photoshop, but considering its cost and an average newbie HTML hacker's budget, we discuss a lower-cost alternative first in the following section.

Photoshop Elements: The amateur champ

At around $150, Adobe Photoshop Elements is an affordable PC- and Mac-based starter version of the full-blown Photoshop (the gold standard for graphics). You can do almost anything with Photoshop Elements that you might need for beginning and intermediate-level graphics editing. The current version of the program is Photoshop Elements 3.0.

This product is for you if you want to add images to your site but you don't want to make graphic arts your full-time living (or your full-time obsession).

To learn more about Photoshop Elements, visit www.adobe.com, select Products⇨Digital Imaging, and then select whichever version of Photoshop Elements (PC or Mac) you want to read more about from the Digital Imaging Products drop-down menu.

If you're really on a tight budget, check out the $100, PC-only Paint Shop Pro at www.jasc.com instead. It does nearly everything that Photoshop Elements does and costs about one-third less.

Professional contenders

If you work with lots of photographs or other high-resolution, high-quality images or artwork, you may need one of these tools for Web graphics.

Adobe Photoshop

If it weren't so darned expensive, we'd grant top honors to Photoshop. Alas, $650 is too rich for many novices' budgets. Wondering whether to upgrade from Photoshop Elements? Adobe mentions these capabilities among its "Top reasons to upgrade":

- **Improved file browser:** Shows and tells you more about more kinds of graphics files and gives you more-powerful search tools.
- **Shadow/Highlight correction:** Powerful built-in tools add or manipulate shadows and highlights in images.
- **More-powerful color controls:** Color palettes and color-matching tools with detailed controls that Elements lacks.
- **Text on a path:** Full-blown Photoshop lets you define any kind of path graphically and then instructs text to follow that path. This provides fancy layout that Elements can't match.

If you need to apply sophisticated special effects, edits, or tweaks to high-resolution photorealistic images, full-blown Photoshop is your best choice. For most basic Web sites, however, Photoshop Elements is more than up to the task — which is why it's the most popular graphics editing tool.

Like its little brother Photoshop Elements, full-blown Photoshop works with both Macintosh and PC operating systems. The current version is Adobe Photoshop CS. It's included in all of Adobe's product suites.

Photoshop CS add-ons and plug-ins provide specialized functions — such as complex textures or special graphics effects. This extensibility is nice because graphics professionals who need such capabilities can buy them (most cost $100 and up, with $300 a pretty typical price) and add them without any muss or fuss. But those who don't need them don't have to buy them and thus don't need to pay extra for the base-level software.

Macromedia Fireworks

Fireworks is a graphics program designed specifically for Web use, so it offers lots of nice features and functions for that purpose. The current version is Macromedia Fireworks MX 2004.

Fireworks is tightly integrated with other Macromedia products and therefore is of potentially great interest if you're using (or considering) Dreamweaver. Simply put, this combination of Macromedia products makes it very easy to add graphical spice to Web pages.

For more information about Fireworks and related Macromedia products, check out `www.macromedia.com/software/fireworks`.

Link Checkers

A broken link on your site can be embarrassing. To spare your users the dreaded `404 Object Not Found` error message, use a link checker to make sure your links are

- ✔ Correctly formatted before you publish
- ✔ Live on the Web after you publish

  Other Web sites may change or disappear after you publish your site. Regularly check your site's links to make sure they still work.

The worst broken link points to a page on your own site.

Many HTML editors and Web servers include built-in local link checkers, and they may even scour the Web to check external links.

Web Link Validator: The champ

Web Link Validator 3.5 is a professional-strength tool at an affordable price ($27). We recommend it because it handles many kinds of links and reports clearly and concisely on their condition.

You can find Web Link Validator all over the Web. A good place to grab it is at `www.download.com` (search the program name to find it immediately).

Contenders

Both of the following programs are pretty good link checkers, They need a little elbow grease to learn and to use, but the price is right: *free*.

W3C Link Checker

This is a utility created by volunteers for the World Wide Web Consortium. You can either

✔ Download it from `http://validator.w3.org/docs/checklink.html`.

> You have a couple of download options:

- • Grab a compiled version for your computer and operating system and run it as-is.
- • Grab the source code and tweak it for your needs and situation.

✔ Use the online version at `http://validator.w3.org/checklink`.

MOMspider

Roy Fielding's MOMspider is a sentimental favorite. It was one of the first link checkers for Web folks. It runs on any machine that can compile *Perl* (every machine we know of), and it has lots of options to do the heavy lifting.

The ingredients are at `http://ftp.ics.uci.edu/pub/websoft/MOMspider`.

HTML Validators

Validation compares a document to a set of document rules — a Document Type Definition (DTD). Simply put, validation checks the actual markup and content against the DTD and flags any deviations it finds.

Typically, a document author follows this process:

1. **Create an HTML document in an HTML editor.**

   Let's say this step results in a file called `mypage.htm`.

2. **Submit** `mypage.htm` **to an HTML or XHTML validation site for inspection and validation.**

   If any problems or syntax errors are detected, the validator reports such errors in an annotated version of the original HTML document.

3. **If the validator reports errors, the author corrects those errors and resubmits the document for validation.**

Sometimes, breaking HTML rules is the only way for your page to look right in older Web browsers. But document rules exist for a reason: Nonstandard or incorrect HTML markup often produces odd or unpredictable results.

Browsers usually forgive markup errors. Most browsers identify HTML pages without an `<html>` element. But someday, markup languages will be so complex and precise that browsers won't be able to guess whether you're publishing in HTML or another extensible markup language. Get the markup right from the beginning and save yourself a bunch of trouble later.

HTML validation is built into many HTML editors.

W3C validator

The W3C has a free, Web-based validation system available at `http://validator.w3.org`.

The W3C validation tool lets you choose

✔ Which HTML or XHTML DTD version to check against your document

✔ Output formats:

- A *terse* output lists only the line numbers in your document, the boo-boos, and a brief description of each.
- A *verbose* output lists great detail about each error and links to the relevant information in the HTML specification.

Built-in validators

Many tools in this chapter offer HTML validation. These include HTML-Kit, HomeSite+, and BBEdit. Use 'em if you got 'em; get 'em if you don't!

FTP Clients

After you create your Web site on your computer, you have to share it with the world. So you need a tool to transfer your Web pages to your Web server.

Web servers do the heavy lifting

A Web server houses collections of stuff like pages and graphics for a Web site. You may have your own server. If you don't know if you have one, you don't. But don't run out and buy one!

A Web server runs special software that's dedicated to presenting and maintaining Web files (among several other Web-related tasks). If you don't have one of these supercomputers, your ISP (such as EarthLink or MSN) can host your pages for a fee. Many service providers include support for Web sites (normally up to 100MB in size) as part of their basic account offerings.

After you select a server host and you know how to access a Web server (your service provider should supply you with this information), upload your pages to that server by using FTP. That means you need an FTP program.

All FTP programs are similar and easy to operate. We recommend these:

- **WS_FTP Professional** for Windows is located at `www.ipswitch.com`.
- **Fetch** for the Mac is located at `http://fetchsoftworks.com`.

Swiss Army Knives

Collections of tools can help you manage and control your Web site. They're the Web version of a chunky red knife with a tool for every purpose. We call these *Swiss army knives.*

- **HTML Toolbox,** from NetMechanic, is the sharpest tool in the shed. This puppy has most of the features we recommend in this chapter, including link and spell checking and validation.

  This convenient little package costs you about $60 per year. If that's not too much to ask, check it out at

  `www.netmechanic.com/maintain.htm`

- **HTML-Kit** supports plug-ins to add functions such as link checks and spelling checks. Most of these plug-ins are free or inexpensive.

  `www.chami.com`

- **Easy HTML Construction Kit** offers a collection of useful conversion, reformatting, and template management tools. It's at

  `www.hermetic.ch/html.htm`

Chapter 21

Ten HTML Do's and Don'ts

*B*y itself, HTML is neither too complex nor overwhelmingly difficult. As some high-tech wags (including a few rocket scientists) have put it, *HTML ain't rocket science!* Nevertheless, important do's and don'ts can make or break the Web pages you build with HTML. Consider these humble admonishments as guidelines to make the most of HTML without losing touch with your users or watching your page blow up on its launch pad.

If some points we make throughout this book seem to crop up here, too (especially regarding proper and improper use of HTML), it's no accident. Heed ye well the prescriptions and avoid ye the maledictions. But hey, they're your pages. You can do what you want. Your users will decide the ultimate outcome. (We *never* say, "We told you so." Nope. Not us!)

Concentrate on Content

Any Web site lives or dies by its content. That a site is meaningful, that it delivers information directly, easily, and efficiently, and the reasonable expectation of finding something new and interesting on each new visit are all pluses. But all of those things (and more) rest on solid, useful content to give visitors a reason to come (and later, to return) to your site.

Never lose sight of your content

So we return to the crucial question of payload: page content. Why? Well, as Darrell Royal (legendary football coach of the University of Texas Longhorns in the '60s and '70s) is rumored to have said to his players, "Dance with who brung ya." In normal English (as opposed to Texan), this means that you should stick with the people who've supported you all along and give your loyalty to those who've given it to you.

We're not sure what this means for football, but for Web pages it means keeping faith with your users and keeping content paramount. If you don't have strong, solid, informative content, users quickly get that empty feeling that hits when Web pages are content-free. Then they'll be off to richer hunting grounds on the Web, looking for content somewhere else.

To satisfy user hunger, put your most important content on your site's major pages. Save the frills and supplementary materials for secondary pages. The short statement of this principle for HTML is, "Tags are important, but what's between the tags — the content — is what really counts." Chapters 2 and 3 cover making your content the best it can possibly be.

Structure your documents and your site

For users, a clear road map of your content is as important for a single home page as it is for an online encyclopedia. When longer or more complex documents grow into a full-fledged Web site, a road map becomes more important still. This map ideally takes the form of (you guessed it) a flow chart of page organization and links. If you like pictures with a purpose, the chart could appear in graphic form in an explicitly labeled site map.

We're strong advocates of top-down page design: Don't start writing content or placing tags until you understand what you want to say and how you want to organize your material. Then start building your HTML document or collection of documents with paper and pencil (or whatever modeling tool you like best). Sketch out relationships within the content and among your pages. Know where you're building before you roll out the heavy equipment.

Good content flows from good organization. It helps you stay on track during page design, testing, delivery, and maintenance. Organization helps users find their way through your site. Need we say more? Well, yes: Don't forget that *organization changes with time*. Revisit and critique your organization and structure on a regular basis, and don't be afraid to change either one to keep up with changes in content or focus.

Go Easy on the Graphics, Bells, Whistles, and Hungry Dinosaurs

Markup, scripting, and style sheets make many things possible. But not all possibilities deserve implementation, nor can Web sites live by snazzy graphics, special effects, and blinking marquees alone. Let your design and your content drive the markup, the graphics, and interaction, and your site will do its job without dazzling visitors so they lose sight of same.

Make the most from the least

More is not always better, especially when it comes to Web pages. Try to design and build your pages using minimal ornaments and simple layouts. Don't overload pages with graphics or add as many levels of headings as you can fit. Instead, do everything you can to make sure your content is easy to read and follow. To keep distractions and departures to a minimum, also make sure any hyperlinks you include add real value to your site.

Gratuitous links to useless information are nobody's friend; if you're tempted to link to a Webcam that shows a dripping faucet, resist, resist, resist!

Structure and images exist to *highlight* content. The more bells, whistles, and dinosaur growls dominate a page, the more distracted from your content visitors become. Use structure and graphics sparingly, wisely, and carefully. Anything more can be an obstacle to content delivery. Go easy on the animations, links, and layout tags, or risk having your message (even your page) devoured by a hungry T. Rex.

Build attractive pages

When users visit Web pages with a consistent framework that focuses on content, they're likely to feel welcome. The important thing is to *supplement* content with graphics and links — don't trample users with an onslaught of pictures and links. Making Web pages pretty and easy to navigate only adds to a site's basic appeal and makes your cybercampers even happier.

If you need inspiration, cruise the Web and look for layouts and graphics that work for you. If you take the time to analyze what you like, you can work from other people's design principles without having to steal details from their layouts or looks (which isn't a good idea anyway).

As you design Web documents, start with a basic, standard page layout. Pick a small, interesting set of graphical symbols or icons and adopt a consistent navigation style. Use graphics sparingly (yes, you've heard this before); make them as small as possible — limit size, number of colors, shading, and so on, while retaining eye appeal. When you build simple, consistent navigation tools, label them clearly and use them everywhere. Your pages can be appealing and informative if you invest the time and effort.

Create Well-Formulated HTML and Test

If you start with solid markup and good content and then work through what you've wrought to make sure everything works like it's supposed to (and communicates what it ought to), you're on your way to a great Web site. But once the construction is over, the testing begins. And only when the testing returns positive results should you open your virtual doors to the public.

Keep track of those tags

Although you're building documents, it's easy to forget to use closing tags, even when they're required (for example, the </a> that closes the opening anchor tag <a>). When you're testing Web pages, some browsers can compensate for your errors, leaving you with a false sense of security.

The Web is no place to depend on the kindness of strangers. Scrutinize your tags to head off possible problems from browsers that might not be quite so understanding (or lax, as the case may be).

As for the claims that some vendors of HTML authoring tools make ("You don't even have to know any HTML!"), all we can say is, *"Uh-huh, suuurre."* HTML itself is a big part of what makes Web pages work; if you understand it, you can troubleshoot with minimal fuss. Also, only you can ensure that your pages' inner workings are correct and complete for your documents, whether you build them yourself or a program builds them for you.

We could go on ad infinitum about this, but we'll exercise some mercy and confine our remarks to the most pertinent items:

- **Keep track of tags yourself while you write or edit HTML by hand.** If you open a tag — be it an anchor, a text area, or whatever — create the closing tag for it right then and there, even if you have content to add. Most HTML editors do this for you.

- **Use a syntax checker to validate your work during the testing process.** Syntax checkers are automatic tools that find missing tags or errors — and other ways to drive you crazy! Use these whether you build pages by hand or with software. The W3C's (free) HTML Validator lives at http://validator.w3.org.

- **Obtain and use as many browsers as you can when testing pages.** This not only alerts you to missing tags, but it can also reveal potential design flaws or browser dependencies (covered in the "Avoid browser dependencies" section later in this chapter). This exercise also emphasizes the importance of alternate text information. That's why we also check our pages with Lynx (a character-only browser).

> ✔ **Always follow HTML document syntax and layout rules.** Just because most browsers don't require elements such as `<html>`, `<head>`, and `<body>` doesn't mean you can omit them. It means that browsers don't give a hoot whether you use them or not. But browsers per se are not your audience. Your users (and future browsers) may indeed care.

Although HTML isn't exactly a programming language, it still makes sense to treat it like one. Following formats and syntax helps you avoid trouble, and careful testing and rechecking of your work ensures a high degree of quality, compliance with standards, and a relatively trouble-free Web site.

Avoid browser dependencies

When you're building Web pages, the temptation to view the Web in terms of your favorite browser is hard to avoid. That's why you should always remember that users view the Web in general (and your pages in particular) from many perspectives — through many different browsers.

During the design and writing phases, you'll probably hop between HTML and a browser's-eye view of your work. At this point in the process, you should switch from one browser to another and test your pages among several browsers (including at least one character-mode browser). This helps balance how you visualize your pages and helps keep you focused on content.

You can use public Telnet servers with Lynx (a character-mode browser) installed for free and that don't require software installation. Visit `www.brain stormsandraves.com/articles/browsers/lynx` for a good discussion of using Lynx when testing Web pages.

During testing and maintenance, you must browse your pages from many different points of view. Work from multiple platforms; try both graphical and character-mode browsers on each page. Testing takes time but repays your investment with pages that are easy for everyone to read and follow. It also helps viewers who come at your materials from platforms other than your own and helps your pages achieve true independence from any single viewpoint. Why limit your options?

If several pages on your site use the same basic HTML, create one template for those pages. Test the template with as many browsers as you can. When you're sure the template is browser-independent, use it to create other pages. This helps ensure that every page looks good, regardless of which browser a visitor might use, and puts you on your way to real HTML enlightenment.

Navigating your wild and woolly Web

Users who view the splendor of your site don't want to be told *you can't get there from here*. Aids to navigation are vital amenities on a quality Web site. A *navigation bar* is a consistent graphical place to put buttons that help users get from A to B. By judicious use of links and careful observation of what constitutes a complete screen (or screenful) of text, you can help your users minimize (or even avoid) scrolling. Text anchors make it easy to move to the previous and or next screens, as well as to the top, index, and bottom in any document. Just that easy, just that simple — or so it appears to the user.

We believe in the *low scroll* rule: Users should have to scroll *no more than one* screenful in either direction from a point of focus or entry to find a navigation aid that lets them jump (not scroll) to the next point of interest.

We don't believe that navigation bars are mandatory or that names for controls should always be the same. But we do believe that the more control you give users over their reading, the better they like it. The longer a document gets, the more important such controls become; they work best if they occur about every 30 lines in longer documents (or in a separate, always-visible frame if you use HTML frames).

Keep It Interesting After It's Built!

The tendency to sit on one's fundament, if not rest on one's laurels, after launching a Web site is nearly irresistible. It's okay to sit down, but it isn't okay to leave things alone for too long or to let them go stale for lack of attention and refreshment. If you stay interested in what's on your site after it's ready for prime time, your content probably won't go past its freshness date. Do what you can (and what you must) to stay on top of things, and you'll stay engaged — as should your site visitors!

Think evolution, not revolution

Over time, Web pages change and grow. Keep a fresh eye on your work and keep recruiting fresh eyes from the ranks of those who haven't seen your work before to avoid what we call "organic acceptance."

This concept is best explained by the analogy of your face in the mirror: You see it every day; you know it intimately, so you aren't as sensitive as someone else to how your face changes over time. Then you see yourself on video, or in a photograph, or through the eyes of an old friend. At that point, changes obvious to the world reveal themselves to you as you exclaim, "I've gone completely gray!" or "My spare tire could mount on a semi!"

Changes to Web pages are usually evolutionary, not revolutionary. They proceed in small steps; big leaps are rare. Nevertheless, you must stay sensitive to the underlying infrastructure and readability of your content as pages evolve. Maybe the lack of on-screen links to each section of your Product Catalog didn't matter when you had only three products — but now that you offer 25, they're a must. You've heard that form follows function; in Web terms, the structure of your site needs to follow changes in its content. If you regularly evaluate your site's effectiveness at communicating, you know when it's time to make changes, large or small.

This is why user feedback is crucial. If you don't get feedback through forms or other means, aggressively solicit some from your users. If you're not sure how you're doing, consider: If you don't ask for feedback, how can you tell?

Beating the two-dimensional text trap

Because of centuries of printed material and the linear nature of books, our mindsets can use an adjustment. The nonlinear potentials of hypermedia give the Web a new definition for the term *document*. But it's tempting to pack pages full of hypercapabilities until they resemble a Pony Express dynamite shipment and gallop in many directions at once. Be safe: Judge hypermedia by whether it

✔ Adds interest

✔ Expands on your content

✔ Makes a serious — and relevant — impact on the user

Within these constraints, such material can vastly improve any user's experience of your site.

Stepping intelligently outside old-fashioned linear thinking can improve your users' experience of your site and make your information more accessible to your audience. That's why we encourage careful use of document indexes, cross-references, links to related documents, and other tools to help users navigate within your site. Keep thinking about the impact of links as you look at other people's Web materials; it's the quickest way to shake free of the linear-text trap. (The printing press was high-tech for its day, but that *was* 500 years ago!) If you're looking for a model for your site's behavior, don't think about your new trifold four-color brochure, however eye-popping it is; think about how your customer-service people interact with new customers on the telephone. (*"What can I do to help you today?"*)

Overcome inertia through vigilance

When you deal with your Web materials post-publication, it's only human to goof off after finishing a big job. Maintenance isn't as heroic or inspiring as creation, yet it represents most of the activity to keep any document alive and well. Sites that aren't maintained often become ghost sites; users stop visiting sites when developers stop working on them. Never fear — a little work and attention to detail keeps your pages fresh. If you start with something valuable and keep adding value, a site's value appreciates over time — just like any other artistic masterpiece. Start with something valuable and leave it alone, and it soon becomes stale and loses value.

Consider your site from the viewpoint of a master aircraft mechanic: Correct maintenance is a real, vital, and on-going accomplishment, without which you risk a crash. A Web site, as a vehicle for important information, deserves regular attention; maintaining a Web site requires discipline and respect. See www.disobey.com/ghostsites/index.shtml for a humorous look at ghost sites.

Keeping up with change translates into creating (and adhering to) a regular maintenance schedule. Make it somebody's job to spend time on a site regularly; check to make sure the job's getting done. If people are tagged to handle regular site updates, changes, and improvements, they flog other participants to give them tasks when scheduled site maintenance rolls around. Pretty soon, everybody's involved in keeping information fresh — just as they should be. This keeps your visitors coming back for more!

Chapter 22

Ten Ways to Exterminate Web Bugs

In This Chapter

▶ Avoiding markup and spelling faux pas

▶ Keeping links hot and fresh

▶ Gathering beta testers to check, double-check, and triple-check your site

▶ Applying user feedback to your site

After you put the finishing touches on a set of pages (but before you go public on the Web for the world to see), it's time to put them through their paces. Testing is the best way to control a site's quality.

Thorough testing *must* include content review, analysis of HTML syntax and semantics, link checks, and various sanity checks to make doubly sure that what you built is what you really wanted. Read this chapter for some gems of testing wisdom (learned from a lifetime of Web adventures) as we seek to rid your Web pages of bugs, errors, gaucheries, and lurking infelicities.

Avoid Dead Ends and Spelling Faux Pas

A sense of urgency that things must work well and look good on a Web site will never fail to motivate you to keep your site humming along. That said, if you work from a visual diagram of how your site is (or should be) organized, you'll be well-equipped to check structure, organization, and navigation. Likewise, if you put your pages through their paces regularly (or at least each time they change) with a spell checker, you'll be able to avoid unwanted *tpyos*.

Make a list and check it — twice

Your design should include a road map (often called a *site map*) that tells you what's where in every individual HTML document in your site and the relationships among its pages. If you're really smart, you kept this map up-to-date as you moved from design to implementation. (In our experience, things always change when you go down this path.) If you're merely as smart as the rest of us, don't berate yourself — update that map *now*. Be sure to include all intra- and interdocument links.

A site map provides the foundation for a test plan. Yep, that's right — effective testing isn't random. Use your map to

- ✔ Investigate and check every page and every link systematically.
- ✔ Make sure everything works as you think it should — and that what you built has some relationship (however surprising) to your design.
- ✔ Define the list of things to check as you go through the testing process.
- ✔ Check everything (at least) twice. (Red suit and reindeer harness optional.)

Master text mechanics

By the time any collection of Web pages comes together, you're looking at thousands of words, if not more. Yet many Web pages get published without a spell check, which is why we suggest — no, *demand* — that you include a spell check as a step when testing and checking your materials. (Okay, we don't have a gun to your head, but you *know* it's for your own good.) Many HTML tools, such as FrontPage, HomeSite, and Dreamweaver, include built-in spell checkers, and that's the first spell-check method you should use. These HTML tools also know how to ignore the HTML markup and just check your text.

Even if you use HTML tools only occasionally and hack out the majority of your HTML by hand, perform a spell check before posting your documents to the Web. (For a handy illustration of why this step matters, try keeping a log of spelling and grammar errors you find during your Web travels. Be sure to include a note on how those gaffes reflect on the people who created the pages involved. Get the message?)

You can use your favorite word processor to spell check your pages. Before you check them, add HTML markup to your custom dictionary, and pretty soon the spell checker runs more smoothly — getting stuck only on URLs and other strange strings that occur from time to time in HTML files.

If you'd prefer a different approach, try any of the many HTML-based spell-checking services now available on the Web. We like the one at the Doctor HTML site, which you can find at www2.imagiware.com/RxHTML.

If Doctor HTML's spell checker doesn't float your boat, visit a search engine, such as www.yahoo.com or www.google.com, and use **web page spell check** as a search string. Doing so can help you produce a list of spell-checking tools made specifically for Web pages.

One way or another, persist until you root out all typos and misspellings. Your users may not thank you for your impeccable use of language — but if they don't trip over errors while exploring your work, they'll think more highly of your pages (and their creator) even if they don't know why. Call it stealth diplomacy!

Keep Your Perishables Fresh!

New content and active connections to current, relevant resources are the hallmarks of a well-tended Web site. You can't achieve these goals without regular (and sometimes, constant) effort, so you plan for ongoing activity. The rewards can be great, starting with a genuine sense of user excitement at what new marvels and treasures may reveal themselves on their next visit to your site. This kind of anticipation is nearly impossible to imitate (without doing what you'll have to do to keep things fresh in the first place).

Lack of live links — a loathsome legacy

We performed an unscientific, random-sample test to double-check our own suspicions; users told us that positive impressions of a particular site are proportional to the number of working links they find there. The moral of this survey: Always check your links. This step is as true after you publish your pages as it is before they're made public. Nothing irritates users more than a link that produces the dreaded 404 File not found error instead of the good stuff they seek! Remember, too, that link checks are as indispensable to page maintenance as they are to testing.

If you're long on 21st-century street smarts, hire a robot to do the job for you: They work really long hours (with no coffee breaks), don't charge much, and check every last link in your site (and beyond, if you let them). The best thing about robots is that you can schedule them to do their jobs at regular intervals: They always show up on time, always do a good job, and never complain (though we haven't yet found one that brings homemade cookies or remembers birthdays). All you have to do is search online for phrases like *link checker.* You'll find lots to choose from!

We're fond of a robot named MOMspider, created by Roy Fielding of the W3C. Visit the MOMspider site at `http://ftp.ics.uci.edu/pub/websoft/` `MOMspider`. This spider takes some work to use, but you can set it to check only local links, and it does a bang-up job of catching stale links before users do. (Some HTML software, such as HomeSite, includes a built-in link checker to check your links both before and after you post your pages.)

If a URL points to one page that immediately points to another (a pointer), you're not entitled to just leave the link alone. Sure, it technically works, but for how long? And how annoying! So if your link checking shows a pointer that points to a pointer (yikes), do yourself (and your users) a favor by updating the URL to point *directly* to the real location. You save users time, reduce Internet traffic, and earn good cyberkarma.

When old links must linger

If you must leave a URL active even after it has become passé to give your users time to bookmark your new location, instruct browsers to jump straight from the old page to the new one by including the following HTML command in the old document's `<head>` section:

```
<meta http-equiv="refresh" content="0"; url="newurlhere" />
```

This nifty line of code tells a browser that it should refresh the page. The delay before switching to the new page is specified by the value of the `content` attribute, and the destination URL is determined by the value of the `url` attribute. If you must build such a page, be sure to include a plain-vanilla link in its `<body>` section, too, so users with older browsers can follow the link manually, instead of automatically. You might also want to add text that tells visitors to update their bookmarks with the new URL. Getting there may not be half the fun, but it's the whole objective.

Make your content mirror your world

When it comes to content, the best way to keep things fresh is to keep up with the world in which your site resides. As things change, disappear, or pop up in that external world, similar events should occur on your Web site. Since something new is always happening, and old ways or beliefs fading away — even in studies of ancient cultures or beliefs — if you report on what's new and muse on what's fading from view, you'll provide constant reasons for your visitors to keep coming back for more. What's more, if you can accurately and honestly reflect (and reflect upon) what's happening in your world of interest, you'll grab loyalty and respect as well as continued patronage.

Check Your Site, and Then Check It Again!

There's an ongoing need for quality control in any kind of public content, but that need is particularly acute on the Web, where the whole world can stop by (and where success often follows the numbers of those who drop in, and return). You must check your work while you're building the site and continue to check your work over time. This allows you to revisit your material with new and shifting perspectives and evaluate what's new and what's changed in the world around you. That's why testing and checking are never really over; they just come and go — preferably, on a regular schedule!

Look for trouble in all the right places

You and a limited group of users should thoroughly test your site before you share it with the rest of the world — and more than once. This process is called *beta testing,* and it's a bona fide, five-star *must* for a well-built Web site, especially if it's for business use. When the time comes to beta-test your site, bring in as rowdy and refractory a crowd as you can find. If you have picky customers (or colleagues who are pushy, opinionated, or argumentative), be comforted knowing that you have found a higher calling for them: Such people make ideal beta-testers — if you can get them to cooperate.

Don't wait till the very last minute to test your Web site. Sometimes the glitches found during the beta-test phase can take weeks to fix. Take heed: Test early and test often, and you'll thank us in the long run!

Beta-testers use your pages in ways you never imagined possible. They interpret your content to mean things you never intended in a million years. They drive you crazy and crawl all over your cherished beliefs and principles. And they do all this before your users do! Trust us, it's a blessing — even if it's in disguise.

These colleagues also find gotchas, big and small, that you never knew existed. They catch typos that word processors couldn't. They tell you things you left out and things that you should have omitted. They give you a fresh perspective on your Web pages, and they help you see them from extreme points of view.

The results of all this suffering, believe it or not, are positive. Your pages emerge clearer, more direct, and more correct than they would have if you tried to test them yourself. (If you don't believe us, of course, you *could* try skipping this step. And when real users start banging on your site, forgive us if we don't watch.)

Cover all the bases with peer reviews

If you're a user with a simple home page or a collection of facts and figures about your private obsession, this tip may not apply to you. Feel free to read it anyway — it just might come in handy down the road.

If your pages express views and content that represent an organization, chances are, oh, *about 100 percent,* that you should subject your pages to peer-and-management review before publishing them to the world. In fact, we recommend that you build reviews into each step along the way as you build your site — starting by getting knowledgeable feedback on such basic aspects as the overall design, writing copy for each page, and the final assembly of your pages into a functioning site. These reviews help you avoid potential stumbling blocks, such as unintentional off-color humor or unintended political statements. If you have any doubts about copyright matters, references, logo usage, or other important details, get the legal department involved. (If you don't have one, you may want to consider a little consulting help for this purpose.)

Building a sign-off process into reviews so you can prove that responsible parties reviewed and approved your materials is a good idea. We hope you don't have to be that formal about publishing your Web pages, but it's far, far better to be safe than sorry. (This process is best called *covering the bases,* or perhaps it's really covering something else? You decide.)

Use the best tools of the testing trade

When you grind through your completed Web pages, checking your links and your HTML, remember that automated help is available. If you visit the W3C HTML Validator at `http://validator.w3.org`, you'll be well on your way to finding computerized assistance to make your HTML pure as air, clean as the driven snow, and standards-compliant as, ah, *really well-written HTML*. (Do we know how to mix a metaphor, or what?)

Likewise, investigating the link checkers discussed earlier in the chapter is a good idea; use them regularly to check links on your pages. These faithful servants tell you if something isn't current, so you know where to start looking for links that need fixing.

Schedule site reviews

Every time you change or update your Web site, you should test its functionality, run a spell check, perform a beta test, and otherwise jump through important hoops to put your best foot forward online. But sometimes you'll make just a small change — a new phone number or address, a single product listing, a change of name or title to reflect a promotion — and you won't go through the whole formal testing process for "just one little thing."

That's perfectly understandable, but one thing inevitably leads to another, and so on. Plus, if you solicit feedback, chances are good that you'll get something back that points out a problem you'd never noticed or considered before. It's essential to schedule periodic Web site reviews, even if you've made no big changes or updates since the last review. Information grows stale, things change, and tiny errors have a way of creeping in as one small change succeeds another.

Just as you take your car in for an oil change or swap out your air-conditioning filter, you should plan to check your Web site regularly. Most big organizations we talk to do this every three months or so; others do it more often. Even when you think you have no bugs to catch, errors to fix, or outdated information to refresh, you'll often be surprised by what a review turns up. Make this part of your routine, and your surprises will be less painful — and require less work to remedy!

Let User Feedback Feed Your Site

Who better to tell you what works and what doesn't than those who use (and hopefully, even depend on) your site? Who better to say what's not needed and what's missing? But if you want user feedback to feed your site's growth and evolution, you not only have to ask for it, you have to find ways to encourage it to flow freely and honestly in your direction, then act on it to keep the wellsprings working intact.

Foster feedback

Even after you publish your site, testing never ends. (Are you having flash-backs to high school or college yet? We sure are.) You may not think of user feedback as a form (or consequence) of testing, but it represents the best reality check your Web pages are ever likely to get, which is why doing every-thing you can — including offering prizes or other tangibles — to get users to fill out HTML forms on your Web site is a good idea.

This reality check is also why reading *all* feedback you get is a must. Go out and solicit as much feedback as you can handle. (Don't worry; you'll soon have more.) But the best idea of all is to carefully consider the feedback that you read and then implement the ideas that actually bid fair to improve your Web offerings. Oh, and it's a really good idea to respond to feedback with per-sonal e-mail, to make sure your users know you're reading what they're saying. If you don't have time to do that, make some!

Even the most finicky and picky of users can be an incredible asset: Who better to pick over your newest pages and to point out those small, subtle errors or flaws that they revel in finding? Your pages will have contributed mightily to the advance of society by actually finding a legitimate use for the universal delight in nitpicking. And your users can develop a real stake in boosting your site's success, too. Working with your users can mean that some become more involved, helping guide the content of your Web pages (if not the rest of your professional or obsessional life). Who could ask for more? Put it this way: You may yet find out, and it could be remarkably helpful.

If you give to them, they'll give to you!

Sometimes, simply asking for feedback or providing surveys for users to fill out doesn't produce the results you want — either in quality or in volume. Remember the old days when you'd occasionally get a dollar bill in the mail to encourage you to fill out a form? It's hard to deliver cold, hard cash via the Internet, but a little creativity on your part should make it easy for you to offer your users something of value in exchange for their time and input. It could be an extra month on a subscription, discounts on products or services, or some kind of freebie by mail. (Maybe now you can finally unload those stuffed Gila monsters you bought for that trade show last year. . . .)

But there's another way you can give back to your users that might not even cost you too much. An offer to send participants the results of your survey, or to otherwise share what you learn, may be all the incentive participants need to take the time to tell you what they think, or to answer your ques-tions. Just remember that you're asking your users to give of their time and energy, so it's only polite to offer something in return.

Part VII
Appendixes

The 5th Wave By Rich Tennant

"YOU KNOW KIDS — YOU CAN'T BUY THEM JUST ANY WEB AUTHORING SOFTWARE."

In this part . . .

This part of the book supplements the main text with pointers to useful resources and summary information. It includes addresses to Web pages that provide complete lists of HTML and XHTML elements, with syntax information and brief descriptions and explanations, and does the same for Cascading Style Sheet (CSS) markup as well. It also holds a glossary of technical terms found elsewhere in the book.

We hope you get to know these supporting members of our cast, and use them often and well!

Appendix A

Deprecated (X)HTML Elements and Attributes

• •

*I*n markup terminology, elements or attributes may be *deprecated*. This means they're still recognized but doomed to obsolescence. If you see (X)HTML markup you don't recognize or can't find elsewhere in this book, chances are good that it's deprecated. (XHTML doesn't recognize deprecated items if you use the Strict DTD, but XHTML Transitional and Frameset DTDs do recognize them.)

Table A-1 lists deprecated (X)HTML elements; Table A-2 lists deprecated (X)HTML attributes (in alphabetical order, for easy reference).

Table A-1		Deprecated (X)HTML Elements		
Element	*Common Name*	*Empty?*	*Category*	*Description*
applet	Applet	No	Inclusion	Includes Java applet in (X)HTML document
basefont	Base font	Yes	Presentation	Sets default font for text to which no style sheet or font element applies
center	Center text	No	Presentation	Centers enclosed text in current display area
dir	Directory list	No	List	Lists style for lists of short strings (like file names)

(continued)

Table A-1 *(continued)*

Element	Common Name	Empty?	Category	Description
font	Font info	Yes	Presentation	Sets size, font, and color for element content
isindex	Single-line input	Yes	Form-related	Prompts user for single line of input
menu	Menu list	No	List	Creates compact list format
param	Object parameters	Yes	Inclusion	Passes "command line" input to Java applet
s	Strikethrough	No	Presentation	Uses strikethrough font for element content
strike	Strikethrough	No	Presentation	Uses strikethrough font for element content
u	Underline	No	Presentation	Uses underline font for element content

Table A-2   **Deprecated (X)HTML Attributes**

Name	Where Deprecated	Description
align	`<caption><img><table>` `<hr><div><h1..6><p>`	Sets alignment at top, bottom, left, right
alink	`<body>`	Sets color for active document links
background	`<body>`	Sets background picture for document body (URL is target)

Name	*Where Deprecated*	*Description*
bgcolor	`<body><table>` `<tr><td><th>`	Sets background color for document body
border	`<img><object>`	Sets width of border around image
clear	` `	Sets side of line break on which floating objects may not be positioned
color	`<basefont><font>`	Sets color for `basefont` (default) or `font` element content
compact	`<ol><ul>`	Special compact formatting for list elements
hspace	`<img><object>`	Sets horizontal margin around an image or object
link	`<body>`	Sets default color for document links
noshade	`<hr>`	Instructs browser to draw horizontal rules without 3-D shading
nowrap	`<td><th>`	Instructs browser not to perform word wrap
size	`<basefont><font><hr>`	Sets size for `<basefont>` or `<font>` from 1 to 7, `<hr>` in pixels
start	`<ol>`	Sets starting number for ordered list
text	`<body>`	Sets text (foreground) color for document body
type	`<li>`	Sets list style (1|a|A|i|I for ordered lists, `disc`|`circle`|`square` for unordered lists)
value	`<li>`	Sets the value for a list item, specified by number

(continued)

Table A-2 *(continued)*

Name	Where Deprecated	Description
vlink	`<body>`	Sets color for document links already visited
vspace	`<img><object>`	Sets vertical margin for an image
width	`<hr><pre><td><th>`	Sets width (percentage or pixels) for object sizing or spacing

Appendix B

Shorthand and Aural CSS Properties

• •

This appendix provides complete coverage of two special categories of CSS properties that we describe in Chapters 8 and 9:

✔ **Shorthand properties** are catchall CSS properties that permit a single selector statement in a style sheet to cover all properties that relate to each other, such as backgrounds, padding, borders, audio cueing, and so forth. See Table B-1.

✔ **Aural properties** relate to how styles help control how text is rendered in speech form (usually for visually-impaired Web surfers). See Table B-2.

Table B-1	CSS Shorthand Properties	
Name	*Values*	*Description*
background	{background-attachment background-color| background-image| background-position| background-repeat| inherit}	Sets all background settings
border	{color|border-style| border-width|inherit}	Sets all border properties around an element
border-bottom	{border-bottom-width| border-style|color| inherit}	Sets all border bottom proper-ties for an element
border-left	{border-left-width| border-style|color| inherit}	Sets all border left properties for an element

(continued)

Table B-1 *(continued)*

Name	Values	Description
border-right	{border-right-width|border-style|color|inherit}	Sets all border right properties for an element
border-style	{dashed|dotted|double|groove|hidden|inset|none|outset|ridge|solid|inherit}	Sets all border styles for an element
border-top	{border-top-width|border-style|color|inherit}	Sets all border top properties for an element
border-width	{length|medium|thick|thin|inherit}	Sets all border width properties around an element
cue	{cue-before|cue-after|inherit}	Sets all controls for auditory cues on text-to-speech rendering
font	{Caption|Font-family|Font-size|Font-style|Font-variant|Font-weight|Icon|Line-height|Menu|Message-box|Small-caption|Status-bar|Inherit}	Governs all types of text display controls
list-style	{list-style-image|list-style-position|list-style-type|inherit)	Governs display of all list style properties for an element
outline	{outline-color|outline-style|outline-width|inherit}	Governs all outline properties for an element
padding	{padding-width|inherit}	Sets padding width around all four sides of an element
pause	{pause-before|pause-after|inherit}	Controls duration of silent pauses before and after element rendering

Table B-2	CSS Aural Properties	
Name	*Values*	*Description*
azimuth	{left-side|far-left| left|center-left| center|center-right| right|far-right|right- side|behind|leftwards| rightwards|inherit}	Describes horizontal position of a sound source
cue-after	{none|URI|inherit}	Defines auditory cue to play after rendering an element
cue-before	{none|URI|inherit}	Defines auditory cue to play before rendering an element
elevation	{above|angle|below| higher|lower|inherit}	Describes vertical position of a sound source in the listening environment
pause- after	{time|percentage| inherit}	Controls duration of silent pause after element rendering (percentage based on speech-rate)
pause- before	{time|percentage| inherit}	Controls duration of silent pause before element rendering
pitch	{frequency|high|low| medium|x-high|x-low| inherit}	Sets average pitch of speaking voice used to render text
pitch-range	{number|inherit}	Sets amount of pitch variation in speaking voice used to render text
play-during	{auto|mix|none|repeat| URI|inherit}	Controls background sound to be played while rendering text to speech
richness	{number|inherit}	Defines degree to which speaking voice will carry (higher numbers carry further)
speak	{none|normal|spell- out|inherit}	Defines method whereby content should be rendered aurally, if at all

(continued)

Table B-2 *(continued)*

Name	Values	Description
speak-header	{always|once|inherit}	Specifies audible repetition of table headers, if any
speak-numeral	{continuous|digits|inherit}	Specifies whether numbers are read as a whole or in consecutive digits
speak-punctuation	{code|none|inherit}	Sets method by which punctuation should be spoken, literally or in the length of the pause used
speech-rate	{fast|faster|medium|number|slow|slower|x-fast|x-slow|inherit}	Specifies rate at which speaking voice renders text; number sets average words spoken per minute
stress	{number|inherit}	Sets amount of inflection used to render stress markers in text
voice-family	{specific voice|generic voice|inherit}	Defines specific voices; can define a generic voice for rendering text to speech
volume	{loud|medium|number|percentage|silent|soft|x-loud|x-soft|inherit}	Sets volume of sound playback

Appendix C

Glossary

$\cdots$

absolute: When used to modify pathnames or URLs, a full and complete file specification (as opposed to a relative one). An absolute specification includes a host identifier, a complete volume, and path specification.

anchor: In HTML, an anchor is tagged text or a graphic element that acts as a link to another location inside or outside a given document, or an anchor may be a location in a document that acts as the destination for an incoming link. The latter definition is most commonly how we use it in this book.

array: A collection of data values in a programming language variable; JavaScript is among the many such languages that support array typed data values.

attribute: A named characteristic associated with a specific HTML element. Some attributes are required, others are optional. Some attributes also take *values;* if so, the syntax is `attribute="value"`).

bandwidth: Technically, the range of electrical frequencies a device can handle; more often, bandwidth is used as a measure of a communication technology's carrying capacity.

beta-testing: When you and a limited group of users test your site before you share it with the rest of the world.

block element: Any of a number of text block markup elements in (X)HTML, like those used to designate paragraphs, headings, block quotes, lists, tables, and forms. Block elements help to organize (or define) text structure in chunks. See also *inline element*.

body: That part of an (X)HTML document that contains the actual document content, especially all text that appears when the document is displayed. Occurs between the `<body>` and `</body>` tags; that is, as content within the `body` element. Also called document body.

bookmark: A reference from a saved list of URLs kept by the Netscape Web browser. Bookmarks allow quick loading of a Web site without retyping the URL. Bookmarks work the same as Microsoft Internet Explorer Favorites.

browser: A Web access program that can request HTML documents from Web servers and render such documents on a user's display device. See also *client*.

bugs: Major or minor errors, mistakes, and gotchas in software.

client: The end-user side of the client/server arrangement; typically, "client" refers to a consumer (rather than a provider) of network services; a Web browser is therefore a client program that talks to Web servers.

Common Gateway Interface (CGI): The specification that governs how Web browsers communicate with and request services from Web servers; also the format and syntax for passing information from browsers to servers with either HTML forms or document-based queries. The current version of CGI is 1.1.

content: For HTML, content is its raison d'être; although form is important, content is why users access Web documents and why they come back for more.

cookie: A collection of data created and stored on a per-user basis to track behavior, preferences, and other persistent kinds of information, across page views or site visits.

CSS (Cascading Style Sheets): A method of coding that allows users to define how certain HTML, XHTML, or XML structural elements, such as paragraphs and headings, should be displayed using style rules instead of additional markup. The versions of CSS are *CSS1* and CSS2, with *CSS2* being the most recent version.

default: In general computer-speak, a selection made automatically in a program if the user specifies no explicit selection. For HTML, the default is the value assigned to an attribute if none is supplied.

deprecated: The term we use to earmark an HTML element or attribute that is to be left for dead by future versions of HTML.

DHTML (dynamic HTML): The combination of HTML, CSS, the the DOM, and JavaScript, used to create interactive Web pages.

DOCTYPE declaration: Tells the processor where to locate the DTD and contains declarations for the particular document. Also called a document type declaration, abbreviated as DTD.

document: The basic unit of HTML information, a document refers to the entire contents of any single HTML file. Because this definition doesn't always correspond to normal notions of a document, we refer to what can formally be called HTML documents more or less interchangeably with Web pages, which is how browsers render such documents for display.

DOM (Document Object Model): A Web standard, defined by the W3C, that allows JavaScript to programmatically access and manipulate the contents of a document. The DOM defines each object on a Web page and the attributes associated with those objects, and defines the methods that you can use to manipulate those objects.

domain name: A unique name that's registered as part of the Internet's vast distributed Domain Name System (DNS), defined somewhere on a nameserver, and can therefore be translated into a corresponding numeric IP address, located, and accessed on demand (essential for any working Web site).

dot syntax: Javascript's notation for separating objects, properties, and methods using periods, as in `automobile.headlight.left` and `document.image.name`.

DTD (Document Type Definition): A formal SGML specification for a document, a DTD lays out the structural elements and markup definitions to be used to create instances of documents.

element: A section of a document defined by a start- and end-tag or an empty tag.

empty tag: An HTML element that doesn't require the use of a closing tag. In fact, the use of a closing tag in empty tags is forbidden.

entity: A character string that represents another string of characters.

error message: Information delivered by a program to a user, usually to inform him or her that the process hasn't worked properly, if at all.

event: A user activity, such as moving a mouse pointer over an image or clicking a link, that a user performs while visiting a Web page.

expression: A specific type of programming construct, such as a JavaScript "phrase" that can be interpreted to return some kind of value (such as numeric, true/false, and so forth).

external style sheet: A style sheet that resides outside of the Web document in a separate, external file.

footer: The concluding part of an HTML document, the footer should contain contact, version, date, and attribution information to help identify a document and its authors. Most people use the `<address>` element to identify this information.

form handler: A program on the Web server or even possibly a simple `mailto` URL that manages the data a user sends to you through the form.

forms: In HTML, forms provide a mechanism to let users interact with servers on the Web. Forms are built on special markup that lets browsers solicit data from users and then deliver that data to specially designated input-handling programs on a Web server.

function: A set of JavaScript statements that performs a task; especially useful when a code fragment or segment is used more than once in a script.

gateway: A Web site that acts as a portal to an entire virtual community, thereby serving as an entry point and a resource map. (This is different from an application gateway, which translates between mutually incompatible sets of communications protocols or data representations.)

graphics: In HTML documents, graphics are files that belong to one of a restricted family of types (usually .GIF or .JPG) that are referenced through URLs for inline display on Web pages.

GUI (Graphical User Interface): Pronounced "gooey," GUIs make graphical Web browsers possible; they create a visually oriented interface that makes it easy for users to interact with computerized information of all kinds.

head: This provides basic information *about* a document, including its title and metadata, such as keywords, author information, a description, and so forth. If an external stylesheet is referenced in the document body, it's also linked in the document head. In (X)HTML documents this part occurs between an opening `<head>` and a closing `</head>` tag; that is, as content for the `head` element. Also called document head, document header, or header,

heading: For HTML, a heading is a markup element used to add document structure. Sometimes the term refers to the initial portion of an HTML document between the `<head>` . . . `</head>` tags, where titles and context definitions are commonly supplied.

helper applications: Today, browsers can display multiple graphics files (and sometimes other kinds of data); sometimes, browsers must pass particular files — for instance, motion picture or sound files — over to other applications that know how to render the data they contain. Such programs are called helper applications because they help the browser deliver Web information to users.

hexadecimal: A numbering system composed of six letters and ten numbers that is used to condense binary numbers. In HTML, hexadecimal numbering is used with elements and their attributes to identify colors for backgrounds and other elements in a Web page; in this context, such numbers are often called "hex codes."

HTML (Hypertext Markup Language): The SGML-derived markup language used to create Web pages. Not quite a programming language, HTML provides a rich lexicon and syntax for designing and creating useful hypertext documents for the Web.

HTTP (Hypertext Transfer Protocol): The Internet protocol used to manage communication between Web clients (browsers) and servers.

hyperlink: A shorthand term for *hypertext link*. (See also *hypertext link*.)

hypermedia: Any of a variety of computer media — including text, graphics, video, sound, and so on — available through hypertext links on the Web.

hypertext: A method of organizing text, graphics, and other kinds of data for computer use that lets individual data elements point to one another; a non-linear method of organizing information, especially text.

image map: A synonym for *clickable image*, which refers to an overlaid collection of pixel coordinates for a graphic that can be used to locate a user's selection of a region on a graphic, in turn used to select a related hypertext link for further Web navigation.

image rollover: A change in image (usually button) behavior that occurs when the user's cursor is positioned over that image (or button).

inheritance: The style characteristic whereby all elements that nest inside any particular element acquire style information from the element within which they nest. For example, changing the body element changes all other text elements that appear within it, thereby changing the whole Web page.

inline content: A word or string of words inside of a block element.

inline element: Any element that controls presentation on an element-by-element basis. An inline element doesn't denote structure. It's a text element (such as the <b> element).

internal style sheet: A style sheet that resides inside of the Web document in which you're working.

IP (Internet Protocol): IP is the specific networking protocol of the same name used to tie computers together over the Internet.

ISP (Internet Service Provider): An organization that provides individuals or other organizations with access to the Internet, usually for a fee. ISPs usually offer a variety of communications options for their customers, ranging from analog telephone lines, to a variety of higher-bandwidth leased lines, to ISDN and other digital communications services.

Java: An object-oriented, platform-independent, secure, and compact programming language designed for Web application deployment. Most system vendors support Java, which was created by Sun Microsystems.

layout: The overall arrangement of the elements in a document.

link: For HTML, a link is a pointer in one part of a document that can transport users to another part of the same document, or to another document entirely. This capability puts the "*hyper*" into hypertext. In other words, a link is a one-to-one relationship/association between two concepts or ideas.

markup: A way of Embedding special characters (*metacharacters*) within a text file that instructs a computer program how to handle the file's contents.

markup language: A formal set of special characters and related capabilities used to define a specific method for handling the display of files that include markup; HTML is a markup language, which is a subset of SGML, used to design and create Web pages.

media types: CSS instructions that govern how pages should be rendered on a computer display, how they should print, and how they should sound read out loud. For that reason, such styles are divided into visual media (for on-screen display), paged media (for print display), and aural (for rendering text to speech) types or categories.

metadata: Specially defined elements that describe a document's structure, content, or rendering, within the document itself or through external references. (Metadata literally means data about data.)

method: In the context of programming and scripting languages, methods describe the things that objects can do (or conversely, the kinds of operations to which objects may be subjected). In JavaScript, method names may be easily recognized because they're followed by parentheses (for example, `click()`, `open()`, and `selected()` are all well-recognized method identifiers).

multimedia: A method of combining text, sound, graphics, and full-motion or animated video within a single compound computer document.

nameservers: Computers on the Internet that translate domain names into the actual Internet location for the resources to which such names refer (such as computers, servers, or other devices and interfaces).

navigation: In the context of the Web, navigation refers to the use of hyperlinks to move within or between HTML documents and other Web-accessible resources.

navigation bar: A way of arranging a series of hypertext links on a single line of a Web page to provide a set of navigation controls for an HTML document or a set of HTML documents.

nesting: In computer terms, one structure that occurs within another is said to be nested; in HTML, nesting happens most commonly with list structures that may be freely nested within one another, regardless of type.

object: In the context of programming and scripting languages, objects refer to named entities that have associated properties (characteristics) and methods (actions that may be performed upon specific objects).

operator: Symbols in JavaScript used to work with variables. These include common arithmetic operations (+, -, /, and so forth) and various kinds of logical (!= or "not equals", || "either x or y is true", and so forth) and comparison (> or "greater than", < or "less than", and so forth) operators.

pages: The generic term for the HTML documents that Web users view on their browsers.

Perl: A powerful, compact programming language that draws from languages such as C, Pascal, sed, awk, and BASIC; Perl is the language of choice for CGI programs, partly because of its portability and the many platforms it currently supports, and partly because of its ability to exploit operating system services quickly and easily.

plug-in: Hardware or software added to a system that adds a specific feature such as plug-ins that allow Netscape Navigator to play video.

properties: In CSS, they are the different aspects of the display of text and graphics, such as font size or background color. In working with scripting languages (and object-oriented programming languages in general), properties describe characteristics associated with named and defined objects.

pseudo classes: Any of four link states that can be modified using CSS: link (normal state, no activity), visited (user has already been to this link), hover (cursor is positioned on the link), and active (user is clicking the link). CSS permits link colors or characteristics to reflect pseudo classes.

relative: When applied to URLs, a relative address provides an abbreviated document address that may be combined with the `<base>` element to create a complete address or is the complete address for a local file found in the same directory.

resource: Any HTML document, capability, or other item or service available through the Web. URLs point to resources.

robot: A special Web-traveling program that wanders widely, following and recording URLs and related titles for future reference in search engines.

screen: The glowing part on the front of your computer monitor where you see the Web do its thing (and anything else your computer may like to show you).

script: A set of programming instructions that activate when an event that you define occurs.

scripting language: A special kind of programming language that a computer reads and executes at the same time (which means that the computer figures out what to do with the language when it appears in a document or at the time that it's used. JavaScript is a common scripting language associated with Web use).

search engine: A special Web program that searches the contents of a database of available Web pages and other resources to provide information that relates to specific topics or keywords, which a user supplies. Also called a crawler.

selector: In CSS, identifies the element to which the style rule applies.

server: A computer on a network whose job is to listen for particular service requests and to respond to those that it knows how to satisfy.

SGML (Standard Generalized Markup Language): An ISO standard document definition, specification, and creation mechanism that makes platform and display differences across multiple computers irrelevant to the delivery and rendering of documents.

site map: A visual guide to a Web site's structure and components that you may build, maintain, and use only for yourself, or that you may implement in (X)HTML as a user aid and navigational tool.

specification: A formal document that describes the capabilities, functions, and interfaces for a specific piece of software, a markup language, or a communications protocol.

statement: A complete command, or other syntactically correct line of code, in JavaScript or some other programming language. JavaScript has such statement types as *expression, conditional,* and *loop* statements.

style sheet: A file that holds the layout settings for a certain category of a document. Style sheets, like templates, contain settings for headers and footers, tabs, margins, fonts, columns, and more.

syntax: Literally, the formal rules for how to speak. But In this book, we use syntax to describe the rules that govern how HTML markup looks and behaves within HTML documents. The real syntax definition for HTML comes from the SGML Document Type Definition (DTD).

syntax checker: A program that checks a particular HTML document's markup against the rules that govern its use; a recommended part of the testing regimen for all HTML documents.

tag: The formal name for a piece of HTML markup that signals a command of sorts, usually enclosed in angle brackets (< >).

template: Literally, a model to imitate, we use the term template in this book to describe the skeleton of a Web page, including the HTML for its heading and footer, and a consistent layout and set of navigation elements.

text document: A data file that includes only text characters from well-defined and usually restrictive character data sets (such as 7- or 8-bit ASCII, or ISO-Latin-1).

thumbnail: A miniature rendering of a graphical image, used as a link to the full-size version.

title: The text supplied to a Web page's title bar when displayed, used as data in many Web search engines.

transparency: A technique for editing images for use on a Web page that permits the image to blend in with the surrounding page background. Whichever color or colors are designated as transparent allow the page to show through.

URL (Uniform Resource Locator): The primary naming scheme used to identify Web resources, URLs define the protocols to use, the domain name of the Web server where a resource resides, the port address to use for communication, and a directory path to access named Web files or resources.

user interface: The overall design of your site. Sometimes Abbreviated as *UI*.

valid: Code that follows all the syntax rules defined in a document type definition, allowing the document to pass through a validator program with no errors.

validation: The process of comparing a document to a set of document rules, in this context a DTD.

variable: A named value in a programming language such as JavaScript that programs manipulate using operators, and/or within expressions.

W3C (abbreviation for World Wide Web Consortium): The international standards body that's charged with custody over the specifications for important Web markup languages, including CSS, HTML, XML, and XHTML, among many others.

Web: Also called the World Wide Web, WWW, or W3. The complete collection of all Web servers available on the Internet, which comes as close to containing the "sum of human knowledge" as anything we've ever seen.

Web pages: Synonym for HTML documents, we use Web pages in this book to refer to *sets* of related, interlinked HTML documents, usually produced by a single author or organization.

Web server: A computer, usually on the Internet, that plays host to `httpd` and related Web-service software.

Web site: An addressed location, usually on the Internet, that provides access to the set of Web pages that correspond to the URL for a given site; thus a Web site consists of a Web server and a named collection of Web documents, both accessible through a single URL.

well-formed document: An HTML document that adheres to the rules that make it easy for a computer to interpret.

white space: The "breathing room" on a page, white space refers to parts of a display or document unoccupied by text or other visual elements. A certain amount of white space is essential to make documents attractive and readable.

WYSIWYG (What You See Is What You Get): Text editors or other layout tools (such as HTML authoring tools) that try to show their users on-screen how final, finished documents will look.

XHTML (Extensible Hypertext Markup Language): The reformulation of HTML 4.0 as an application of XML 1.0.

XML (Extensible Markup Language): A system for defining, validating, and sharing document formats.

Index

• *M* •

• *Q* •

• *R* •

● *X* ●

Notes

Notes

Notes

BUSINESS, CAREERS & PERSONAL FINANCE

0-7645-5307-0

0-7645-5331-3 *†

Also available:

- Accounting For Dummies †
  0-7645-5314-3
- Business Plans Kit For Dummies †
  0-7645-5365-8
- Cover Letters For Dummies
  0-7645-5224-4
- Frugal Living For Dummies
  0-7645-5403-4
- Leadership For Dummies
  0-7645-5176-0
- Managing For Dummies
  0-7645-1771-6

- Marketing For Dummies
  0-7645-5600-2
- Personal Finance For Dummies *
  0-7645-2590-5
- Project Management For Dummies
  0-7645-5283-X
- Resumes For Dummies †
  0-7645-5471-9
- Selling For Dummies
  0-7645-5363-1
- Small Business Kit For Dummies *†
  0-7645-5093-4

HOME & BUSINESS COMPUTER BASICS

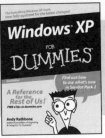

0-7645-4074-2

0-7645-3758-X

Also available:

- ACT! 6 For Dummies
  0-7645-2645-6
- iLife '04 All-in-One Desk Reference
  For Dummies
  0-7645-7347-0
- iPAQ For Dummies
  0-7645-6769-1
- Mac OS X Panther Timesaving
  Techniques For Dummies
  0-7645-5812-9
- Macs For Dummies
  0-7645-5656-8

- Microsoft Money 2004 For Dummies
  0-7645-4195-1
- Office 2003 All-in-One Desk Reference
  For Dummies
  0-7645-3883-7
- Outlook 2003 For Dummies
  0-7645-3759-8
- PCs For Dummies
  0-7645-4074-2
- TiVo For Dummies
  0-7645-6923-6
- Upgrading and Fixing PCs For Dummies
  0-7645-1665-5
- Windows XP Timesaving Techniques
  For Dummies
  0-7645-3748-2

FOOD, HOME, GARDEN, HOBBIES, MUSIC & PETS

0-7645-5295-3

0-7645-5232-5

Also available:

- Bass Guitar For Dummies
  0-7645-2487-9
- Diabetes Cookbook For Dummies
  0-7645-5230-9
- Gardening For Dummies *
  0-7645-5130-2
- Guitar For Dummies
  0-7645-5106-X
- Holiday Decorating For Dummies
  0-7645-2570-0
- Home Improvement All-in-One
  For Dummies
  0-7645-5680-0

- Knitting For Dummies
  0-7645-5395-X
- Piano For Dummies
  0-7645-5105-1
- Puppies For Dummies
  0-7645-5255-4
- Scrapbooking For Dummies
  0-7645-7208-3
- Senior Dogs For Dummies
  0-7645-5818-8
- Singing For Dummies
  0-7645-2475-5
- 30-Minute Meals For Dummies
  0-7645-2589-1

INTERNET & DIGITAL MEDIA

0-7645-1664-7

0-7645-6924-4

Also available:

- 2005 Online Shopping Directory
  For Dummies
  0-7645-7495-7
- CD & DVD Recording For Dummies
  0-7645-5956-7
- eBay For Dummies
  0-7645-5654-1
- Fighting Spam For Dummies
  0-7645-5965-6
- Genealogy Online For Dummies
  0-7645-5964-8
- Google For Dummies
  0-7645-4420-9

- Home Recording For Musicians
  For Dummies
  0-7645-1634-5
- The Internet For Dummies
  0-7645-4173-0
- iPod & iTunes For Dummies
  0-7645-7772-7
- Preventing Identity Theft For Dummies
  0-7645-7336-5
- Pro Tools All-in-One Desk Reference
  For Dummies
  0-7645-5714-9
- Roxio Easy Media Creator For Dummies
  0-7645-7131-1

* Separate Canadian edition also available
† Separate U.K. edition also available

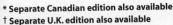

Available wherever books are sold. For more information or to order direct: U.S. customers visit www.dummies.com or call 1-877-762-2974.
U.K. customers visit www.wileyeurope.com or call 0800 243407. Canadian customers visit www.wiley.ca or call 1-800-567-4797.

 WILEY

SPORTS, FITNESS, PARENTING, RELIGION & SPIRITUALITY

0-7645-5146-9

0-7645-5418-2

Also available:
- Adoption For Dummies
  0-7645-5488-3
- Basketball For Dummies
  0-7645-5248-1
- The Bible For Dummies
  0-7645-5296-1
- Buddhism For Dummies
  0-7645-5359-3
- Catholicism For Dummies
  0-7645-5391-7
- Hockey For Dummies
  0-7645-5228-7

- Judaism For Dummies
  0-7645-5299-6
- Martial Arts For Dummies
  0-7645-5358-5
- Pilates For Dummies
  0-7645-5397-6
- Religion For Dummies
  0-7645-5264-3
- Teaching Kids to Read For Dummies
  0-7645-4043-2
- Weight Training For Dummies
  0-7645-5168-X
- Yoga For Dummies
  0-7645-5117-5

TRAVEL

0-7645-5438-7

0-7645-5453-0

Also available:
- Alaska For Dummies
  0-7645-1761-9
- Arizona For Dummies
  0-7645-6938-4
- Cancún and the Yucatán For Dummies
  0-7645-2437-2
- Cruise Vacations For Dummies
  0-7645-6941-4
- Europe For Dummies
  0-7645-5456-5
- Ireland For Dummies
  0-7645-5455-7

- Las Vegas For Dummies
  0-7645-5448-4
- London For Dummies
  0-7645-4277-X
- New York City For Dummies
  0-7645-6945-7
- Paris For Dummies
  0-7645-5494-8
- RV Vacations For Dummies
  0-7645-5443-3
- Walt Disney World & Orlando For Dummies
  0-7645-6943-0

GRAPHICS, DESIGN & WEB DEVELOPMENT

0-7645-4345-8

0-7645-5589-8

Also available:
- Adobe Acrobat 6 PDF For Dummies
  0-7645-3760-1
- Building a Web Site For Dummies
  0-7645-7144-3
- Dreamweaver MX 2004 For Dummies
  0-7645-4342-3
- FrontPage 2003 For Dummies
  0-7645-3882-9
- HTML 4 For Dummies
  0-7645-1995-6
- Illustrator CS For Dummies
  0-7645-4084-X

- Macromedia Flash MX 2004 For Dummies
  0-7645-4358-X
- Photoshop 7 All-in-One Desk
  Reference For Dummies
  0-7645-1667-1
- Photoshop CS Timesaving Techniques
  For Dummies
  0-7645-6782-9
- PHP 5 For Dummies
  0-7645-4166-8
- PowerPoint 2003 For Dummies
  0-7645-3908-6
- QuarkXPress 6 For Dummies
  0-7645-2593-X

NETWORKING, SECURITY, PROGRAMMING & DATABASES

0-7645-6852-3

0-7645-5784-X

Also available:
- A+ Certification For Dummies
  0-7645-4187-0
- Access 2003 All-in-One Desk
  Reference For Dummies
  0-7645-3988-4
- Beginning Programming For Dummies
  0-7645-4997-9
- C For Dummies
  0-7645-7068-4
- Firewalls For Dummies
  0-7645-4048-3
- Home Networking For Dummies
  0-7645-42796

- Network Security For Dummies
  0-7645-1679-5
- Networking For Dummies
  0-7645-1677-9
- TCP/IP For Dummies
  0-7645-1760-0
- VBA For Dummies
  0-7645-3989-2
- Wireless All In-One Desk Reference
  For Dummies
  0-7645-7496-5
- Wireless Home Networking For Dummies
  0-7645-3910-8

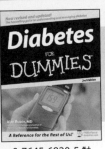

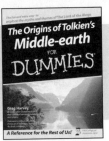
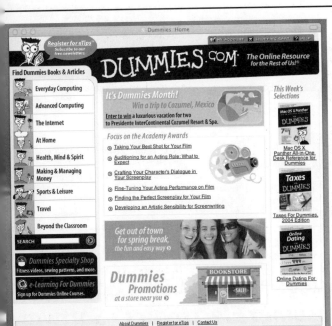